TRUTHS,
& DISTORTIONS

Why Mankind is suffering:
Hidden Truths revealed!

An Insight into Humanity's misadventures in the World of Matter

Dictated by Evolved
Masters & Teachers
In the 'Spirit World'

Channelled by
French Medium
BRIGITTE RIX

CON-PSY Publications

First Edition

© Brigitte Rix
2012

Published by
CON-PSY PUBLICATIONS
P.O.BOX 14, GREENFORD,
MIDDLESEX, UB6 0UF.

ISBN 978 1 898680 60 4

Other books by Brigitte Rix:
'I'm Not Dead: I'm Alive Without a Body' (2011 & 2012)
'Get by in French: BBC Active' (1998 & 2007)
'Pas de Problème' (2003)

ACKNOWLEDGEMENTS

My loving and respectful thanks to my very patient 'Spirit Masters' who asked me to take time to listen to them on a regular basis, so that they could dictate their book. It is an honour for me to be the recipient of their revelations and to help such Evolved Teachers offer them to Mankind. Their work taught me mind-boggling but fascinating and exciting facts. I feel very privileged to be their humble messenger. All my love and gratitude to my daughter Anne-France for her help, patience and artistic talent with the cover and to my son Jim for his support and suggestions.

And of course all my gratefulness to my very dear friend Stan Pattison, for his great patience, understanding and caring help, giving me more time to focus on my work for Spirit.

To my dearest friend Hazel Moore in Kent, who magically appeared in my life at the right moment: my warmest and heartfelt thanks and love for her encouragement and kindly, conscientiously and enthusiastically devoting long hours checking the manuscript.

I could not have done without you, Hazel! You have a very special place in my heart and life. You are a wonderful spiritual lady!

My appreciation too to Matt Gough and Brenda Gibbons for reading the early stages of this book with interest. Warm thanks to my publisher, Candy Taylor of Con-Psy Publications, for her help and work to ensure the publication of this book. Finally, all my love to my beautiful cat 'Lady' for patiently and 'purringly' keeping me company during those long hours at the computer!

****

TRUTHS, LIES & DISTORTIONS

Acknowledgements

CONTENTS

Introduction

PART 1
UNDERSTANDING THE FUNDAMENTAL

PART 2
WEIRD & WONDERFUL

PART 3
FEARLESS LIVING

PART 4
IMPROVE THE WORLD

§§§

Please visit my website for further knowledge:

www.italkwithspirits.com

INTRODUCTION

Am I potty, deluded, or a fake? Definitely not! Hundreds and hundreds of people can vouch for my sanity and honesty. This book is not 'about me', as I am just the messenger of these teachings, but here is a bit about me to show you that I am a normal person and to explain how this book evolved.

MY BACKGROUND

I am a mum of two and a French language teacher by profession, now retired. I live in York, UK and you can find me on Facebook. But I am also a genuine clairaudient medium and probably have been all my life - yet I only realised it properly in 1983! I then made sure I trained to polish my mediumship ethically and safely in order to give people personal messages (at no charge) that provide evidence of life after (and before) death.

Ever since, when I am very relaxed and 'tuned in' to their fine frequencies, I have been able to converse with numerous people who have lost their flesh bodies - but who are still alive! They have kept their personalities and emotions and are fully aware of who they are in the World of Mind and Light, which we tend to call the 'Spirit World', or other names such as the 'Hereafter', 'Paradise' or 'Heaven'.

I can also receive automatic and inspired writing. I hear the words at the very same time as my pen feels compelled to write them down at high speed. I receive answers immediately to any question that I ask. Because the answers have provided so much new information that I have never heard before, go beyond my weak grasp of scientific knowledge and have often been the opposite of my own beliefs and expectations, this has proved to me, time and time again, that this information is not coming from my own mind or subconscious! I sometimes argue with my communicators because of my own limited understanding of these astounding concepts, but they remain so patient with me and calmly do their best to explain things in various other ways.

THE BOOKS

This book is just one of many of my conversations with Spirit. I have decades of writings that I am now able and devoted to sharing with the world. It has taken me years to type up the thousands of handwritten pages! Then, in 2011, I published a diary of conversations with my loved ones and my 'Spirit teaching Guide', who are alive in the Afterlife. Its title *"I'm Not Dead: I'm Alive Without a Body"* stems from my own mother's comments, days after her passing, as she marvels at the wonders of being still alive and pain free! Her enlightening 'travelogue' reveals what it's like to painlessly leave your body at 'death' of the flesh, what life is like after we die and what activities we can do in that 'Other World' where what you think about will manifest in front of you.

The book you are now holding was **written down exactly as it was dictated to me at the request of very knowledgeable and evolved Energy Personalities** (also called '**Spirit Teachers**'). As they say, they are no longer focused on the physical world or their physical form (which we call the flesh body), they are now Energy and Mind, though they have previously lived on Earth at some time or other.

Over several years, these individual 'spokespersons' came close to me to unexpectedly start dictating profound thoughts and facts, most of which were unknown to me! As I marvelled at the mind-boggling contents, they asked me to make sure 'their book' was made available to the public. They told me that if I wanted this knowledge, I had to share it and not keep it for myself. Their fascinating and inspirational facts and revelations are explained simply and **provided in all sincerity and for the good of Mankind.** Their book purposefully avoids obscure or complex scientific angles and jargon, as the Spiritual Teachers want the information to appeal to and reach the general public.

HOW THE TEACHINGS CAN HELP YOU

These Evolved Masters want to encourage Humanity to open its Mind, to understand where it has gone wrong and to help itself by using its Mind Power. The profound knowledge within this book can help people who are seeking the Truth, to avoid being brainwashed by manipulative authorities or religious leaders. They will get the courage to enlarge their vision of events and even **challenge** entrenched, unfounded or distorted man-made dogmas or theories.

This book does not impose any dogmas, but offers hope, a greater understanding and long-awaited answers to profound questions which have puzzled and frustrated Mankind, who chose to create arguments, wars and religious rifts.

May you read this with an open mind so you can truly grasp Reality and your Life Purpose, discover your own inner strength, rid yourself of fears, improve your health and learn **why you are on Earth and why this Earth exists.** Above all, I hope these teachings help you to realise that you are more than what you see in the mirror - you are a special Being!

****

PART 1

UNDERSTANDING
THE FUNDAMENTAL

"All great Truths begin as blasphemous"
G.B.Shaw

Medium's comments or questions to her communicators are
shown as (*BR* + *plain italics*)

Chapter 1

BASIC FACTS AS TOOLS

AURA & ENERGY BODY

1.   Everyone and everything alive is and has an Energy body!

Some of its colourful layers (the 'aura') can be photographed with sensitive cameras or apparatus, such as used in Kirlian photography.

2.   You are NOT your flesh body! Your Energy body is the 'Real You', the 'driver' of your flesh.

Many sensitive (psychic) people have observed this Energy body 'fly out' of the physical one at the time of 'death' of the flesh body.

3.   Your Energy body is indestructible and eternal, unlike your flesh body, which it uses as its vehicle to allow you to experiment life on Earth.

4.   Your physical body's health is affected by, and reflects, any emotions and traumas felt by the multi-layers (such as emotional and mental levels) of the Energy body.

5.   The vibrations of this Energy body are far superior and faster than those of your body of flesh Matter. That is why human eyes have difficulty with seeing it. It has been labelled 'Spirit body'.

THE BRAIN IS NOT MIND OR SPIRIT

1.   The brain is only flesh, it dies and decays. The brain is NOT the Mind! The Mind, emotions and personality of the owner of the 'corpse' never disappear! They carry on existing, separate from the flesh brain and body at a faster vibrational rate, therefore being invisible to the majority of people.

2.   Every single living Being is a 'Spirit' Being, with a Mind of his own, before choosing to be born on Earth to temporarily experiment life in a flesh body. When the '**flesh** garment' dies we 'return home' to our normal state as a 'Spirit' Being.

COMMUNICATING BETWEEN THE TWO WORLDS

1.   The means of communication between the 'Spirit World' and the Earth World is **Thought.** People in the 'Spirit World' need to learn how to communicate with Earthlings and **choose** to link with us.

This can be and has been **proved** millions of times over the centuries, by gifted and highly sensitive people, such as prophets, seers and genuine mediums.

2.   A medium is a 'human telephone', receiving these messages. Genuine mediums can relay comments, conversations and evidential proof transmitted by those who survived death of the physical body.

3.   People gifted with a heightened sensitivity to such vibrations can see them; they are '**clairvoyant**', i.e. 'clear seeing'.

'Departed' people can learn to recall what they looked like on Earth and project that image with their Thought power for clairvoyant mediums to see them. One can develop this gift.

4.   People gifted with a heightened sensitivity to those fast thoughts and sounds received from the Minds of people in the Spirit World are '**clairaudient**' (clear hearing). One can develop this gift.

5.   Eminent and distinguished professors, scientists etc. have tested, analysed and verified such contacts and **recognised their veracity.**

6.   Conclusive evidence of even just one person's survival means **everybody, including 'Animals', survives** physical death! If one person has evidently survived, why wouldn't everybody survive?!

LIFE IN THE AFTERLIFE

1. Life for anyone in the Spirit World is affected by their mental attitude. Your thoughts, attitude, desires and regrets create your surroundings.

2. Like on Earth, there are teachers devoting their time to inform people to help them progress. Some teach within the Spirit World, offering constant guidance and support. Others choose to help Humans on Earth by being their invisible 'Guides', or helpers, inspiring their protégés without infringing on their free will.

Everybody has one main **'GUIDE',** or 'door keeper', from birth, as well as some other helpers. Those 'guides' and teachers are thoroughly **trained** to do this work.

But if the Human on Earth refuses to pay attention to, or ignores the advice of, what he may label 'his conscience' and acts against the only Universal Law, the Guide cannot force him to behave better. That one Spiritual Law is: *"Do not harm ANY other living Being (including 'Animals' of course). And when one is in need, try and help if you can."*

3. The Afterlife world is made of pure Energy and vibrations, yet that world **feels real** to those living there, just like a dream feels real to the dreamer. You realise that colours are vibrations and emit sounds! Thoughts become visible! The physics of the 'Spirit World' is far superior to, and beyond, physics known on Earth!

SPIRIT? - HIGHER SELF? - SOUL? - HUMAN?

1. All Humans have a physical body of flesh. But this is only their outer 'visible' appearance. They also ALL have fundamentally an Energy Body, the vibrations of which are superior to the flesh 'casing'. Every Human **is** an 'Energy Being' consisting of the intrinsic Life Force we call 'Spirit'. When the flesh body 'dies' and decays, the **Energy/ Spirit/personality carries on existing.**

Everyone and everything living are made of that 'Spirit' Energy/Force, in the same way as a diamond is basically made of the substance 'carbon' throughout. Each such Energy/Spirit Being is and has a **'Higher Self'**: The overall rough 'diamond piece of rock'.

2.   All Beings have an Urge to exist, improve and evolve.

In the same way as each individual facet of a diamond can only sparkle after being chiselled and polished, the 'Higher Self' of a **Spirit Being polishes each of its own facets** through experiencing various challenges and expanding its knowledge. One school for this learning is the Earth.

Each life that the Energy/Spirit Being experiences in a physical body, with the challenges and hurdles encountered, helps the polishing of one of the facets of its Higher Self.

The part, or facet, of the Higher Self focusing on a particular personality (e.g. a man) during a particular life which **he chooses** to experience is the **Soul** of that 'man'.

3.   For the Higher Self of an Energy Being to sparkle at its best and throughout, it needs to undergo **many** experiences and lives. Therefore each life chosen and lived by all its various Souls adds to and expands the overall knowledge and experience of the Higher Self. **A Higher Self is composed of a huge number of facets.**

Going to temporarily live in a flesh body is called 'Incarnation'. *(From the Latin 'carn': flesh and 'incarnate': made flesh).* **Reincarnation** means going back to incarnate again and again as a **totally different** person and gender.

None of this is compulsory. But all Beings have a built-in Urge to discover more, create more and expand their experience and knowledge! It's the Joy of Creativity!

****

Chapter 2

MY EVOLVED SPIRIT MASTERS - TEACHERS

INTRODUCING SOME OF MY COMMUNICATORS

In these countless conversations with the Spirit authors, who bring Knowledge, my occasional questions and responses are distinguished by italics and begin with 'BR'.

I am not always told which of the many spokespeople from the Spirit World, are dictating their book to me at the time. Each of these Spirit authors have linked up with many other evolved Minds, so they all insist that individual names do not matter. As they all say: "It is the message which matters, not the messenger".

But some of the communicators relented and accepted to be 'labelled' by a name and say a few words about themselves.

• **'Silver Arrow'** - *My Guide and 'Door Keeper'.*

The personality talking to you has always been your main guide and leader, 'Silver Arrow' as you call him. He is the mouthpiece for others. When others speak, it is with his permission for safety and reassurance to you. So, we'll say it's me talking but the **Knowledge ALSO comes from others**, as we pull together to give you facts which can be of interest or use to you.

One of them, calling himself 'Man by the river'- or 'River Man' as I call him - wanted to say this about himself:
• **'River Man'**

I have indeed been many other 'people' on Earth, as well as elsewhere, over the aeons that I have existed. I am still in progression, because sharing my knowledge is part of 'creating myself 'as I expand my knowledge by learning to share it and answering your queries. This might stretch the extent of my knowledge, as I have to search for more answers. So I learn more and extend myself and 'create myself' more.

BR- Please give me an idea of some era when you have existed?

My life as a 'scientific person' is not very useful to know about. It was no more amazing than what I know now. My life as a scientist reigned in the years when the Dukes of Normandy came to England and you felt you were not happy with the state of things.

BR (Rather confused and surprised) - Could you repeat please?

As I said, my one life as an 'Earth scientist' was not a marvel. That is not where I learnt all my 'knowledge', as you say. I had a great interest in scientific things but was not particularly brilliant. It is only when I came to the Other World, as you call it, that I learnt more and more. My life on Earth was during the conquest of that land over the water from Normandy, as it is called now. You knew of me then.

BR (Amazed) - Did I? How?

You knew me because we worked and travelled together. You had a similar interest but were not very knowledgeable either. We both tried to learn more. Eventually I came here but you went back to Earth many times after that because you wanted to carry on with that experiment - discovering other facets of the life you chose to create out of Matter. *(He will explain this point in more detail further on - BR).* You loved playing with Matter and had that thirst to find out what can be done or experienced. You had the same longing as me, that is why we have so much in common, you see!

BR- A silly question, but do you recall any names?

I had some obscure name (I don't recall it) and was not what you call famous - neither were you. We were both dilettantes, wanting to learn for the pleasure. A search in medieval books may have led you to my name because I was known enough to have my name in print, but would it make much difference? It's only a name.

I had a practice as a medical man, you see, with quite a lot of knowledge of science of those days, but the knowledge was no way as extensive as now! All in all, no real need for a name because I am currently your 'River Man', who is now even more of a scientist, having discovered the **real Laws of Physics** from this point of view of Reality.

Since then I have made many more discoveries from this world and **you** wanted to know more about that Earth you have been living on. So we pooled our resources together to try to answer some questions - such as those about Creation!

BR- Who do you mean by 'we'?

The 'we' is because I see things as they were, as a kind of film of explanations. (I know the modern words, you see, because I learnt them to try to explain things to you!).

Explanations come from the Source of Knowledge pooled together by all those who have been there or are there. Accept the fact that '**that** Time' still exists as 'now' and one looks over such a creation as if it is happening now. I am simply being the **mouthpiece** for all this information to be channelled to you in as a clear a way as we can make it - considering you have to try to understand what I am saying without blocking it because your brain rejects it.

So I see it for real and 'live' it, to pass it on to you. Hence the 'we', which makes you think I was there. I was in a way, probably, because we all were, being all Beings of Light who have evolved and are still evolving. That makes me happy, to discover more and more and to pass it on for those who search too.

My life as a 'Spirit person,' as you call it, is a constant dream of fulfilled desires, lovely discoveries and constant achievements, leading to more questions, discoveries, results and so on!

The substances of Matter are different in my world. **I do not have Matter of atoms and molecules!** I have Matter of Light and vibrations of infinitesimal speed. If you could see what I see, you would be so amazed you would not want to do anything else than study it!

You could never satisfy your thirst for knowledge because there is always something new to discover! Hopefully, people on Earth will also be happy to know our 'secrets' of Knowledge.

My friend, you and I are inseparable. You and I will never part because we are made of each other. Aspects of a whole. You have a side I have not; I have a side you have not and we need each other to be complete.

BR- Which sides?

Explaining that will take a long, long time but you can know we have an opposite side to our present nature, which you and I complement by being that other side to our companion.

Just as light needs darkness to exist, darkness needs a lack of light to justify its own name. So are we. You have sides of your personality which have taken me a long time to develop, whereas they are in you. I have aspects in me which are second nature but which you struggle to develop.

BR- Which ones?!

The sole aim of **your** being on Earth is to help others - teach them, love them, heal them; that is **why** you have come. You may not be 'the best' teacher or healer of your times but you have all the qualities to be used for the good of Humanity and 'Animals'.

My side is similar but I have that quietness of Mind in me. You are 'action power'. I am peace for reflective meditation within. Between the two of us we can combine the

23

exchange of Knowledge - encouraging each other to develop that other aspect lacking in depth. You have the fire, I have the peaceful water within me.

A man is different from a woman physically - yet their Souls could be alike. All we can do is combine our Souls as one, to grow together, to help each other become better at the opposite side of our nature.

Let us join more often and you will feel my peace and I will feel your fire and burning desire to help others. We can boost each other in that way.

Praise the day you were born, praise the day you were 'born to Spirit' in a way, as you broke the silence between our two worlds the day you heard us properly and the day we heard you well. *(29-01-1983)*. Praise those days as **Birth** days in both senses; you were 'reborn' to us, we'd lost you for a while because you had no idea we were here! You found us again and you were brought back to us in a way. That's why we found that day to be so joyful; we could not stop celebrating and being happy!

Mighty Powers will fall if they don't look for the Truth, with their deeds and thoughts. Look for the Truth everywhere you go and in whatever you do and hear. **You must be prepared to stand for the Truth** and have arguments with people. So be brave, learn to stand up for your beliefs!

As Truth is upheld, lies will die out because all those around you will learn to open their eyes to the **facts that are hidden behind mountains of false information.** Will you be prepared to stand up for what you know to be right?

BR: Well, of course! Though no doubt I'll face a lot of opposition from the closed-minded world!

As you talk we will be there. You have the backup of those who have the Truth. No one could let lies slip in, in front of such a barrage of Truth.

Produce leaflets and information to let people grasp

24

what you know. You may want to specialise in one particular field, i.e. the Truth of life after Earth life. You will know what to say to them. All you have to do is be the mouthpiece for our information to come through.

Make the world understand that these teachings here are **not repetitions of what others have already written**. We will be giving you **'new' information,** yet not so new, as it had been given long, long ago in a totally different form.

Mankind rejected it then, because in those days the rulers kept the knowledge hidden from the people - who mostly could not read or write. Then leaders distorted it to suit their means and that is why it never reached the crowds.

We will give you a little at a time, so that you can process it both in your Mind and on your machine. All will depend on how much time you are prepared to give to all this, how much time you can sensibly spare too, as we don't really want to rule over your life and prevent you to live also!

If you wish to enjoy yourself a little here and there, there is scope for it, as you are on Earth after all to enjoy life too, not to be 'enslaved' by us. But bear in mind the importance of this work please.

We had been meaning to teach you long ago but **your Mind had to be made ready to accept that kind of Knowledge and information**, as it would be no good to us if we told you things that your Mind would reject. **This book is very important and urgent because it has to coincide with others coming out**, you see?

You cannot feel relaxed if you have not achieved your goals and these are some of them: Goals of publishing mighty works worth reading, for the world to be inspired, uplifted and taught! But it will be tough, we know… so please do your side of the bargain, we will do ours. Your other book about your communications with your mum talking from our world (*) is important too!

25

We cannot wait any more for Mankind to pay attention; it has to be flooded with information to make it sit up and think: "There must be something in this!"

(* Note - *Mum's book that he refers to is 'I'm NOT DEAD: I'm ALIVE without a body', describing years of genuine communications I received directly from my mother, father, husband, 'Spirit Guide' and other people - all in the 'Spirit World'. My mother first contacted me, **26 hours after** her 'passing over'! This 'travelogue', humorously narrated by my mum, describes her step-by-step journey following her passing from Earth into a whole new world of mind-boggling discoveries of the Afterlife.*

*It provides astounding and comforting genuine **insights** into exactly what happens when we die and life afterwards. Additional individual fascinating and reassuring accounts by other loved ones and Spirit 'Guides' are included. Our flesh body dies but not our Mind, personality and love for those still residing on Earth. We are **not** 'judged' by a deity, we analyse our own recent life and learn from it*).

'The Thinking Man'

One voice for many, but in fact mine too. I was a priest in one life, a Quaker minister in another, a diligent worker for 'peace within yourself' before you expect it from the world outside'. I am a profound thinker, as you call it. It makes me very pleased to hear you agree with my thoughts and suggestions and would like to see them put into action.

BR- Do you wish to tell me what your name was?

Pleasant as a name may be, it has no bearing on the message put forward, so why worry about a name!

BR- I do not worry!

All right, so why 'bother' about a name?

BR- Have you talked to me before? Or will you do so again?

Thoughts are constantly sent to you for you to process within and absorb. I often guide your thoughts towards more spiritual ways of thinking, to make sure you don't regret having missed out one day. **You are on my list of people I care about and guide**. You can say I am a 'guide', but one of many.

I help those who want to think spiritually as I know what pleasures linking to the Inner Side of oneself can bring and you also have others working on that side of things too, so you are not left alone struggling to find your inner balance. We are all here to guide you.

BR-How are you known in your world, apart from your light?

My world knows me for what I am now and was before and will be hopefully after. **No name is needed** here; we see each other's way of thinking and we know what the levels are. **We can read the thoughts** - the Light, the Being himself within! No need for outer labels but you would like one for me, wouldn't you?

BR- Well, it would make it easier to differentiate…

What about 'The Thinking Man'?

BR- Are you the same as the one I call 'River Man'?

A thinker. He is a very profound thinker who is modern by my standards, as I go back in time with my beliefs and preaching. You can rest assured I am not He. He is a good man too, of course, but not the same thoughts are expressed by him or me, though **we agree** with each other.

BR- So, I have Silver Arrow, River Man, Yourself…

My little friend, all that matters is **what** we teach you and tell you. Who says it does not matter too much, does it?! Because what we pass on is Universal Knowledge, the Law of the Spiritual World and the way of living which suits best someone wanting to achieve a lot in this work between the two worlds. So why be concerned about who says which bit? We are 'all in it together', as you so aptly say sometimes in your world.

Let it be known that **no one here disagrees with the others** because we all know the laws and the basis of spirituality and life in the Spiritual World, which should be reflected in life in the material world, if only Mankind made the effort to remember where it comes from!

'Brother John'

My dear, we have said it before, the spokesperson is only a speaking Mind into your Mind. All those around have as much to say as one single one, or even more, as **all Minds meet to gather and bring information to yours**. We are all happy to talk to you because you want to learn.

My 'voice', so to speak, to-day, can be labelled 'Brother John' but that is not what is important. **The message counts, dear, not the messenger!**

BR- I know, but it gives me comfort to 'label' you all - you are my real friends who teach me so much!

You can rest assured we shall always be your friends and we'll all meet again one day, in more real circumstances as you call it, though we do meet at times when your body has a rest but you usually don't remember in the morning, do you?!

You can take comfort in our presence, which will be eternal, as your and our Minds blend and will make one creative learning/teaching Mind Power out of our joint resources and interests.

The 'Learned Gent' - *Another Teacher was introduced by my Guide.*

We have here a gentleman who wishes to speak to you. He is **a very learned personality.** He learnt a lot on Earth; he has also studied a lot once he got here. So you can feel 'honoured' in a way to have his attention.

He has been in our world for a long time now and knows more than most of us. He has a special interest in the

28

way **Mankind has distorted what was originally the Truth of existence on Earth.** The Truth being that one is always a Spirit, **no matter what shape** or body one has chosen to have within that particular 'span-time' on Earth.

It is of utmost importance to listen and not talk; let him tell you what he has to say, then you may be able to ask him a question. If you interrupt, you cut his flow of thoughts and his link to wherever he gets his information from.

****

Chapter 3

HOW SPIRIT TEACHERS OBTAIN INFORMATION

REACH HIGHER VIBRATIONS

BR- How do you get answers to my questions?

As we talk, please make sure you keep calm, relaxed and focused on what we are saying. **We have to tune in ourselves to much higher vibrations** from where more detailed information can come through. So we need to pay great attention to what is being 'said', or rather what information emanates from these levels. Levels that we can reach with our Minds if we do listen within intensely and thoroughly.

We attempt to answer your questions to the best of our present abilities. If we acquire more we'll be able 'later on' to add to this. It's all a matter of intense focusing and of purpose of Mind, of 'Thought Querying Mechanism'.

We have indeed **access to far greater Knowledge** than you could think of, as that is where we get it from. We ask as we reach further and deeper into the Realms of Knowledge, the layers of more and more refined vibrations that contain much more subtle insights than you could envision. So we reach them and find the answer to your queries and gladly bring it back, both for ourselves if need be and for you too, of course. It is a lot more complex than you may ever imagine, as the Knowledge provided is forever malleable in the sense that **it can be reached at various deeper levels.**

Once you get to one level and describe it or obtain that type of information, the **next level reveals itself**, being even more concise or complex! That then allows access to the sub-layers, one at a time, or else several at a time, which then makes things even more intricate to absorb, remember and grasp. You see what we mean? It's not just a question of

30

plucking an answer out of a box within reach of our hands and giving it out! We all have to work at this, all the time, to improve our efficiency at polishing our perceptions within. It's **all done and received within our individual selves.**

As we work as a group to help **you**, we have to **pool together** what we have individually received and grasped, as our joint comprehension is more likely to be correct than just one individual's. This is said to make you understand how it works and how it is not as easy as you may have imagined. It is within the grasp of many, of those who endeavour to polish that aspect of our world where **Knowledge is constantly available and accessible** but only **to those who make the effort** to work at attaining it.

SEEK, WANT AND FIND

There is no law saying: "You cannot learn that". **Nothing is refused to the mind-seeking.** None is 'forbidden'. Because all are One in the ultimate Reality! All Beings and Minds are fundamentally ONE big, gigantic, endless and limitless Mind Power. Not many personalities, Mind powers/forces/Energies.

So the 'divisions' which are categorised by some as 'Humans', 'Animals' or 'Beings of Light' or 'Angels' etc. are just **labels** which Humans can vaguely or more exactly grasp. The labels make more sense to their limited way of thinking. But the Truth or, if you like, the Reality is that ALL are One big, endless Mind Force.

Therefore, we can all link to everything else. It has no barriers as such. **It is the inner Energy and Force within the individual 'personality' or Being, rather, which has its own limits.** They are not bound by anything except their own lack of expansion and self-awareness. They have to want, to seek, to feel the urge to find out more. They need the desire to experiment with 'new' (to them) ways of sensing, feeling, absorbing what is available and comprehending it all as well!

31

That's why we have to work at it if we want to get better and better, absorb more and discover more! It's no good saying: "This is how it is" if we (or anyone else talking to Earth people) have not delved deeper and deeper and even more deeply!

As you know, there are often pieces of incomplete information given out by some Beings who communicate with you, Earth people. That is a shame because some recipients will believe firmly what is given and the claim that "The Spirit World has spoken..." Yet those bits of information may be right at a certain level, **but** there may still be more underneath that has not been studied and absorbed. So this has done you more a disservice than a service, as **their limited absorption skills have transformed a limited view** into a 'final and authentic' piece of news and information.**This is what WE want to avoid doing!** So we all pool together as **Seekers of eternal Knowledge**, so that the question you ask spurs us onward and more deeply into the search for us to find and receive more details.

You can always ask us questions. We'll do our best to reply and see whether we can find answers for you. You can trust what you hear from us and you'll see you won't go wrong. We do not try to con you and we do not impose our own individual, ex-human ideas.

We are here to teach the Truth obtained from even higher levels of Understanding and Knowledge. There is a **great** need for more Knowledge to be given out to the world you live in. Because they have none or nearly none in general.

****

Chapter 4

THE LADDER OF UNDERSTANDING
TO BE READ IN THE ORDER GIVEN, STARTING
FROM THE BEGINNING

*As dictated by my Evolved Teachers living in the World of Mind and Light, to outline the essential points which **they will explain in more detail** throughout their book. Thus answering the question:*

"Why are we on the Earth?"

1. All Beings are 'Spirits'

The main thing people need to realise is the fact they are Spirits themselves, whatever their shape or colour of skin! They need to have that firmly in their Minds... and then we may get a bit more sense out of them!

It's no good Humans imagining they are only Beings made of 'material flesh' and come from a physical world and nothing else, because they will have no idea what we are talking about! If people understood that **each of them is a pure Spirit Being, who has chosen to come** to the Earth world they know of and live in, then they'll comprehend better what we are teaching for their own sakes.

2. Everyone and everything is Energy, everywhere!

The 'invisible world of 'Spirit', as you call it, is the same as the invisible air you are all surrounded with when on Earth. If you doubt the air you are in then you doubt yourself! You have air all around and even within you. You need to use that as a comparison to see yourself as a 'Spirit', an Energy Being.

You are surrounded with Energy, everywhere. You **are** Energy and have Energy within you that keeps you going and alive... until the Energy decides to leave the envelope of the flesh body. This will then be like a balloon deflating itself, or a tyre, or any other object that needs air to give it shape, solidity and continuity. If you take the air out, you no longer have the object you expect to see.

If and when the Spirit Being (and its Energy) removes itself from the flesh shell by sheer will, it will leave that casing as a floppy unworkable 'thing'.

3. Energy carries on existing - it can't be destroyed

This is a well-known fact in physics! It is not difficult to comprehend. All that is required is to **accept it**. So we need people to want to open their minds and think: "Right, let's assume or accept for a moment that this is correct."

Therefore, if you are all Spirit Beings, not only are you all 'alive' now in your physical world of flesh but you as Energy Beings will then be **alive in the world of Energy and Mind**, which you call the 'Spirit World'.

4. Thinking means creating!

Once this is accepted you'll proceed to understand that the World of Mind, Light and Energy is a **world pulsating with Life** as it constantly creates and creates. Why? Because every single thought becomes automatically visible and perceivable to its creator, who is the Being thinking it, whether by accident or wilfully.

As you realise we **all think constantly**, you can see why we say this world of ours is pulsating with Life and constant Light, from the Energy emanating from all those thinking (therefore creating!) Beings!

5. ALL BEINGS THINK... so create around themselves!

If we push the boundaries of understanding further, we can then make you understand that the Beings in our world are not so dissimilar to those in yours after all, as they all have **the same Power of Thought!**

The Power of Thought is the power to create. This is what everything is about - creating! Why create? Why not stay as we are, as things are?

Because Life is never static. Nothing in existence is ever still and stagnant. Everything you see and even do not see has a continuous momentum, an exhilarating desire to move on, move out, expand and extend itself towards more possibilities!

There is a built-in Urge in everything and everyone created to be more, to be better, to be different, to add to itself and to go beyond the present limits and boundaries. That is what 'progress' is. The progression of ideas leads to more ideas as they self-seed and procreate more and newer ideas. It has always been and will always be so.

Accept it or at least consider it, to be able to understand further propositions and demonstrations.

6. Can 'creation' come out of nothing?

If you can imagine a vacuum, a totally empty vase, or gigantic recipient to be more exact, you need to think: "How could anything be created in it unless you first put something in it, which would produce some object or mixture?"

As far as most of you know, it is impossible in your Earthly world. It may happen to your eyes in some rare cases but if you use your mightiest microscope you'll see that at the atomic or sub-atomic level there would have already been something or things present, which would trigger the apparition of that mysteriously created new 'thing'.

35

7. Self-creation without a trigger?

Is it really 'self-creation' or is there an Energy behind it, which creates it, whether you see it or not? This is the mighty question. Could anything self-create without Power of some kind giving it 'life', so to speak, giving it enough vigour so that is becomes sustainable and keeps existing?

It is **not possible without a trigger** and that trigger is what we want to talk about now. All life has a 'starting' and trigger point (unless you wonder what started the 'point'!). As all this is intermingled, you will have to comprehend one mighty fact which cannot be proved by a+b = c but by us telling you **what we know** from our eternal world of existence in Light and Truth.

We know for a fact there is only one 'sea of eternity'. That sea, or ocean, or **realm of eternity is a gigantic and limitless force of Mind Power made of what you would label 'Energy'**. This is what bathes everything, this is what everything and all Beings consist of.

8. Creative Thought Power has always existed!

It is THE basis to everything! An 'ocean' of eternal Thought Power which has always existed and will exist forever. It cannot be destroyed or removed and **it never had a starting point!** It has simply always been! Since this is tremendously difficult for Human Beings to grasp, we do understand if you find it hard to conceive. But we'll ask that you do us the honour to believe us on that point as well.

No one can prove it to be different, no one can prove we are 'wrong'since no one on Earth has ever seen the supposed 'beginning' of all things. As we place this firmly on the next step of understanding more, we'll go further and stipulate the following point.

9. Built-in Urge to expand

That **self-creating Thought Power is not content with just existing** because (like everything else has!) it has the **built-in Urge** to do more, to expand, to multiply and to create.

It is an unquenchable Urge, a thirst to be on a self-reproducing move. Yet not 'self' in the sense of 'cloning' itself, but improving, changing, adding aspects to it. Just for the joy and curiosity of Creativity! The purpose of this is not understandable to anyone who thinks creation and creating is for a self-serving purpose, for selfish aims!

10. Joy of Creativity

Such an Urge to expand and multiply can only possibly be understood by artists and musicians. It is a built-in desire for 'more' and 'different' and the fun of discovering what can be done. That leads to the fact that **any such creations will have a life of their own because they'll have the same built-in Power within** themselves! So they'll go on doing the same!

11. Open your Mind - discover a new angle?

We know we now have reached a point when people's Minds are exploding at the thought of trying to grasp such huge and mind-boggling concepts! But is it a reason for us to stop explaining? Or would it be better if we carried on and gave the reader the benefit of the doubt and the chance to see whether they can catch up with our thinking and explanations?

Shouldn't we keep going along the path of **true facts**, which need to be brought out in the open? Even if they are very difficult for those who cannot conceive anything beyond 'an egg and sperm make a third creature' or else nothing is acceptable? So, for those who are brave enough to carry on giving us a chance to explain more, here it is!

12. Creative Life Force: NO beginning. NOT a Being.

That Life Force, built in everything imaginable, **had no starting point. It has always existed**. But that is a very difficult concept and idea to grasp, absorb and accept!

This is why so many religious leaders had to generate in people's Minds the image of **a** 'benevolent Being', superior to anyone and anything, who can create all that exists yet 'himself' has never been created by anyone else! That is back to square one, which we explained ourselves previously.

There is and was no beginning because eternity has obviously always existed. **The Eternal Force is a creative Force, not a Being!** A mighty power of 'electric light' may be an easier picture for some people? But there is definitely not a personality, 'a father' or any other 'Being'! We cannot stress this strongly enough because the moment you attribute happenings to **one** 'Being' of any type, you cause yourself more problems than you realise! This is because, as often happens, you cannot make things stick or come to a sensible conclusion or explanation!

So, no single Being! No start. But a bathing, **all pervading 'sea of Thought Power', which is therefore automatically creative.** As this fact sinks in and is hopefully accepted, we add the new dimension of **each new creation** being a 'Being' on its own merits, which has ways of thinking and creating too!

13. All filled with this Creative Power

So the Universe is filled with such Power constantly creating and recreating itself. That applies to **each of you Human Beings now existing on Earth!**

Yet none, or few, are aware of it...which is a shame! Because grasping this would speed up your evolution and your understanding of your own human race if you could just, for a moment at least, consider the following facts:

• You have **not** come to Earth because an egg and a sperm met, nor has that created your complex personality!

• Nor is it because a Being from elsewhere, whether a god or a 'Martian', or other ET, has decided to make you be there!

14. Why are you on Earth, then?

You arrived here because you chose to be here, for whatever reasons you picked! This is indeed a very complex and 'debate-creating' issue, but we can only tell you **this is why you are on Earth**.You have not been sent, you were not obliged! **You have always had Free Will** to do so!

15. When did you decide?

If it was not within the sperm and egg mixture then it's obvious it must have been BEFORE! If/since it was before, then **you must have been a thinking Being**, **but without a flesh body.** You existed as a thinking Being BEFORE you were born on Earth, **before the conception of the physical body you now inhabit**. And that is the conclusion we would like you to come to.

You have chosen to experience life on Earth as an experiment! How can you do that? In whatever ways this current life presents itself, so that you could learn or do certain things. Why? **To suit your own personal development as a Being of Thought Power.** You are a Being who is in charge of its present and its future, by activating your Mind Power and your Energy centres, built in your own Self.

16. Your Real Self is a Being of Energy!

This Self is beyond the material, Earthly flesh body.
This Self is a Being that cannot die, since it is an Energy Being!

39

Energy never dies or disappears. It can only change form or intensity, but never vanishes! So, we have got an Energy Being:
- who can think for himself
- has choice and free will
- and who decides to go on Earth for a while, to experience life there, for various reasons only known to himself.

17. Where does 'he' come from?

He comes from the invisible world of Energy, which pervades everywhere and everything. This invisible world is what you may call the 'Spirit World', or heaven, or various similar labels. But the basic truth is: **Any Being** who materialises in the physical world of the Earth has 'his' **starting point in that world of Light and Mind Power.**

18. No one is 'just a flesh Being'!

'He' takes with him, to Earth, the **same powers** he had and has (as an 'Energy Being') in that world of Mind. But he has the added challenge to use them **to manipulate the flesh body** of **his** choice. "Why 'a body of his choice'?" We hear you say. Because there is no reason for going in a vehicle of flesh designed by someone else!

19. Who and what created the flesh body?

Each Being on Earth, owner of his physical body, designed it as a vehicle to navigate his way and live in the physical world. As an Energy Being he constantly uses the built-in Creative Power of his own Mind. Therefore the **thoughts of each Being on Earth have designed** and created his own physical vehicle in the first place!

"What?! Created his own flesh body?!", you may say. Well, yes! **Beings of Light are made of 'Mind power'.**

This automatically means Creative Power and the best designer is the one who will be using his own tools to create for himself a means of transport to drive him around his Earthly life! A vehicle to survive the ups and downs and most of all **to reflect the way he wants to project himself** physically, visibly.

Deep within each of you, driving the flesh body, is the Light from the Being you really are. The true 'You'. The original You. Yet it may not always be visible to your human eyes That's where you come from. The idea, the thought power of your own Self, your Higher Self, your own Being of Light transformed, or **disguised, as a Human Being** in a flesh body!

20. Your flesh body cannot last forever but YOU can & do!

Your disguise as a human body can then be discarded, like a garment, when (for whatever reasons and at whatever age you choose) you, the Real Being of Mind and Light, leave it, 'fly out' of it, to return to the eternal peace and freedom of the world of Light and Mind.

That's **all it takes to get out of it - a thought**! The thought: "I don't want to stay any longer in that vehicle".

Your Higher Self knows it is best to go in the long run and on the grand scale of eternity, for your own deeply set reasons. Even if it means others left on Earth may be sad that you will no longer be visible to them. Yet **YOU will still exist as an invisible Being!** Though many people sensitive enough to the vibrations of your Energy Being should be able to sense or see you. And you will eventually be able to meet up again with all those you care for, who were left behind temporarily - as well as those you loved who had 'passed over' before you, yet are still alive and will 'receive' you joyfully when you arrive! Of course!

****

41

Chapter 5

ONE UNIVERSAL MIND: AKASHIC RECORDS & UNIVERSAL 'FACTS BOX'

ACCESS TO UNIVERSAL KNOWLEDGE

We (who speak to you) know the true facts about the Creation of your physical world, **from the knowledge stored in the eternal Universal Mind,** which is a kind of memory stored at high levels - like a big safe that one can access when required, as long as it is for good use - not bad.

When accessed, it feels like Light pours over us with facts becoming transparently clear and understandable to everyone who is searching.

That is why I love to go delving into it when I have my quiet moments. I know I can reach those facts if I am in deep concentration - opening myself and my whole Being to better comprehension of the Reality of things - of everything! It can only be done with a very quiet Mind and Soul, in search of Truth and increased Knowledge. Some people also refer to this 'Facts Box' as 'the Akashic Records'.

ONE MIND FORCE: CREATIVE POWER

The origin of the Universal Mind cannot be defined because no Time exists, so Time is 'Now all the time'. The Mind **is**. The Mind will be.

This 'original' Power of Mind did not have a beginning, since it was already there. Moreover, this eternal Power of Creative Force that is called 'Mind' by Humans is **not** a personality.

(NOTE - Some readers may feel this chapter is hard to grasp. Please do not get put off! Simply read it through and

move on to the next ones, in order. You will discover fascinating new topics as you go along. Thank you. BR).

We could try to draw the plan of creation as a kind of eternal 'mass', not solid and not limited by edges or anything; it is ever growing and glowing with powerful Force. It is not a solid ball or blob, it is **a throbbing and shimmering 'mass' of intense inner activity made by the Creative Mind-Power** which it actually is...

If you sense it as a 'mass', you'll feel more what it had as its contents and consistency. This mass is throbbing with 'actualisation in the process of being achieved but has not given birth yet', if you see what we mean!

From its inner core, the Power pours out as a huge mass of effervescent sparkles of Creativity. It **sends 'shoots' out of itself** and around itself. Each spark in it is the start of something new!

That boundless mass has **immense potential within** and that potential is raring to go and make itself actualised into some kind of more 'solid' reality, so to speak, but it won't necessarily be 'solid' as you think of it.

That 'mass' of Power has always been in existence. We cannot see how Humans can imagine it could be created by anything or anyone since **this mass is THE Source of all creation**!

ONE MIND: SOURCE OF ALL MINDS/'SPIRITS'

All other Minds stem from that one Mind. So everything everywhere and every Being is 'One', **on the Universal scale!**

So what exists, has existed, will exist and does not exist (probabilities), is ONE 'Centre Point'! That Centre Point is the Mind which some Humans may call 'God', but **it is NOT a personality!** It has the **power of creating more Energy** all the time and can also retain the knowledge and memory of what is to be and what has been - because there is no 'Time', as such. So, since all is 'now' in the Now, then the 'Mind Box' is also the 'Mind Power', which creates new things and yet remembers what is in existence!

All other Minds are **what you call 'Spirits' and are transformed into Beings of flesh - or into other Matter!** But really, nothing exists separately: The multitude of shapes in all the worlds and universes are all in only ONE 'MIND'. So the **'Universal Mind' is a memory store and a creative power.**

For example, when the decision to create the Earth was taken then ' The Mind Mass' spurted out various shoots which were Thoughts in 'steps', coming out of creative Minds/'Spirit Beings' - Thoughts which 'took shape', we could say, to multiply their own thoughts of creation.

A Mind is never still, is it?! A Mind constantly creates around itself. As explained before, myriads of other Thoughts shoot out of it constantly, which are Minds too.

Mind and Thought are the same in a way, as **Mind creates Thoughts which are living Minds of their own**, as they create their own creation too. An amazing circle of mind-boggling happenings! Yet true.

In a way there is not really 'one' SINGLE Mind, because **it encompasses All That Will Ever Be and Has Ever Been!**

Your Mind and mine are part of that eternal Mind. We all create things and events because we are all from the same Source. That Power resides in everything and everyone it may help to create. The Force is and has always been latent, like a sea of Mind Power or a lake. Out of this 'lake' spring up and sprout (like little buds) the Thoughts of having new types of 'creatures', of Being, of Souls to make it more exciting. To have a goal, a creative goal that is useful, as all goals have to be useful, have an aim.

Everything is an experiment. Everything is Creation and Creativity. Everything is exciting and is an attempt at discovering and improving on the discovering, i.e. attempts to progress. **Progress is Creativity made better.** If progress in one direction leads to making things worse in another, then it is a failure in that direction.

SUMMARY OF CONCEPTS

We know it is very hard for Humans to grasp those points. We can try and sum this up, if you want:

- Knowledge of the true facts about the creation of the physical world is stored in the eternal Universal Mind.
- There is no 'Time' **so Mind has always existed. It just** IS.
- That Universal and Eternal Mind **is a creative power.**
- It constantly creates more Energy all the time.
- It retains memory of what is to be, or what has been.
- But it is not a single Being!
- Yet there is not really 'one SINGLE Mind', because it encompasses All That Will Ever Be and Has Ever Been.
- We all create things and events as we are all from the same Source.
- All Minds are what you call 'Spirits' and can be transformed into Beings of flesh, or other Matter!
- Everything is Creation and an experiment in Creativity.
- Creativity is used to improve on the discovering: **That** is Progress!

****

Chapter 6

NO BIG BANG

BR- Can you comment on the 'Big Bang Test' in Geneva?

You want to know about the (physically non-existent as such) 'Big Bang', as they call it? We are aware of experiments on that subject. But it is important to realise that no one will ever manage to reproduce such a **non-existent event** because we ourselves did not produce it in the first place, when we, of this World, had to work on the creation of many a 'Universe' (you could call it) or more precisely, many a place of physical appearance, but all of different appearances!

If there had been a/one Big Bang, there would have been 'someone' creating these two 'balls' or forces banging each other.

BR- Couldn't it be Energy exploding and expanding?

Energy has to come from somewhere. That somewhere **existed already** before anyway and the creation of those 'balls or energies exploding in mid-air' is not going to give either evidence or proof of the so-called 'Original Creation'!

The SOURCE IS NOT A VOID

Matter you are made of on Earth is a very selected array of vibrations, which all have their place, so that the results are correct and well-balanced to produce bodies of various sorts. But the Life-giving Energy comes from the Source, the Spark of Life which we all have in us and which is in this World of Light. It bathes everything else everywhere, it must be remembered! The Spark of Life, for anything to be 'alive', has to be of such a degree of intensity that no one could possibly imagine it, or grasp what it is and how it operates, because it is not functioning with terrestrial or man-made means. **It is not a visible way of giving Life, it is a 'self-combustion' way of giving Life!**

INTENSE UNDERLYING POWER

Self-combustion implies **power within oneself**, to produce enough Energy and force to ignite the inner fire, to create the Energy necessary for the next step. No one could understand that, as you do not have it on your Earth! But we could say this: Imagine a non-existing candle suddenly appearing in all its splendour - you would think it is a 'miracle', wouldn't you?! Yet if that candle turned out be the reflection of another candle, which itself was more real, because it was solid to the touch, you'd wonder how it happened! Well, this is what we are trying to explain.

There is a current of mighty 'electrical Power' constantly underlying every single thing (we say 'electrical', only to simplify things to the extreme! It's not the right word) all over the 'Universal Web of Nothing' at the 'origin'.

We have, therefore, a gigantic, infinite web of 'electrical' Power, not visible, not used yet, but very, very potent, which could ignite anything touching it because it **would explode at the slightest vibration.**

If that Power was made to react to another such 'electrical' vibration of possibly a slightly different kind, then the reaction between the two would be gigantic (or even 'ginormous', as you like to say) and the results would be unpredictable or possibly predictable in some direction, depending on what is known.

That's what the 'problem' is - a Creation of intensity impossible to fathom out and producing even greater intensity! When these waves of forceful concentration gather at a pace no one can keep up with in order to measure them, they will create waves of Energy 'all over the place'. These waves will bounce against others and each other and create even more waves of similar or newly-formed Energy! That is what we are trying to make you understand!

ENERGY FIELD ALWAYS EXISTED

Those Energy bands and fractions and particles, as they bash each other and create little ones which become bigger, have been imagined as one single Big Bang! But the truth is **those Energies already existed before existing as 'solid'**, so who or what created them? They came from the **unified Thought Power** of those Beings wanting to create Physical Matter! Here, wanting creates! Wanting on Earth should create too, but do you always see it as such? It's another question!

ENERGY HAS A GOAL

Perhaps, what you call Energy is not what we call Energy? We use that word because it is a word you would understand in your vocabulary.

We have a Field of Power and inner strength from 'Thought' which is the fundamental basis of all that exists, eternally exists! Nothing has started it. There has ALWAYS been THOUGHT. Why? Because it is so! **Why** should there have been a 'beginning' to it?' is a good question! We do not see why.

There has always, eternally been and will be THOUGHT POWER! That is a massively **powerful blend of all possible vibrations** one could imagine and beyond! That Power is what we call 'Energy'. **The vibrating and pulsating flow of intention and sensing a direction, which has a purpose in the end,** as all things have a purpose. Nothing exists that does not ultimately have a small or large purpose! This is, therefore, what Energy is in our eyes.

The flow of Power has many variations of colours which you know are frequencies of vibrations of different

48

kinds. We know we have difficulty using your human words to explain all that because **we do not see things with words, we sense all happenings** and they do not have such labels.

So if you can be patient and try to see what we are trying to express, it would be very good for us and for you.

There is just Truth in what we say, as you know. All is said from the deep inner desire to make you understand what is difficult to express and very difficult to understand, as we are both standing at opposite ends of a wide, multi-dimensional spectrum of vision of what constantly happens... but also constantly changes, shifts and blends for more Creativity to take place!

WHAT IS A THOUGHT?

A Thought is a piece of Energy made by a thinking Mind. A thinking Mind is a self-creating Energy Force. Self-creating can mean creating by itself, without anyone else's help. And Self creating may also mean creating itself.

So there is this 'double-sided word', for creating itself more and more every 'time'. It has an urge expanding outwards and also creating outwards expansions and variations (like waves bashing each other and creating other little or big waves, some half-broken, others long rolls of water). Therefore, we have this simplified picture of two pointers --< which means: A same thing can do two things at the same time.

That is what that 'Sea of Mind', that eternally lasting and existing major Force does: it exists, has always existed and is at the same time a source of Energy, constantly changing and multiplying itself. That means the build-up is phenomenal and not describable. As the Thoughts produced themselves, they reproduced and 'fathered' more variations, commutations and permutations. The tremendous range widened, broadened, spread and intensified. The 'original' Thought (if ever there was one!) had long lost its 'original' shape or pattern (if we

49

could use such meaningless words, in such a complex and complicated explanation - but weak in a way!).

We cannot easily find words which you would have in your head, to be able to explain the nearly unexplainable to a Human Being!

As it cannot be seen or touched, it is not within the senses of an Earthly person and even mathematicians or other scientists would find it difficult to convey what is in fact a non-explainable subject, unless you have experienced it from this end - **our** end!

So, to come back to your query: Any Big Bang?

CREATION NOT FROM BIG BANG

The 'Big Bang' talked about by so many scientists has nothing to do with the real Creation of this physical world you are in!

You are **not** the residue of 'big banged' particles osmosing with others or exploding into others to create the minerals forming Matter from an amoeba to a donkey! No! You are not that.

You are the results of thought-out processes which were first worked out 'mentally' here, in our World of Mind and Light, then they were put to the test by creating them both in our world and in the physical world which (it had been decided) was to be created for a very interesting and intriguing experiment!

But **the source of those Thoughts came from Beings already in existence before** the particular creation of these waves of Energy, which will result in sparks of Life being 'breathed into' **any** living Being, from a tiny microscopic alga or moss to an amoeba to any other Beings!

Those (creative) Beings have always existed, as there is no death in the World of Light and Energy! All changes, but it might not change as you may expect it!

50

So why worry about so far back in so-called 'Time', since you cannot, not one of you, grasp the enormity of the process?

To have **Beings who have always existed as Light and Thoughts of a magnitude no one can grasp** in this puny world of material activities is beyond any Human comprehension!

BR- So there was simply One Thought Power at the 'origin'?

That idea has already been explained many a time, hasn't it?! **One underlying Energy field and vibrations of unimaginable magnitude is the only answer to Reality!**

If some people want to call it a 'god', or a 'giant', or a 'dwarf', or any other name, that is their preogative and own ideas. But this has **not** been and is not 'A Being', as such, as you would call or think of a Being, whether powerful or not! It has to be comprehended that the only One Mighty Force is the Universal Power (i.e. all over). **That Power has Life within itself.** That means **as it intensifies itself, it will shoot out creative Thoughts!**

****

51

Chapter 7

MINDS CREATE UNIVERSES

BR- I saw a TV programme on Professor Stephen Hawkings' search for the 'Origins of the Universe'. It seemed to hit a wall, concluding: "Matter just appeared"! Can you comment on this please?

The laws of Physics in your world are totally different from the laws of Physics in our world. We cannot use words that you Humans use because they would mean nothing to us! We can only explain as best we can, to make you understand fundamental facts.

NO PHYSICAL 'START'

The 'origin' of the physical Universe was NOT a 'Big Bang'. Why? Because **where would all that 'exploding Matter' come from** then?! Whatever was and is created, wherever, all that has to do with the **Power of myriads of Minds** (in our world), who **joined together, with the intent to create something.**

Please keep an open mind and read our explanations over the following chapters instead of rejecting this outright! It is a complex subject to try to explain between the two worlds, reaching you over the differences in points of view and in conception and understanding.

NOT JUST ONE UNIVERSE

The Universe you all 'know of', or are more or less aware of, is not the only one that exists! It's only one of many, many 'millions' of such possibilities. So we have a job trying to put across such little details as well as big ones.

We can underline the fact that since **everything that is**

created comes from Mind Thought Power, it is not a visible, tangible thing. What you see at your end is an end result, a physical manifestation, eventually, but you forget that what happened 'first' is and was not visible or tangible!

A spark of Thought is **not** tangible. It is Energy indeed but where did that Energy flash come from?! It will NOT be found in your realm of the physical, for one good reason:
No physical Being or Force created the physical world!

It has been and is being created from the accumulation of powerful creative Thoughts, of Ideas, of 'Emotions', coming from many, many 'billions' of Minds, who have always had an interest in creating 'things'- in creating, full stop! That's what **Creation is about: The joy of Creativity**, action nonstop, action from the moment a Thought is sent out, as it will never stop!

No one is ever able to stop a Thought in its tracks once it has set off, because the Power of its momentum cannot be turned off. That Power can only possibly be directed one way or the other, but it cannot be switched off... and that's something very difficult for Humans to comprehend.

CREATION: A BUILT-IN URGE

What is Creation? Why was there, and is there, a Creation of things around you, as you are now? All that has to do with **the Will and the Urge, within anything and everything**, to appear in a physical manifestation! It is the physical appearance of those who want and wanted to be there, as explained before. It is to be found in every little speck of anything visible, or even invisible, to you on your Earth and around the physical Universe as you know it.

The physical Universe is **only one** manifestation of many possibilities, in the flesh or in the other ways to make oneself visible or tangible, or 'real' as you call it, in the physical world. But it is NOT the only way!

There are as many other ways and 'universes' and creations, as there are ideas popping out of Creative Minds! That should say a lot, shouldn't it?

So the best answer to your question is: To exist physically (i.e. to come into what you call 'existence') it has to come **from outside** that physical state. It cannot come from within, otherwise you could not find the so-called 'starting point' you all look for!

You'll have to accept that the physical Universe surrounding you all has been and is being **created by Beings beyond the realm of the physical,** touchable world you know. It had to be so! Otherwise how could it have come into being?!

ROOT: A CREATIVE URGE & THOUGHT

The **'starting point'** of the Creation was (so to speak) one single 'idea', which was an Urge. That 'Thought' was something like: "What can we do to make things different? What else could be invented?"

You see, we can't even find the right words to put across a fleeting Thought which had probably germinated in several 'Minds'. But it does **not** mean that 'one Mind' is 'The Grand Creator' of all Universes, as many want to see it!

It came from many Minds in a way, let's say, like in a kind of 'conversation' possibly, an exchange of ideas, to try to make you understand that it is not so much the single Thought of one individual but the resulting Thoughts out of a mix of many Thoughts and ideas.

Some took shape and other Thoughts followed and then more Thoughts from intelligent active Minds led to more ideas and so on. There is and was NOT just one Being's Mind, 'sitting on a throne' activating all this!

MIND: PURE FUNDAMENTAL CREATIVE ENERGY

A Mind has no boundary, no limitations, no time set within or without. A Mind has Energy, pure unadulterated Energy. That means it **is** vibrations. This is why we have difficulties in explaining this at times.

So, a Mind has a tremendous Power and **THAT is what started the world you know of**. Just that Mind Power. Not a physical explosion. Not a god sitting on a throne.

It is a Mind Thought Power constantly and eternally renewable, because it is never exhaustible. It has to be an eternal Power to have the 'strength' to withstand constant shifting and changes, yet to be constantly moving forward

A Mind does not stop 'thinking, a Mind is an engine forever 'on'. It has no need for fuel of any kind; it has its own built-in fuel! THAT is what you all need to understand.

A Mind has what it needs and it creates what it wants and even what it may not want, because the moment it thinks, the thought itself is on its way to be created!

There is nothing visible, physical and tangible. It has to be grasped and pondered about and accepted as an eye opener; a way to comprehend things previously not understood for centuries because you all tried to perceive what you could not see.

How can you understand with mathematical equations or drawings what you cannot even conceive as an invisible Thought?!

You all need to apprehend that the Mind Power constantly creating and re-creating that world of yours (and **many others** going on!) has no starting point itself; it is **an Eternal Power which resides, at different degrees of intensity, in everything created by that 'eternal' Mind Power, which is not a personality!**

YOUR THOUGHT ENERGY ANSWERS YOUR 'PRAYERS'

You cannot talk or pray to that eternal Power, forever existing! You can 'pray' and talk if you wish, but you will not make that Fundamental Energy change something from 'its own will'! It will be **your creative Energy from your Thoughts which will possibly activate** anything towards an alteration of circumstances or other wishes!

You all need to understand that the biblical or other religious ideas of a 'man sitting on a throne' in so-called 'heaven' and ruling the Universe, was the only way those who had understood (or possibly partly understood) the Truth could put it across to the mass of people who would not grasp these ungraspable concepts!

As we are Beings from that World of Thought and Mind, we have difficulties in explaining to you in the physical world, ideas which are often beyond your understanding, scope or grasp! It is very difficult, but it is necessary to say: Think again! You cannot keep banging your head against walls of miscomprehension, which you'll never break down, because you **Humans look for a physical thing**, a physical source. Even if it is infinitesimal, it is still physical!

Yet the 'source' so to speak (if you have to have one!), is not that at all!

Recap: As explained before, the start of the physical Universe around the newly called 'Earth' was **an idea,** an Urge built up into **many** ideas. Ideas are Thoughts, remember.

HOW ATOMS WERE CREATED

Thoughts are Energy beams of very great intensity and range of action. So, Thoughts accumulated as other Minds joined in the 'new idea' or ideas. They used their immense knowledge of vibrations at fantastic speeds and range and other 'physics factors' (let's call them).

That's how the resulting atoms used to create Matter were formed... 'Matter' as you Humans know it and see it somehow!

The physical world can only do so much in any direction. So, Matter has its limitations too! **The physical world is not as powerful as the Mind world.** Because the Mind world can constantly alter itself, at any 'split second' (as you'd call it) because Mind Power has no limitations whatsoever!

That is what Creation is all about: Mind Power has no limits; it can create what it wants, thinks and tries. It only has to **put INTENSITY into it to bring it to existence**, and that's the difference between the physical results which are Matter.

We can try to explain more, but it will never be in the same way as your physicists try to solve their equations, or even their discoveries, as they begin to probe more into the gigantic or the tiny, minuscule aspects of what you all see as 'Matter' - or even Energy forming Matter.

There will eventually be a point where you will all have to accept that the 'Invisible' (to your eyes and instruments) has created what you are looking for and that Invisible 'resides' in the World of Light, the World of Mind! Not 'Light' in the same way as you see light on Earth, as that is limited too!

The Real Light we are talking about is **the Light created by positive Thoughts, positive Minds.**

When Minds are positive, they create beautiful Energy, which is brilliant and therefore creates bright positive results.

Creating the physical world has to do with MIND POWER, not just a dot or a blob of Matter, or even 'Energy', which most of you assume is physical somehow.

To start from 'nowhere', it cannot be physical! It has to come from the world of Eternal Mind Power.

TIPS FOR PHYSICISTS

How can physicists be helped to understand, you will ask? Well, it is fairly simple, as well as very difficult!

Simple, if they want to open their Minds to the fact that there **is** something beyond the visible, or even minutely visible, or invisible to their machines.

Simple, if they want to accept there is something beyond what can be repeated by their equations and all that kind of thinking! Then they will obtain some kind of understanding that **what they have thought to be the 'truth' was not always right.** If they want to pursue down that avenue, they may reach other conclusions and gain more comprehension of the reality of events in the physical world.

It has not been sufficient for some to talk of a 'god' doing it, as that was not provable and was too unreal and unmanly, even, to accept that.

It was not sufficient either to say such and such explosion of Matter created what you have now, because where did that Matter come from?

When they delve deeper into the infinitely small and discover atoms and subatomic activity, they are still dealing with some physical things, even though a lot of it is reaching the level of Energy. But will they ever accept that Energy as such has always existed? And will they accept that the Mind Energy is what created things? And will they **search for the Source of that Mind Energy,** which is not really calculable or seen with the strongest of microscopes?

All this boils down to **understanding that there is a World of Mind** - pure, unequivocal Mind. And that World is where we, who speak to you, 'reside'.

We are **not** your Mind; you *(BR)* would not have any of that knowledge anyway; you were not brought up to think that way! We are totally separate and independent entities, Beings of Light and Mind Power, who have endeavoured and are

58

trying to explain to you all, especially those who are not scientifically minded, that **the world is not what you've been told it is!**

The Earth has been designed as a place to try a few experiments, by those who created it and by those who inhabit it. It is so simple when you think of it, but it has to be seen from the correct perspective.

That is what has been missing for such a long time - that we had to come through and try to put across our message.

WHY ARE YOU ON EARTH?

You have a reason for being on the physical Earth, because you have **chosen** to be there, after coming first from our World of Light and Mind! **You are the result of your own Mind experiment,** if only you could understand it better! You and all Humans could not exist on Earth in a flesh body without first having **visualised it, planned it and wanted it**, as it is for your own particular purpose.

The laws of the physical Universe are difficult to understand for the average Human, so imagine how much more complicated it would be to try to explain the laws of our World of Mind! It is not really possible. The nearest we could get to it would be to say: You have a big bubble of air which has limits around your Earth, yet you don't feel it or see it until you get there with your machines. You'd get to know, for example, there is no more oxygen, after so far out. But you could not see it as a limit, a boundary.

This is the same with the 'lines' between this world and the Universe. You cannot expect to see everything in a physical way because **not everything is physical**, that's the point!

If it was all physical then there would be no problem explaining it; you'd only have to measure it and calculate distances and have photos of it etc. This is different because the substances we are talking of and dealing with are not tangible or measurable in the same way. This is where Understanding has to come in! If you don't understand that there is a World of Mind which can create and **can WILL any kind of Matter into desired shapes** then you'll never be able to grasp what it is all about!

This is why the invention of a 'god' was the nearest Mankind could get to, because Humans cannot comprehend anything not physical.

Yet you do understand about emotions and feelings, so maybe you should go down that line of explanation? In the same way as Thoughts, emotions and feelings have an influence on your flesh body (if you have understood that, of course), then the resulting influence of Mind over Matter should be more obvious and acceptable.

ETERNAL & ENDLESS MIND FIELD

Therefore, accept **there is and has always been a gigantic and endless 'ocean' of Mind vibrations**. What has always existed is that 'sea'/space/expanse of vibrations, which are Mind/mental vibrations, always there and channelled into myriads of results, which will never stop existing or being created. This is the wonder of Creation.

We do not agree with the word 'god' because it goes against the fact there is **not one** single starting point as a 'personality', no matter how you describe it/him/her.

It is important not to limit your vision and under-standing in such a way. **The moment you narrow it down to one personality, you create boundaries and therefore rules!** As for those who do not believe in a 'personality', that is the atheist and scientific hard core, then they are on the right track, but they do not comprehend it has to be from a Mind World. Not from one Mind but from a mental sea of **vibrations which have the power of creating what is 'thought'!**

These are your Human words. There are no real words for us, you see. We cannot always explain everything in words because they have limitations. The nearest to make you understand is: An 'ocean', an environment, a 'space' of **mighty powerful vibrations, of intangible existence, has the power to make things happen, come into existence**.

How did Spirit/Mind Beings come to exist? Permeating everything, seeping into the basis for everything the Mind World (or 'Spirit World' if you prefer) is in and into, everything. So the 'original' (not right word!) conscious Mind Beings **that have always been in existence** are 'shapes' (if you like, but wrong word!) creating themselves out of the **intensity of Thought** in various 'places' (wrong word!) or levels of vibrations (still not quite the right word!).

As we said before: **Mind self-reproducing. Urge 'to be'**, to become, to exist, actualising themselves. A Mind is the wrong word. A Mind is not *'a'* mind, it is a Force Power which permeates through every conceivable and unconceivable Being and thing, to use your word. If there was **one** Mind, that would limit its power.

Mind, as 'spiritual existence of vibrations', is a pervading state which has always existed and cannot be 'split' into categories or 'boxes' or bodies. That 'state' is a powerful, eternally creative state. It is on the move, on the go constantly, because it has the impetus to do so, which has always existed and therefore cannot be stopped either!

That state creates and recreates itself in various, unbelievable and unconceivable (to you) ways! The millions of billions of myriads of achievements can be consolidated in putting more effort and **'intensity of creative desire'** into each, if wished.

So, the Mind State, or **the State of Existence called Mind** on the great scale of real Existence, is what needs to be understood, grasped, guessed at and comprehended.

It is no good trying to compartment things, Beings, states, because this Mind State is through and into and the cause of every possible thing and other states and vibrational levels and so on! We cannot do more than this to help you all grasp what we are talking about.

As long as no one wants to accept that Mind-State, there will NOT be any positive, successful or correct results in your search, you Humans. The moment **you grasp and accept that there is this pervading, underlying 'state of existence'**, you will start to understand.

MIND GRAVITY

That Creative Force - **'Mind'- has Gravity within itself,** so to speak, because as it creates one thing or other, it has to shift its intensity from one to the other.

The **intensity differential** will create some waves of various 'electronic' (and other such human words) manifestations evidential to your measurements. That perception of your world is one aspect which **you call Gravity.** It has no word in ours, because we do not see or sense 'Gravity'. We know it exists simply because it is a resulting force from other forces and inclinations.

What happens when one 'creation' spreads its effects on others around it is what we call 'Cause and Effect'. It is part of **putting into 'existence' what is 'thought' first.** Thought either by individual Beings of Mind, or by the Mind Force reaction to its own Self and its built-in Urge. Its own creative power, which is **a constant Urge for creation,** has these effects on and on and on! It is not stoppable and why want to stop it? It is the 'fun' and wonder of Creativity and Creation!

As we talk to you, the simple words we use are to try to make your brain and own Mind understand and convey to the rest of the world what is in existence in the 'Invisible-to-the-instruments' side of what Reality **is.**

62

WHAT IS REALITY?

Reality is the fact that all vibrations of all possible kinds are relentlessly (and have been and will constantly be) **created as a surge and Urge of Creativity, from the 'ocean' of Mind,** the State-Mind or the Mind-State, whichever words you want to use as a mental picture of whatever we are trying to put across.

It is a non-visible, 'non word-able' state, a power of an unimaginable magnitude, which has its effects continuously changing and multiplying and shooting off in myriads of other states of existence! There is no need to want to understand the minute details of each of these, as they are far beyond the scope of anyone's Mind or intelligence or brain absorption.

YOU CREATE!

What matters is that you all grasp that **you all have Mind Power within your Self,** your own latent and basic Being, your own Real Self. Your Real Self is not the flesh body you see, as that is only a garment of the Self.

Grasp there is a wider, much wider concept to the basis of Creation of **any** kind! Any kind! That is all we can try to say now.

We think we have exhausted the power of your words… and if we tried to use more 'scientific' words, as you call them, they would be of no avail, as scientists have done well (some of them) but still not grasped what we are trying to put across.

So why use words which would have no meaning in either of our worlds, yours or ours.

You have what you need now to transmit that to the population of the Earth which wishes to try to understand beyond the false and distorted, or limited, or misconstrued, concepts which some Humans have tried to impose on the rest of you over the centuries and millennia!

63

The Truth is simpler in a way, once you have all understood what has been displayed, explained and sketched in the words above.

Good luck with your inner search. That is where you'll have the inner conviction in the end! Because that is where **we** reach you better to make you all understand. We can thus bypass the brain and the words you know or don't know and make your Soul and Spirit grasp what your Mind will comprehend.

****

Chapter 8

GOD, DEVIL & HELL?

What Mankind of all ages has been calling 'God', or even many gods of all kinds, simply shows that **Humans were aware they 'came from elsewhere' originally.** If they had not known that within themselves, no doubt they would never have invented such an extraordinary idea of some Invisible single Being existing forever and creating them, would they!? Who would have thought of that?! So they felt within, some remote, vague, or else very clear at times, knowledge that **their existence rested on the existence of some 'Superior Force'** beyond themselves as physical Beings. But because over aeons they lost the link, or forgot it, that fact got distorted and rearranged.

Mankind should be ashamed to have possibly (some people have) believed in some 'superior power', gods, or other, and still not done more good than harm! Why should Men complain when one tells them their 'god' has no origin outside themselves? Why couldn't they accept that what has usually been believed, in various forms and different names for aeons, is in fact **a simplified 'image'** and symbol **of what they have within,** if only they looked better? What you think of as a separate 'God Almighty' is only **the very wonderful Creative Force you are made of.** Why couldn't people be delighted to think they have the Creative Power and the Caring and Compassion of that' god' within themselves?

What you are made of is **pure spiritual Light**, within a flesh body. A body which you, with the help of others, have created for an Experiment, as we said before, for the sake of expanding your knowledge of the use of Matter, for the sake of discovering new avenues in the world of Creation and Creativity.

Life could NOT have existed if there was not that Spiritual Spark to give life to everything that exists.

Life is a Spark of Spirit. Life is **the Light of Spirit,** to be more exact.

Life has always existed. What is Life?

The fact that someone or **something exists in a sustainable way and can survive in its surroundings,** not just for a second - for longer! **Life has different aspects elsewhere**. But Life you know and I have known is the one on Earth. So let's talk of this one for now.

Life had to have its origins beyond the Earth's shape, because it had to provide the stimulus to get everything going. If there had not been any spark from outside your physical world, how could it have got started? That's how things began, as explained before. All **thought out by Beings outside the physical environment.** But the Life Force of these 'Spirits' had always existed and that's what Mankind finds difficult to understand.

The Life Force (which gave and gives Life) is the Intelligence, the Creativity, which offers everything it created a direction, a shape, the millions of 'bits and pieces' which forms them. That hugely powerful Inner Creative Force is what **has always existed** and you could not find this easy to grasp. Once you understand this, then you'll understand that **all of you have the Power within you,** all of you have always had it and will have it forever, as **you all are this eternal Creative Power!**

MANKIND FORGOT ITS LINKS

Saying that is **not** what some people may call 'blasphemous' or insulting to a god or Creator! It can only be thought so by people who cannot open their Mind to something which they had not thought of before.

All that is asked of people on Earth is to think this: **Do you think it is wrong** of the 'Spirit World' to ask those in a flesh body **to remember their spiritual origins and to ask them to link back to this?** After all, those Spirit Teachers reside there! They know it is true!

It is not an insult to an **imaginary single Being**... who would have a lot to answer for, if it/ he /she was the only cause and reason for your existence and all the troubles you may encounter!

Why should it be 'blasphemous'? It may only be considered so by those who want to go back to old tales! Tales that had been created and **drilled into people** by leaders who were trying to put across deep concepts which the folks they dealt with could not have grasped- being totally ignorant of and ignoring their spiritual heritage and origins. That's because Mankind had sunk to such depravity or selfishness that the Light within them was nearly extinguished.

LEADERS INVENTED 'GOD' SYMBOL

Those leading men had to INVENT the image and the explanation of a leading figure/'father' who would 'punish' people, or reward them, for the sake of trying to get those forlorn Souls back towards the Light. But you modern folks have seen enough, heard enough Teachers with wise words and should realise that all this is not correct.

If Men had not lost the link they had right at the beginning, they would not have to be reminded that each of them is a 'Spirit' and only a Spirit! The body has nothing to do with the creation of the Spirit as the Spirit has always existed.

You have ALL always lived in a world of Light before coming to Earth. You have always been part of a world of Light, 'going back' to times which you could not possibly figure out, because Man's Mind can't grasp so far; it's not within its power, especially having been ensconced in a Flesh body.

Only a 'Spirit' in the Spirit World can begin to comprehend that Time has not got the limits Mankind has given it.

So, if you can just begin to comprehend that you are and will always be a 'Spirit Being', you will one day understand why you are here on Earth, instead of being in our world of Light and Caring.

That's the world where understanding each other is normal, where acquiring knowledge is exciting, where creating with one's Mind is not only normal but a tool which those here want the ones on Earth and elsewhere to be reminded of. **Then** you may start to comprehend what we are talking about!

This is why Mankind is so shaken, confused, ill at ease with itself. Why doesn't it accept that it is still linked to the world it came from?

Whenever a **good deed** is done from the bottom of your heart, each one of you, you do it because **you have let your Real Self come through.** You've let what you call the 'god side' of you come through.

Of course, we could carry on letting you think there is a big god, a Jehovah, or Allah, or whatever, sitting on a throne, ready to 'bash you' on the head if you do wrong. But why do that in these days of modern technology and inventions, when you have learnt to do so much out of Matter?! You have used your Inner Knowledge, your intuition and your inspiration, to create modern machines, many of which have been good for Humanity, have helped or improved Men's lives, so not all is bad of course!

Therefore, it would be **wiser to try to think with new, updated information instead of being stuck in the rut of distorted 'facts' and theories and being manipulated by others who are against your Free Will.**

SCIENCE IS LIMITED

Of course, at the other end of the spectrum, you have some individuals who work to improve, or so they think, Mankind's life on Earth and they try hard. They have 'Science' on their side, that's all they know. They have strong beliefs and they are right to try and test what they do.

Unfortunately, you can only test physical things with physical things. You **cannot really test spiritual things with physical things**, because that involves totally different levels of existences and vibrations. It will take you a long time, in your terms, to find or invent and create objects able to really help you discover what the Spirit nature of Man is. So, what can be done?

Well, to start with, open the door of your Mind with the thought: 'What if there was some Truth there? What if there was something we did not know or could not prove yet?' (After all, even your cosmologists recognise there are errors of logic in their theories and calculations).

Then this attitude may, with practice, open the door wider and allow your own Spirit in (Yes, scientists of modern ages, you too are Spirits who have chosen to come into physical bodies but have forgotten where you came from!). Then the Spirit within will do the rest.

YOUR CREATIVE POWER

All of you who wish to carry on believing in 'a father figure' looking after you may do so, of course, without any harm done to you! To those who object to that 'invention', or 'image', we'll point out that indeed the real creation and **Creative Power has always resided within everything alive,** as stated before. Nothing and nobody was created by an imaginary Being. Of course, to get to details it would take a very long time to explain how everything which exists has and is a Spirit. But here are the main points:

69

Look within to find your Truth.

If you feel happy with other aspects learnt from elsewhere, that's absolutely fine because **what matters in the end is that you find your own source** and origins, you see. So the sooner you find these, the better you'll become if you need to improve, because 'the Source' (whatever you call it) consists of and is the Spirit Power, the Life Force, the Creative Force. You are not at the mercy of, or depend on, anyone. You are a Creative Being!

Combine this with the **desire** to create new things, to discover and expand your own Self and then you'll find why your Spirit within is constantly trying to expand, to create, to love."Why love?" You'll say. Because at the base of every creation there is the desire to make something beautiful, new, interesting and to look after it.

If you create something, whether a cake or a car, a toy or a child, don't you feel like looking after it? (A 'child', in fact, has created himself, being a Spirit and choosing to use the wonderful 'machinery' of the human body to form its flesh body. But this is another lengthy discussion, yet relating to what was first said earlier!) *Note: See following chapters. BR.*

So yes, Creation and Creativity is 'LOVE'; the love of the painter for his paintings, of the mother for her child, of the female animal for its babies. The love of Creation. Who would have thought, or not thought, that love and Creation were linked?! It's worth pondering upon...

All that matters in the end is that all of you, whatever so-called 'religion' you follow or rebuke, do look into the fact there is something inside you which you cannot fathom out, or touch, or cut, or analyse, but you should know you have it. Those of you who think or feel they have not got any of 'that' will have to work much harder of course, but **you will have to look for the Spirit within if you want to find balance in your physical life, bodily and mentally.**

70

Once you **acknowledge the existence of a superior Inner Side to yourself** and start trying to listen to it, THEN and only then, the world will start sparkling a little more, because you cannot hide the spark of Spirit Light once it is allowed to shine again!

Please do not deny yourself the joy of discovering within you something which has always existed since 'the beginning of eternity', which in itself is a concept difficult to grasp! Have faith in the Real You, let it shine and Life on Earth will be better for all, if you all do it.

IS THERE A DEVIL?

We could talk about '**the devil**' if you like. It is another **figment of Mankind's imagination,** just like their gods!

We cannot justify the existence of a 'nasty Being' coming from the world of Spirit, as nothing nasty comes from our world, whatever level you can think of.

If there are so-called 'nasty Beings,' it is those who have been on Earth and have not followed the pathway set out by the laws of this (our) world. They created nastiness out of their own selfishness and desire to enjoy the physical pleasures offered by the flesh senses; but there is NO one single 'nasty Being' called 'the devil'!

INVENTED & SYMBOLIC

The '**DEVIL**' is a symbol of the 'bad' side of Mankind, created by themselves by not doing what they should or could. It has been invented by those in charge of leading the crowds towards a more rightful path, but it got out of hand and they turned it to their advantage too often.

The 'devil' is the representation of Mankind falling off the right path and surrendering to the pleasures of the Earthly flesh body, instead of keeping the link between the two aspects of its dual personality, as has been discussed before.

SEEING A DEVIL? NO, IT'S A THOUGHT FORM!

Many **people believe in it as a real figure, so they may even see it**! **That** is another example of the **power of one's Mind** - showing you **what you fea**r, showing you what you want to see, showing you that you can create whatever you think about if the desire, or intense fear and other feelings inside you are strong enough to **trigger** their (visible to you) creation!

That's all that can be said: A 'devil' does **not** come to fight you or bargain for your Soul with a 'god'. This is all fable and fairy tale! It might have worked in a way at some point, to try to stir the population back to a more spiritual path, but unfortunately, as always, it has been exaggerated!

HELL: A STATE OF MIND, NOT A PLACE

When one thinks of '**hell**', as taught by the Churches, it is supposed to be a place of torment and fire and burning inside you. Yes, it is... but it is not a 'place' as such, as you know now, it is a place **within the Minds of those who have done wrong.** 'Wrong' being against the one law of Earth travel: "You shall go and travel side by side, without hurting others and with readiness to help those in need."

The 'hell' they talk **about is a state of remorse**, an inner feeling which **cannot be removed by anyone**, or be set upon you by anyone. It is how you, as a person, feel about what you as a Spirit in a flesh body have done, when you were on the Earth pathway.

If you have accidentally hurt someone, you may feel terrible guilt. That is understandable but you should be able to be healed by explanations and conclusions. However, hurting others, whether People or 'Animals', by wilfully, nastily and selfishly desiring to hurt, destroy, endanger or ruin them, will give **you** more 'hell time' than you can imagine!

It is an inner feeling of remorse if and when you eventually open your eyes to what you have done and sincerely regret it! That will be when the 'hell time' will start, so to speak, when the realisation of the terrible deeds hit you and open your eyes to **what havoc and horrors** or whatever you, yourself, all on your own, caused to others!

A last example: A man who kills because he wants something another has will rest in inner 'hell' for a long time. No one can remove it for him, no priest, no 'god', no prayer to a 'god' to remove it… until that man realises what he has done and works at somehow trying to repair the harm done.

It may not always be possible but there are ways of atoning for it, by sheer hard work of the Soul towards a more righteous and spiritual way of thinking and living.

'ALL THAT IS'

No 'devil'. No 'god'. Each Being is only one Soul who has the chance to do right or not right **if it follows its built-in Inner Guidance,** which is eternal and pure. Simple, isn't it?

Each Being is a Soul, yet all belong to the One Core Mind. **Each of you is a Soul and a Spirit with a Mind linked to all other Souls, Spirits and Minds, thus creating one mighty fireball of Creativity called 'All that Is',** if you must put a label to it somehow.

ANGELS ?

An 'Angel of Mercy' is **not** a winged Being, it is a Peace loving Being, who loves to come close to those wanting peace in their Mind. It is a Thought Power with a caring, compassionate attitude as a Being who wants to help those on Earth.

No Angels float around with wings or feathers on them! It is a **figment of Mankind's imagination**, but we find it hard

73

to make some people understand that! This has been invented by Mankind and some will actually see such 'feathered Beings' **because** that is what they want to see, or expect to see, or hope to see, or **subconsciously** would be amazed to see! Therefore, this may happen, because as you think, so it appears! **Your** Mind will have created it!

But a fish tail on an Angel might not look as nice as wings, so wings are what they see! It is not important really, it does not make that much difference! Yet it is sad to see people engrossed in their beliefs and visions, which they would fight to their death for and yet are not correct!

No Being floats around with wings here, first of all because that would make them 'matter object' - a wing is an object made of Matter (= feathers). So it is illogical to want to see them like that. **An 'Angel' has no gender, no wings, no flowing dress, no long golden hair,** or whatever! It has **nothing Human,** if ever they exist.

What is possibly perceived by some is the aura and **Energy of loving Beings,** who may **not** have ever come to Earth but who want to help those who do go there.

It is **a kind of Being who cares,** as we all do here if we are at the 'right level'. That means excluding those so 'Earthbound', for example, who can't think beyond their old Earthly activities.

If the right amount of compassion and care is felt towards others who are not here, it is quite normal to want to help them by appearing, going closer to them and to support them with one's own Energy. That is what 'Angels' are.

STATUES MEANINGLESS

Statues of marble won't do justice to the beauty of Love and Compassion emanating from these Beings who want to help or teach Mankind better ways to go back to the original plan.

Make Humans understand that no matter how many statues they make, it will not make Mankind better; it has to come from inside every man on Earth, every Being, so that the Will has found its way on the right path again. Once the **Will to do good only** is set, then the rest will follow.

No Angel, with or without wings, can change the state of the Earth or of Mankind!

****

Chapter 9

CREATION - PART 1

As we said before, the whole idea of coming to Earth had and has always been to create a place for Spirit/Energy Beings, dressed as Humans in Flesh, to **discover what their Spirit could do** to control the Earthly physical environment surrounding them. The Law of the Universe being: "You can try what you want, as long as you do not hurt others", there is a gigantic scope of experiments that can be undertaken!

FREE WILL BUT...

If all had listened to that law, there would never have been any wars or illnesses! But **the Law could not prevent People from doing wrong** for one good reason: **They all wanted Free Will**, freedom to do as they chose. And that's where things can go wrong!

Should Mankind have chosen an easier path, like being advised on how to proceed at each step, it could have avoided doing wrong things. But it could also become very bored with being told exactly what to do all the way, with no allowance for its own creativity or ingenuity! So the Law was set as is.

EARTH & HUMANS: PROTOTYPES

The Earth was not created in seven days! It had to be thought about and conceived in such a way as to provide vital lifelines to those living there, so that their bodies functioned properly to keep them alive. If it had been different, you could have had something very unlike the Earth, working in totally different ways, which **you** would not recognise!

Therefore, because it is as is, some laws had to apply. The laws of physics and chemistry to start with, to be compatible with the ones we have here too. This means its Creation was thought out over a very long 'period', aeons, as you'd call it.

BUILT-IN MIND WORLD FIRST

It firstly had to exist, all formed and 'perfect' in our Mind World! Yes! Designed and created here initially! It was actually built here, by us of this Energy World, as the replica of what was going to be projected onto the physical world.

After it was tested here, we could **send it into a World of Matter by projecting our thoughts to the Matter world, so that the emergence of the Earth took place.** So were the Beings who were to live on it! They needed to test the ground they'd go to before they actually **projected themselves** into it by means of birth. To be 'born' that way was not necessarily the best way to do it, but it caught on because it is a most imaginative and creative way to create a Being, really out of Matter. Others had eggs, or seeds, but this **Human Creation was a masterpiece of engineering at its best**, so to speak.

After all, they could have been 'born' all adult and got on with it! It was the **challenge of creating a small Being from nothing** except eggs within other flesh bodies which was considered an exciting, novel experiment!

DESIGNS & TRIALS

When the world was created, it took many **millions of Minds to put together ideas** of what could be, or should be, done! When those 'first ones' started thinking up the idea of creating a new kind of world, they had to design various ways of producing diverse energies and orchestrate a wide gamut of vibrations, so that these would react as planned and made themselves visible in a way called 'atoms' and 'Matter' on your Earth. They had to be visible, usable, interesting, accessible and useful to any Being on Earth.

An environment without the right vibrations to respond to the Beings there would be pretty useless. So it had to match what was needed, which was having such density, vibrating range and scope that the Beings could react, blend, flourish, enjoy, survive and be part of it.

As they worked out the first plans, there was a **need for trials,** as one cannot organise or create something without testing it first. So they had **mini-environments and 'mini-people' testing it.** How it happened was very interesting and exciting to do! Then, gradually, lots of other Beings also decided they'd like to take part in the new Experiment.

But in order to 'perfect' things' there had to constantly be new experiments and trials! That's why, on the whole, there have been millions and **millions of trials and discarded efforts,** or else 'improved upon' efforts. Some have been found as **'fossils'** but their origins were usually **misunderstood or 'diagnosed' wrongly** by your researchers!

MATTER IS NOT SOLID

Matter has a secret: Matter has nothing really solid within itself, yet it does appear solid. That is its secret.

Why does it look solid? Because when its vibrations are set in such a way that they vibrate at the correct rate, their combination results into a solidification of the 'atomic particles' which they are 'made of', in a way. Yet that is not one hundred percent true as they are still vibrations and particles at the same time, if you see what we are trying to say?

As you look at Matter with a microscope, you Humans see a dot here, a blob there, a 'solid' impression or so you think! But as **we** look at Matter from here, we see Matter very differently. (That Matter we talk about is your Earth Matter, as there is different 'Matter' in other worlds but not made of the same things!).

ILLUSION

An analogy: If you can imagine a plain white sheet of glass, painted white, the glass under is transparent but the paint covers that transparency. So, if you scratched that paint, you'd see the real glass underneath it, instead of thinking there is a white surface in front of you.

The glass is the equivalent of an atom identity, that is the glass is invisible to the eye when hidden by the paint but visible when you remove the paint. When **we** look at your Matter we **look through** the glass, unhindered by the 'paint'.

You people have got the 'paint' (symbol for Matter) produced by **layers of atoms vibrating at a certain frequency** which causes your eyes to see things much slower and 'thicker to your eyes', thus **giving you the impression of 'solidity' and physical Matter**. The paint is the illusion. The real thing is 'transparent', see-through, not blocking the view like paint does.

Another example is this: The antenna of a radio picks up radio waves floating about, but if there was no antenna you would not know there are radio waves flowing across the air, because you cannot see them. So why believe they exist?

You believe, in the end, because you hear the sounds of the radio. But the sounds are not solid, are they?! They are noises and noises are not 'Matter', so how come noises exist? Yet they do, because the vibrations they are made of come from all those waves carrying them, yet all these things are intangible and invisible.

So Matter has the same kind of properties. You have atoms and vortexes of Energy which roam around, at full or various speeds, to create some paths of Energy along which other 'atoms' circle or float.

When all these Energy points meet, there are some collisions at times, which means more Energy is dissipated in other directions, which in turn create more concentration of 'Matter' to your eyes! But to us it is not so, as we see between the waves and the rays: **the particles are non-existent really, because they are in fact bundles of Energy.** All this is heavy to explain in words when the general feeling is to do with energetic dynamism.

TEST TRIPS

As Mankind became created more like what you now expect to see on the Earth, the results came from **many millions of experiments** to do with trying out myriads of possibilities.

The logical way had to be a body as an easy vehicle for the Spiritual Beings to experiment with and to use to explore that new kind of world they had not been in normally before. So they needed some constant revision for practice, but also for improvement of that vehicle.

Facts and suggestions were brought back to our scientists by the first 'explorers' (whose discarded unsuitable flesh vehicles may have turned into fossils eventually!). Subsequently, more 'discussions' and **new alterations stemmed from that...** and more ideas and improved or new creations were the result, tested by the next batch of pioneers.

So you see, there was not one day of Creation, nor even seven days! There were 'aeons' during **which Mankind got itself a self-made environment projected from their Minds here** on to that 'space' where the eventually called 'Earth' took place.

It was built by adding various 'cosmic concoctions', you would say, which we think are very suitable for such an environment. Concoctions which have been made of various

80

types of Thought vibrations, also **using knowledge accumulated elsewhere** in other realms, where what you call physics and chemistry are the norm and have been for even longer than your Earth has existed!

An Earth had to exist for Beings to be there, exploring and having a physical body. But the Earth was not the important part - **the trip was what mattered.**

THOUGHTS CREATE MATTER

The idea of going there was **to manipulate a different type of vehicle!** Manipulating your Thoughts here in our World and creating things or situations was normal and achievable.

(BR- As experienced and confirmed by my mother, father, grandparents and husband Dave after they passed over, as related in the book they too dictated: 'I'm Not Dead: I'm Alive Without a Body').

But having **to use your Thought Power to create all these intricate little parts of what you call 'Matter'** so that they could come together, in order to create what was to look like something visible and solid, 'feel-able' and enjoyable, **that** was the Great Achievement, constantly renewed and constantly worked upon!

What amazes us here is that you **Humans do not know you've done it yourselves,** individually and as a large group!

Some Humans imagine an explosion creating bits of Matter that eventually produced intelligent, emotional and thinking Creatures! How wrong! Or some 'god' personality who decided to make you 'in his image', which is even more complicated because people then imagined various human-looking gods. The **fallacy** got bigger and bigger!

DESIGNING BODIES

The 'Man' one sees nowadays has been worked on for centuries and millennia. There have been many types of 'Humans' over the ages and it had to be so, because Energy Beings who wanted to come to Earth as 'People' had to find the best way to live there.

One could not produce overnight the design and creation of a body as a vehicle for the Spirit Beings wanting to be 'Humans', compared to the ones designed for Spirit Beings wanting to be 'Animals', compared to the Beings wanting to be 'Plants' and so on...

So it took a 'long while' from your Earth point of view. But it had its benefits because it allowed to find the right shape for the most suitable vehicle (if there was such a thing as 'the best') for this unusual endeavour of being a free Spirit but **in charge of a body of flesh** in the world of Matter.

We know it sounds strange anyone may want to do such a thing but seen from here it is, and was of course, an exciting venture, because the goals are different! Therefore, the challenges are various and diverse and **the results will constantly change according to the states of Mind** of the individuals designing it for themselves.

So, the creation of a 'correct, suitable body' was and still is very important, but it was **not** done the way you Humans think, or at least some Humans!

NO FISH EVOLVED INTO A HUMAN

The idea of a 'fish' finally evolving into a Human is not only far-fetched, it is laughable, we must say! (*Referring to Darwin's theory*). The laughter is on our side, because **we** have got the facts! The facts are these:

The 'Man' you know is not the shape of the 'first man' on Earth. The first Men were created as you would create a 'first vehicle' - trying one wheel, two wheels, three wheels, four wheels, trying one engine, two engines, trying this shape, that form etc. So the first bodies were **not** perfect at all (if we are to think that the present body is so-called 'perfect'!), because they had to be tested for the conditions in an Earthly environment.

'Animals" bodies were designed for and by Spirit Beings wishing to come as 'Animals'. They did not want to become 'Humans'. And vice versa.

An Earthly environment means the body has to breathe, to walk, to act as wishes, to be healthy, not to break down, to be supplied with what it needs and to receive repairs when needed.

It had to be done right, otherwise the 'Spirit Being' using that vehicle would not achieve its trip's goals and would be disenchanted and... dispirited! (Ha ha!). So it meant trying various combinations and that required testing it 'for a while', then coming back (to 'Spirit World') or trying again new things here and there. We use 'simple talk' to help you all get an overall idea, rather than the 'technical facts'.

We cannot give you very 'detailed details' for the good reason it was a 'long time ago' in your way of thinking. Moreover it is to do with Matter creation, i.e. with **creating things which you call Physical Matter, out of our way of doing things from here.** This had a lot to do with **visualising** the possible components, with the chemists in our realm playing and **mixing myriads of possibilities** and chemical elements, etc. So we can't say: "This is exactly how or what we did".

The main results were various experiments undertaken at **all** stages, to shape the possible physical creatures which would 'house' the Spiritual Beings wishing to live there for a while. The aim was to **experience the sensations of the physical senses**, compared to the sensations and emotions of our own world here.

So that means: **There was no 'fish' becoming Ape or Man!** The theories about Earth Creation all started as fairy tales and people believed them. Some did anyway!

CREATING PHYSICAL SENSES & FEELINGS

Earth life was not that easy to devise, because Earth life was going to depend on and via sensing things! Senses are made out of a body of flesh Matter which has to function in a totally different way from the way a spiritual 'body' (if any) exists and functions. So the smallest detail of Matter for creating a 'body' of senses had to be worked out too!

No small feat of engineering for the **millions** of Minds who pulled together to suggest, test and confirm or reject ideas and experiments. It was not just a question of make a body, jump into it and work out what was right or wrong and start again another time! It had to be felt, weighed and we had to examine the problems and find a solution. Each time it necessitated a very delicate operation, with infinitesimal changes at times, so that the balance and equilibrium of every part to the smallest could fit in with the rest!

NO 'FIRST' MAN

The notorious 'First man' does not and did not exist, sorry! **There was NO 'First' Man:** there was a batch of lots of little half-made, half-tested, then fully tested, then rejected, bits which could be called 'a Human' at some point or other, but that was all.

It had to be felt on Earth as well as here. It had to be **sent on Earth, felt with the physical senses also,** otherwise a Mind devising it could make mistakes, thinking it would work when it does not! And each time a **'report' was brought back to our scientists, with comments on how to improve it.**

The Beings who 'tested' those part-Human bodies were Beings from here with a Will to live on Earth (or at least

84

to try out these experiments) for the good of all those who would want to go there one 'day'.

Therefore, they'd be involved in the workings of the Flesh; **they had to project themselves towards or into that flesh Being,** to see and sense what was happening, if anything. The feelings had to come through the physical senses so that they felt 'real' to the Being of flesh. That's how a Being from here would go there and do what was needed.

When he decided **to come back** to report, he simply **turned his attention away from the flesh body** and focused back to his own real world of 'Spirit World'. He would then describe or explain to our scientists what he had experienced, but the flesh body would then collapse, since it was without its 'driving force' operating it! And that is what is called 'DYING' by Humans nowadays. **'Dying' is only a change of focus** for the Being of 'Spirit World' back to its original home, having been on a trip in the Flesh to the world of Earthly Matter. That's all it is!

So the agony of worrying about 'death' is really sad, because you don't worry when you think of a nice picture then go to another one, or you sleep at night and dream, then wake up in the morning with a different world in front of you, do you?! That's all it is.

As we were saying, the 'testers' would report to those involved with them in the modifications and recreation of the flesh. What was made? All sorts. Not only 'Humans' as you'd call them, but **all sorts of other shapes and creatures** which could live in many different places, or levels, or types of conditions. 'Levels' in the sense of **being able to use their physical senses and also their 'still spiritual' senses** at the same time.

That was a more difficult combination if the inhabitant of the body was not very good at manipulating both; it still is even now!

So, where is the 'first Man' and the 'first Being' or 'amoeba? Well, there were so MANY MUTATIONS and permutations, all at the same 'time', so to speak! Where did it start? Hard to say, really. **No one actually 'evolved from' the other one**, that's for sure! They were created together, more or less.

There was not a point of an amoeba becoming a fish becoming a bird or monkey etc.! There were lots and lots of little Beings of all types, trying out many things so it meant they overlapped, or lived at the same time, for various durations. It all depended on what they were there for and on how good their 'vehicle' was. A mutation or change from one type of Being, which slightly changed 'second time round', say, was simply because a planned and wilful improvement could be **made as the Being involved with it would have reported.** Then the change was made and the Being might have gone back to Earth in its 'new improved' vehicle, only slightly different from its 'original' one.

So who or what was first? The Earth for sure. It had to sustain its inhabitants and passengers. Then Plants and Beings came together, more or less, as the first 'travellers' were **only** coming to test the vehicle and **pop off soon after**, no doubt.

It's only once some 'models' became more stabilised as a satisfactory design that they spent 'longer time' there and lived off the Earth produce, to keep the flesh going and remain actively involved in their developing the flesh senses.

The fellow Beings of these first travellers were of all types: 'Humans' and also 'Animals' (and birds and fish etc. as you'd call them now). They lived near and with each other, or ignored each other if need be.

BODIES MADE TO MEASURE

All were involved in developing the new vehicle they were creating themselves. Because you must realise that **each Being,** who wanted to live in that body of flesh**, had 'his' own wishes too!** Some (as 'time' went by) wished, for example, to become very rapid in their 'vehicle' and needed extra long legs or more stamina. Others wanted to be extra light and fly above the Earth because the air around it had its own fascination to them, they could feel it on their own flesh unlike 'flying' with one's Mind here.

The body or the vehicle was **fashioned to match the personality and aspirations of the Being** wanting to use it in his experimental journey, during the great adventure of the Earth trip. Therefore, it had to be 'manufactured' to suit the Being going there and no one could tailor it better to its own satisfaction than the 'driver' himself, so to speak. **That's why no one comes on Earth in a body he/it has not chosen for himself/itself**. (BR- *Very important point taught by evolved, knowledgeable Spirit personalities!*).

He who wants to learn how to crawl does not choose a fast racing car, he chooses legs, or paws, or a centipede body. He who wants to feel water on himself does not choose to fly in the air, he goes into water and obviously lives like a water Being, so he needs a body suitable for life on or in water! Always the same from the 'early days' to now and to forever! **The choice of the body is to match the goals of the trip**. Otherwise it makes the trip unsuccessful or hindered.

If the body of a vehicle is unsatisfactory, the Being can decide to leave it behind, come back here and devise for himself a better suited body elsewhere. (BR- *That can be a reason for a stillborn or a child's death.*) What is the problem?! You people change cars or other vehicles according to your needs and journeys! Why couldn't a 'Spirit' Being change too? After all, the journey and goals have far more reaching consequences than what you'd do on Earth for Earthly pleasures!

So there you are, bodies to suit their owner, or driver. Environment to suit all, so that they can all replenish their energies from Matter to Matter! No good having just a Spirit/Energy body if you live in a physical Flesh body - they won't help each other as well as match for match. Where is the problem in understanding this?

Dinosaurs, Giants, tiny shells etc.? They **are all experiments**, trials. They had their way and their mark for a while but were not ideal in the long run! Also, the Beings who had chosen to try those shapes out have **long gone elsewhere** since, to do other things, possibly been back in a different form. They may or they may not, it all depends on their choice and wishes.

BR- Why did dinosaurs come? Why were they so big? How did they disappear? Was there a catastrophe?

As you well know the world was not 'created in seven days'! It has been such a tremendously long process of evaluations and improvement which Mankind has no idea of whatsoever!

So if you want to find out why dinosaurs existed and 'disappeared' (as far as you are concerned) then we'll tell you, we are shown 'visions' of what happened. We look into the Memory or Facts Box of all those happenings, which are still alive, so to speak, whose vibrations still exist and always will, but which have no longer surfaced to your human senses. That's because the reasons for them to be there are no longer needed, or available, or wished for.

So to answer your questions: We can tell you that the main point of their coming was just being part of the 'big Experiment' of the creation of the world of Matter of the Earth. It was not so much for the fun of it (which it partly was) but to see what could be done on what scale. Remember, those

88

'designers' in our World **had no idea of the dimensions needed to exist in that new world!** All had to be worked out and tested and either accepted or rejected.

Until you knew it was no good, you could not reject it, could you? So that's what happened there. If they had stayed longer, there would have been more problems for them or the other creatures could not have survived one way or the other. They could have been trampled upon or eaten or simply not got along with them.

There were a few 'human type' people at the 'same time' but they were experiments too. They were not numerous because all that was still at the investigational level. So the 'designers' did not send too many then. It was still hit-and-miss and trials.

This is why they came: To try the world of Matter in a size which, further along, had to be reduced for the sake of all those around and for themselves. It was very awkward to live with such large bodies.

We know they did exist for some long 'periods' of your time but that was because the whole thing had been juggled and tested. And though there were some good points in being so big, there were bad ones too.

Good points? Not to be trampled upon by anyone else (unless bigger than you!). Easy to see around to look for food, for higher vantage points and power to walk, move and swim without too much effort. But the bad points overcame the minor good ones: To feed such a size was long and difficult and constant to start with! They existed for as long as was needed to adjust things from our point of view here. It may feel like such long periods to you but to us it was of no consequence. Time is not felt the way you do and there were no time limits, no deadlines.

They did not 'disappear' in a big bang or an explosion or a big freeze of death by snow and ice. There was no need for

89

them to suffer the discomfort of being killed by the cold or an explosion etc. It was simply a question of **willing themselves out of the flesh body** like it has always been! So there was **no need** for dramatic happenings.

The reason they went out of human sight is because the 'operators' organising and playing with the creation of those material bodies had decided that after all, the experiment with huge bodies of that kind was not very successful in the end! There were ways of doing things in a different manner on a smaller scale without having those huge things around! It was better to 'minimalise'.

So the fact they reduced sizes was the reason why dinosaurs and the like were shown, or saw themselves, that it was not such a good idea on balance! Those who were there came back of their own will in their own time.

But no one else decided to go back to Earth in that 'disguise', in that flesh outfit. There were other options, plenty of them. Everything was possible!

If it looked like they all died in one big' freezing period,' it could have been that there was such a period and the then residents decided overall to leave at that time. There is no reason why it may not have happened like that. But always, always **remember the creature chooses to come to Earth life and chooses to leave by itself. No one forces it to do it.** So until it is ready it won't come back to this (our) World.

So why have some bones been found of 'a bird looking like a fish', or 'a fish looking like a bird', or 'a man looking like an ape', or an ape looking like a fish, if ever it did?! (Ha ha). Simply for the reasons stated above!

The more details could be changed, the better the vehicle. So fine points were altered, the vehicle improved and hey presto, the new shape appeared, even perhaps near the old physical shape! But having been enhanced, the Being in it may have chosen to stay longer on the Earth to enjoy it, as well as

90

testing the new vehicle... until it got either worn out, or he got fed up with it! So he came back home here.

All that took a lot of 'years of Earth time', of course, as the Earth depends on the cycle of sun and seasons. But does it matter? The whole idea was to have that adventure tested and improved and enjoyed when the goal was reached.

THE EARTH FEEDS BEINGS

The first thing created was the Earth, because it had to be the resting, feeding, sourcing place for those inhabiting it.

The composition of the Earth elements has far reaching implications in the fashioning of Mankind itself. **The Earth minerals and other components had to be useful to the Beings** on it, therefore they had to be created with the greatest care and forethought. THIS is very important in order to understand the rest.

The Earth Matter was to be the basis of what and who would be on it, since it was to **sustain all** those who would live there and eventually 'die' too and come back. Therefore, we had to work out very carefully the composition of every smallest particle, so that each one had its use and each one succeeded in its mission. Those **components had to be absorbed by Plants, then passed on and sustaining the Beings eating the Plants**.

The Earth particles had a life of their own too, as they had to survive and renew themselves too! No good having particles disintegrating themselves after a while and none replacing them! Or else how could the Beings of the time cope and survive with non-existent Earth material at their disposal?!

This is why, as said, point one was the 'as perfect as possible composition' of the Earth itself. That was a great adventure in itself, creating a world built out of unknown constituents, to make it habitable for Beings who have never

91

lived in such a place! Everything was unknown, leading to unidentified future facts because, as you know, **all you can invent has possibilities and ramifications!**

Visualising and inventing in our Mind does not necessarily mean we are creating the correct thing for the **myriads** of possibilities ahead! It was indeed a GREAT adventure and experiment, which had to be worked out as carefully as could be as there were, after all, no deadlines to rush things through! We had all the 'time' in Eternity to make things as well as could be made or thought out.

EARTH POSITION CHOSEN

When the Earth reached an acceptable shape and composition, it had to be positioned in a 'place', as you'd say, which had to be suitable for its purpose. A world too hot or too cold would have impaired the ideas which had germinated in the Minds of those creating these new ventures. So, the **whole systems of stars and planets were created** too.

The Earth was not the first one created, though you must remember we talk to you in words and of 'phases' you would understand being a Human. There **were other worlds created too** and other stars and planets, as you call them, because the whole system had to be balanced for each to help others. Actually there is no 'Time', as such, so we make it as 'past' and 'present' for your own sake of understanding, but it was not really like that.

ASTEROIDS BALANCE

As the Earth was created for Mankind, 'Animals' and Plants to live on, there had been a few upheavals around it, which means the conglomeration of Matter to make it 'flew out' at times until it learnt to settle down properly.

What happened to these pieces of Matter is what you call '**asteroids**' and other flying pieces of rocks in space but we know that these pieces exist and they could have been destroyed or removed but were not. Why? Because they were and are part of **the necessary link between space and the Earth Matter.** The link was **needed to maintain the balance within the 'void'** where the Earth had to be situated.

It's of no interest to astronomers because they do not know these facts or would not understand but we thought you might be interested to realise that **these asteroids and other parts are indeed part of a plan to keep the Earth balanced on its path around its own sun.** You would not think they have any significance, yet it is of great importance and they have their part to play! Unfortunately no one has understood that so far. People assume those rocks are simply flying around because they have nowhere else to go or have 'fallen out' of their own planets.

Your Earth's balance and equilibrium is very delicate and has to **constantly be monitored from here.** It has been so for millennia but who knows that? No doubt they'll say 'God' has to do it?!

NET SUSPENSION SYSTEM

The Energy from one world would help another. The Energies from several would assist others further. The worlds we are talking about are **worlds of Energies manipulated in ways unknown to Mankind** so that the Energies they provide can be used and reused and attracted from one to the other. That way all those webs of Energies could be **a net-type suspension system!** A system on which each star and planet and other physical Beings could **depend on and be helped with.** It is quite intricate and no doubt nigh impossible for you to understand, I guess, but that's what it was all about.

So, as we said, the Earth had to be thought out very carefully for it to accept, welcome and make its residents comfortable... and be able to survive itself on its own, for it

93

had to be the resting place for its inhabitants! The Matter needed for the Earth had been created one way or the other. Then there was the 'small' matter (ha ha!) of creating Beings, i.e. vehicles for the 'Spirits' who wanted and still want to go there, to try out the Experiment of Earth life, as they called it.

FLESH SENSES RULE!

Sadly, it looks as if the goals or goal posts were gradually changed or worse, **the flesh senses became so much the goals that the personality forgot or ignored his own Spirit origins!**

Why? Because focusing so much and **so intensely** on the Earthly/physical senses shifted their attention, focal point, concentration, away from the **original idea of using BOTH** the senses of a 'Spirit' driving and experiencing a Flesh body, with additional senses from the Flesh body. They forgot the first ones and let the second ones rule! That was the start of many a problem!

When one is at the top of the hill going down steeply, one can only fall down at high speed and it is often, or usually, difficult to stop once one is moving, isn't it so? Well, those who erred like mentioned did just that. They blinded themselves with the Flesh senses, forgot their inner knowledge conveniently, let the physical rule and **shut the voice inside** saying: "Where are you going? Why are you off track?".

But that's where the Free Will all wanted at the start had to follow its course; one starts a race as one wants it and if one finishes into a wall that's one's fault and own doing!

What else can be said now? You know most of the rest anyway. **Mankind has too often left its spiritual heritage locked away out of its Mind and now often pays the price for its own man-made mistakes.**

Chapter 10

CREATION - PART 2

The laws of Physics (as learnt on Earth) have got much to be desired! If only one could explain to your scientists on Earth that, seen from here, those laws are far different from what they think they see!

Let's look at atoms and their effect on what you think of as 'Matter'. When an atom attaches itself to another one (so to speak) it starts forming a 'molecule', or that's what you call it. But if you looked at atoms seen from here, you'd see that the link between them is more an 'electrical' link than a physical one.

Then when you see the effect of the magnetic force playing between them, you'd realise there is so much more than some people think. As you watch two atoms move together, you'd see a kind of dance - they repel or attract each other. When more join in that ballet, then the effect is absolutely amazing!

DESIRE CREATES ATOMS OF MATTER

When atoms have been formed by the sheer power of desire, because someone wanted something to happen, to be created, the force and intensity put into this desire will have a marked effect on the result.

If the force is desperately strong, it will affect the creation of these atoms much faster and more powerfully than if the desire was weaker.

When the Power of Creation is used properly to its full, the result is something which one could not guess at - it has to be seen to be believed!

SOURCE OF LIFE

Our view is from within into within; we can see 'deeper than deeply'. That's why **our scientists here can work in a different way to yours on Earth,** apart from not being blinded by the limited or lack of knowledge which affects those on Earth!

Life on Earth began many 'millions of years ago'. Life was **not** the pile of rubble you are led to believe it was. It was not a heap of dust, ashes or torrents of lava. It has had that stage at one time, yes, but 'Life' was **not** an injection in all this chaos, to create atoms of amoebas, worms or whatever out of dust!

Life came from outside the Earth, onto it.

Life has no source on Earth.

Life came from the World of Mind Power and Light (or 'Spirit World' as you call it) because it has **its source there as a Force and a Light**.

Life is the vibrations which create everything living.

Life is an outside Force, working from without, into an organism of flesh or Matter, to 'give it life', to make it alive and real. Without that, the organism would not exist. It only exists because the sparks of the vibrations which create Life have been injected into it.

It had been decided in this ('Spirit') World, that we would have **an experiment,** on this 'pile of earth', to see what could be done and how Matter would be used to promote the development of Beings suitable for the environment.

When a few Beings in our world decided to go and live there, to see what it was like, it was agreed by all in charge that those 'creatures' would not be alone, they would abide by the laws of Nature and they would be helped too. Because no one can cope on a desert-like place without some support. So our team here backed them up.

BR- Were they People, 'Animals'?

'Animals' came too. All forms started more or less at the 'same time', whether People or 'Animals'. They wanted to be created **to see what they could do with that new 'armour'** (the physical body) **to live in a world of Matter**. It was an exciting adventure!

The love poured from our World on to these Pioneers was immense because they chose a big adventure to further the cause of using Matter.

We knew that these Beings, adventurers of a new kind, were attempting something they had never done before and they needed support for it. It has always been given, it has never let them down.

EFFECT OF WILL ON MATTER

Using that type of Matter has been a new venture, in a way. 'Matter' is not just what the Earth provides you with. There are myriads of **different types of other 'Matter' elsewhere,** totally different and unrecognisable to you!

Life, as Earthlings know it, is a pale reflection of what we can see here. If you knew what Life really is, from the 'days' of Creation onwards, you would see **a transformation of the energetic Power of that Life Force into a fuzzy mass of flesh, of atoms of all sorts** of things, Plants, 'Animals', Humans…

It sorted itself out into 'categories' to be recognisable, but it needed not. When a new 'person' was created, the Energy behind it all was phenomenal and amazing!

We watched from here to see how successful it was becoming. We would observe masses of atoms taking shape into different parts of inner anatomy!

We would wonder how the Will of the 'person' would manage to emerge intact out of this shamble of atoms and inner structure! **The Will is what makes the body form itself**.

97

So we wondered what the Will wanted to achieve, how well it would do it as classification began. But **all were created for the fun and the experience.** Everything was done as an experiment and 'The Experiment' seemed successful!

EXCITING EXPERIMENT

When the older generation of the Earthly 'pioneer travellers' passed over back to our world, we could ask them how they'd felt and what was right or not.

It has been quite an arduous task for these pioneers because nobody before them had been there and done so! Once they set the pace and showed the road, **many more wanted to go and experiment with this new type of Matter!**

The creation of everybody and everything was a really exhilarating new venture full of promises and developments. When the Earth world was started, it was only a fantastic new place to go to, **to find out what it was like to live outside an ethereal realm** into a different shape and literally feel everything around the Self...

Our perception of this 'beginning' is that it was not really a beginning in that sense, but **a continuation, another aspect of being a Spirit in a different 'place'.**

Life as you know it, as 'Beings of Flesh' or various types of substance, seems very difficult to grasp when one is on the Earth itself. But seen from here, we can work it out much better. The astounding feat of creating such an incredible amount of types of Matter is what fascinates me.

Here we understand that the worlds of the Earth and the stars are only a 'false aspect', a wrong impression given to people on Earth. If we could explain to you that what you see is only a tiny particle of what Life creations really are, we would do a great job!

THE WILL TO LIVE

Life has a primary aspect and some secondary ones too. Life as a primary aspect is the fact that **when 'atoms' get joined together, they cannot come apart on their own,** unless the force combining them is made to leave and release them. The union is caused by many factors from the point of view of Physics, but the main pull is provided by the force of vibrations of different types of atoms. Life has vibrations running through it all the time.

What we call **Life is vibrations which can create Matter at will and the Will is what matters. If there is not a Will to create Matter and keep it together, the whole thing will collapse.** As the Will makes the vibrations stronger, then the Will has also the power to release the strongest link ever.

For a 'Person' to be created, say, **they need the Will Power to want to have a physical vehicle** and to **produce** a series of vibrations to keep the whole 'concoction' working. Also, the personality has to be happy to have that vehicle because the moment the vehicle is not suitable enough, then the Will shall diminish and fade... and the pull will become so much weaker that no one could keep it together by other means!

(Losing the Will to live is what we call 'death'. BR)

It HAS to be the Will of its own creator. **Each personality is its own creator** that provides the 'electrical forces', the powerful vibrations which will keep those atoms together, so that they can work in a synchronised fashion to emit more vibrations for the 'mechanism' to work.

The EARTH

What do you think created the Earth itself first, before putting People or others on it? If no one wanted to live on Earth, there was no need or use for the Earth itself to exist!

So it was **necessary to have an Earth wanted and needed. For that, it had to be made an exciting project** for those going there to live and find out about and cope with Matter!

Those Beings had to have reasons to crave for it, therefore the project had to be really well thought out in advance, so that the whole thing would not collapse into nothingness!

ECOSYSTEM

The main concern was that People who were created out of that type of Matter had to be able to **survive** long enough for the experience to be useful!

As they were to live there, they had to have a body which could **replenish itself and father its own new vibrations**, for Matter to keep going along the same lines as before. So, there was to be a whole **Ecosystem**: i.e. if bodies were to survive, they had to find their nourishment, their supply of Energy directly from the Source itself - that is, the source of the same Matter they were made of.

Therefore, **that source had to be the Earth**, so that the replenishment did not stop and could continue constantly at will. All that was needed was to construct a whole, well-balanced environment which sustained itself and sustained others depending on it. This is what we mean by an 'ecosystem', where all in it helped each other to survive, for the good of themselves and of the others.

PLANTS ARE SPECIAL

'Plants' had their say too because a Plant is a 'Spirit' too, who decided to feel the Energy of the Earth at ground level, so to speak. It wants to use it and energise itself more, be what a Plant wants to be - part of the natural environment. When 'Humans'/People came, some Plants were already there.

100

Plants were happy to eventually serve as food, because Mankind had wanted to have a link with Nature too. Eating a Plant was all right, as it has **no nervous system so it feels no pain** and has a given Energy which would sustain the Earthly Being back to its roots.

The Plant Energy was an even better link for the person or Animal to feel bonded to his new world of Matter. When you come from a 'Spirit World' where all you have is a Spirit's form, oozing spiritual Energy and vibrations, but nothing really tangible and solid, it is rather difficult to feel your feet on the ground; you have the impression that you don't belong there! The only way was to infuse, absorb and imbibe the Earth Energy, in such a way that you could feel better linked and balanced with it.

So **the Life Force of Plants was vital to that attunement to the Earth and the re-balancing of the flesh creatures into Humans or 'Animals' who** came from a spiritual, ethereal realm, where nothing was as tangible.

DUAL PERSONALITY: LINK BETWEEN TWO WORLDS

Yet the Source could not be a spiritual source only, because would you want to live in two worlds at the same time?! No, there had to be a gap - a bridge, yes, but a division, a gap, a chasm in a way - so that there was a separation and a difference between the Matter of the Earth and its dwellers and the one from the Spirit bodies and world.

All that was needed was a simple 'magic wand' to help the division, so that those in one world did not feel constantly pulled between that world and the other. It required the creation of a physical body, all operating, self-governing but **needing a link with its origins and creators** - those from here, in our world. So we thought the best thing to do was the creation of **physical flesh which lives from the Earth,** the plants, the soil, the air, the water etc. Yet **the Soul** wanting to

101

be in it **could still link up with its origins,** by **remaining quiet** when it wanted, to mentally switch off from one world to the other.

It would be too much of an effort and also confusing if one's Mind kept jumping from one world to the other and constantly moving back and forth! Therefore, to sum up: One's Mind had to settle for one world, concentrate on it. Then if it wished, it'd be able to switch back to tune into its origins, by being quiet and cutting out noises and visions and feeling the other aspect of itself.

That's when the idea of the Dual Personality came to be a design with a real attraction to it. An idea at first, but with polishing and trying to improve it at each go, the whole thing became real and we created the wonder of living on Earth and also having a link with the original world, the Source.

A concept not thought out by 'one personality', but by many, many millions of Souls who wished to participate in **that extraordinary adventure:**

* to be a solid Being with senses which can register through the body of flesh

* yet be also a Being of Light, a Soul and a Spirit, who can do without a solid body and be a Mind.

THAT wonder is what people now have completely lost! They cannot grasp that sense of awesome marvel we had here when the idea, the project, was launched as a fun idea, as a prototype, an exciting aspiration and attainment!

When all was ready for it, the Earth was actually created and existed. 'Plants' too had their say to be 'Plants' because they wanted to be the providers to help those coming to stay, to be alive and well functioning according to the new laws. Then the stage was set for the wonder of the physical life in this particular world to get going.

As centuries and millennia evolved, the lives coming to be lived were more or less interesting and different. Each

102

Being had 'his' own particular problems or experiences and his own tale to tell when he came back here, at the end of the trial journey.

EASY 'DEATH'

The end was not painful at all, the end was simple. Anyone who wanted to come back simply had to **remove its Will, detach its thoughts, from the flesh vehicle!**

Then the vehicle of flesh disintegrated quickly enough, for lack of the support provided by the wishes and thoughts of the Soul who had wanted to be in it and use it.

(*This is a clear definition of bodily 'death': Losing the Will to be physical, deciding the experiment is over and* **wanting** *to return 'home' to Spirit World. BR*)

TRAP OF THE FLESH

Unfortunately, as aeons passed, people developed a greater sense of belonging to (and identifying with) that flesh body! Instead of seeing it as vehicle, it became in their eyes a tool for pleasure not for experiments. It **became a reason** for being and existing, not a device for trying something new!

That Will to want more from the physical senses led to more troubles than anticipated, because those senses were feeling frustrated if one did not constantly feed their needs... And those desires, if not fulfilled, were causing pain and discomfort!

As the body of flesh became more demanding, the Soul felt deprived of its own fulfilment! **The Soul wanted to express itself, yet the physical body was taking over** and blocking the expression of the Soul! That is why as needs of one side are not met, the other side of the personality suffers so much.

So **dis-comfort and dis-ease set in** and **people started to suffer** whereas they should have been happy forever, with a

Spirit of Light within a Flesh Body to guide them through a more physical and solid world than they had known.

That's where the **origins of the 'Adam and Eve story'** come from: **The dis-union of the Soul and the body** when it should have been one collaboration, not a fight between themselves. A disappointment in a way, after such an exhilarating adventure at the beginning!

WATER

You may be intrigued to learn about another part of The Experiment: The creation of water, rivers, oceans, air, sky, etc.

You know what water is but do you know that it has a 'Spirit entity' within itself? It has but no Human will ever really grasp it properly! As water lives its life, it has the joy of being fluid and free flowing. That fluidity and freedom, the moulding round everything is what this particular 'type' of spiritual 'Being' chose. Those Water Beings are very 'fine' Beings, in the sense of having not so much Mind power as 'feeling/sensing power'.

Difficult to explain! If you could imagine the feel of a feather touching you compared to a thought floating about, that's the difference. A feel, a sensation. **That Spirit type of 'personality', that entity, likes to have that fluidity.**

Many People think they have seen those Water Spirits. They call them 'ethereal Beings' etc. but you know **it cannot be real Beings in the sense of 'Human types'** because that's not what was created at all.

The Water Spirit Forms like to appear in that 'liquid shape', which they imagined and created out of their own wish and desire for fluidity. They provide the water used on the Earth right from when it was first formed, as water has helped the creation and sustenance of other Beings and forms of life on Earth and that has always been acceptable.

So, the water Spirits chose to be used to fill what became oceans and rivers, also People's and 'Animals" bodies, as well as Plants too. Their goal to be useful was and has certainly been achieved, but the lack of it on Earth at times in some places makes up for the immense amount provided elsewhere.

BR- But some of it is useless, for example, salty water?

Lots of reasons cause what are problems now on your Earth; you have to understand that it had not been created with that purpose in mind!

The lack of such convenience in a desert is **not** 'aimed at depriving people', but why do they choose to be born and live there? Couldn't it be their choice or fault for being there? All members of Mankind and Animal-kind can move away from where they are because they have the choice as to where to go, being mobile.

As they learn their 'lessons', as they discover new ways or none, they are still **choosing to be part** of that famous Experiment and long-standing project. So that's where their problems started in the first place - their choice, their desire and their wishes!

BR- Could you explain Dr Masaru Emoto's discovery that frozen water crystals display changes when specific, con-centrated thoughts are directed towards them and the fact that water seems to 'remember' and to reflect mood and even written words! (See Note *1) (My Teachers replied with alacrity!)

Make yourself comfortable, my dear, because we'll have a lot to say on this! You'll have to start with understanding the fundamental truth about water!

Water is not just that strange, 'magic' liquid you all think of. It has a **special inner substance** which cannot be defined by human terms, which has indeed an incomparable way to mimic what it sees or rather comes into contact with! It can multiply its own inner cells, if you see what I mean?

BR- Not really, could you explain more?

By that I mean it has constituents which are so fine and refined as to be invisible to human microscopes and the like. Those constituents are of 'spiritual vibrations', that's why they cannot be seen. We mean if you were here, you could observe them, because you would be able to tune in to that level of very fine and refined vibrations, which cannot be captured by man-made instruments.

So, as we were saying, the water you drink has far more properties and abilities than you'd ever dream of! For one good reason to start with: It has been and is still being made by 'Spirit Beings', as it appears on your Earth.

BR- So, it's not just H₂O? Why?

My child, H_2O is only a man-made way of dissecting what they could see in it or what they think it is made of. Of course there are gases blending which can create that, but is it sufficient? No. Why hasn't anyone put tons of H_2O together and therefore have gallons and litres of water for the deserts to be watered with, for thirsty people to be fed with? No. Mankind cannot make water. This is why it is so precious. It is impossible to create water if you don't have the 'facilities' and skills **we** have here in our world of Light and Love! You can always try but will not succeed.

That's all that can be said.

We know what would be lacking even if they managed to make a little drop. There is something which cannot be defined in words.

BR- Please try? And also, how can words on paper influence water crystals?

What is intrinsic to and built in water is the ability to blend and merge with what it encounters. It can absorb all sorts physically, of course, but even more so, **it can send out emanations and vibrations towards what it is surrounded with**. That capacity is to do with what you do when you send

106

your 'aura' out towards others. The water you see in front of you, whether the sea or a glass of water, is not a still object, a dead end, a 'thing'! It has tremendous life!

If you use real, fresh water from the mountains (so not adulterated and poisoned by various chemicals or pollution), you will see the difference, if you **let that water in the sunshine for a while... it will 'grow'** more beautiful. I mean its inner abilities, its spiritual properties, its inner gifts will grow! So, what it can then do is transport much more, copy much more and most of all pick up many more vibrations than before. It's only to be tested and it would be seen. This is why the essence of flowers, inspired by our world to the doctor who started them, are indeed vibrational influences put into pure water which expands their properties. The pure water multiplies the power, the properties, the gifts, if you like, which the plant has within itself. It needs very little of it to do so.

BR- Why is 'little' better?

The more it is diluted, the more you get to the very essence of the original subject, i.e. the flower. As you Humans dilute the drop of essence of the flower used for medicinal purposes, you reach the core of the 'goodness' because you enhance the property by putting it in pure 'spiritual water' with its own abilities to copy and magnify what it has within itself.

BR- Why doesn't it work with more essence? The water could still do it.

Take this example: A little stone has no hope to be diluted into a powder by just being looked at or put in still water if it is not rubbed and knocked about. It has to be broken up first to be turned into powder. A flower essence is obtained by having water from the mountain receiving petals of the 'magic' flower, correct? So, when the petals send their energies, their vibrations into the water, they give out a lot of vibrations, all mixed up.

107

As these vibrations blend into the vibrations of the water, the two create a 'super vibration', a model, a 'template vibration'. When the template is present, it can be diluted even more. That means more vibrational properties of the **water** can blend with it and dominate that little drop of the flower, in order to give it more power. **It is not the flower giving itself more power, it is the water carrying that essence, which can then use its 'super power' to enhance the drop of original flower essence. It is a question of intensity.**

If you want a very good result, you increase the intensity and level of vibrations of the 'thing' which has the power to do so (= water) over the thing which will receive it or it is taken from (= the flower).

We have a dilemma here: Mankind cannot think in terms of vibrations like we do here! You see, all we are aware of and sense is vibrations! Our whole world is made of vibrations. So we have to explain to you, who don't know much about vibrations, what happens when vibrations of one kind are mixed with vibrations of another kind! That can be a headache, you know! Except we don't really have a head, so there is no ache! We mean, we need to find ways to explain and again, when it is not clear enough for a human mind to understand as the person is awake.

In your sleep, we can teach your Soul and Spirit - they will understand! But come to being awake, the mind-activated brain feels it has to slot any subliminal knowledge obtained during sleep time into niches it has and into which our 'new' facts will not fit! So there is that problem.

Of course, there is also the problem of 'human logic'. How can something divided into smaller and smaller pieces, or parts, become as strong as, or even stronger than, the original?

This is because it has been 'infused', 'inflated' by the spiritual vibration of that magic spiritual creation - water!

108

As water gives out (when it can, i.e. if it is not polluted) those spiritual powers mentioned, it can then infuse them into what it touches and thus multiply what is in front of or in it! But it will also better it, improve it! Because you can't beat spiritual powers or Power from the 'World of Spirit', as you call it, as its power, its potential, its force and properties are phenomenal! You will not be able to replicate that on Earth.

Think how 'just' the power of Thought, well used, can make things happen and create! Then it is not difficult to begin to grasp how the power from Spirit, included in **water as an amplifier and improver,** can work well!

BR- Fantastic indeed! Can you explain why water is influenced by words on pieces of paper? I can understand music influencing it because of its vibrations. But written words, not spoken, baffle me. Spoken I grasp, because of vibrations of thoughts and intentions, but I don't if (in Emoto's experiments) they are just pre-written and stuck on a jar, in various languages yet not spoken.

An example might help you grasp this better: A child has no concept of words when he is a baby. He has no words in his head in whatever language. If he had no mother or father etc. no one to speak to him, ever, he would never speak in words. He may make sounds and those sounds could try to copy the noise made by objects or others around him but obviously no words would form in his head. He is not born with words in his head, in whatever language. This is because **words are a man-made invention** which started aeons ago, when people started copying or symbolising objects, actions and emotions. Fine.

But now we'll talk about **water** and pieces of paper with words written on them. Those words in whatever language were written by someone who has put his thoughts on the paper as he wrote or typed or stuck them on, yes? His **thoughts will never die out because they are pure Energy.** Agreed?

As that Energy is embedded on and in the paper, whether it is stuck on or put in front of the jar of water, then **the vibrations stay there,** they will not disappear, they are 'living things', as you know. So what happens?

The water in the jar senses, picks, receives those Energies or vibrations and guess what... it **has the power to amplify them** and increase them automatically!

As it receives a 'bad Energy' from a nasty word, it fills itself with it, because that's the way it is made, the way it works and reacts! So if it is filled and imbued with all those unpleasant Energies from 'awful words', it will react as 'suffering' from those negative Energies! It will, therefore, show itself to those who can see it, as affected crystals, instead of pure beauty, balance and harmony, as is the usual formation from pure water. All Energies have the growing Power of Life within themselves, i.e. they can constantly multiply themselves, always expand and extend their power.

So, you have crystallised water parts, crystallised because the cold of the 'freezer' make them do so, or the cold of the weather outside, of course. If they are surrounded with, imbued with and bombarded (therefore affected!) by disharmonious sounds, or words which are vibrations of thoughts, then they will automatically react to those Energies. Purely and simply. That's what water vibrations can do... and so can all Beings made of Spirit power, which all are made of!

You cannot get away from the fact that absolutely everything in the whole Universe (and other universes too) consists of vibrations with a tremendous power. **A power for absorbing, but also increasing itself.** Therefore, whatever it receives, or is in contact with, it imbues it with its own harmony, strength and eternal force. You cannot escape from that, so it needs to be implanted in human Minds who can take it. Those who can't will have to wait until they can absorb this fundamental and irrefutable fact... and that's it! So simple when you know why and how, so hard when one keeps one's head in the sand, hidden in a cave with the door closed...

(Note *1 – Masaru Emoto 'Hidden Messages in Water' and many other books. www. masaru-emoto. net).

SKY AND AIR

The **air** you are surrounded with was a brilliant experiment! What a clever and astonishing idea to have created that substance which can inflate things as well as lungs and gills etc. and be weightless and yet be heavy! The creators of that substance had great ideas behind its creation: the lightness was provided to be part of the Earth environment and also part of the Beings living there. Not only for People and 'Animals', but Plants too need air to live.

As the Beings from this world brought air into action as a creation, they built it with such care and love that it has a certain 'texture' and feel to it other things don't have. You can feel air move, yet not be wet or damaged by it. Of course, such occurrences as storms or tornadoes are exaggerations away from the norm. I was talking of air around you, breathing it. You cannot notice it and most probably forget it! So be grateful to have this air around and in you because you would not be alive without it: it keeps you going!

'AIR Spirits' are not so much 'Spirits' as you may imagine them (a thinking personality), but a fine piece of Mind Thought **produced by others who had thought of WATER** as being their 'medium' for materialising themselves! Water does flow and moulds itself around things and so does air, you see. The same type of 'thing', we could say.

Why should the air, water, sky, stars etc. be of interest? Because Creation has never really stopped and **the world** (as you know it) **is constantly being created**. But, of course, there are also so many worlds all over, visible and invisible to you. So why discuss them? Because **the world you know is one of**

111

many special 'inventions' from our side and you, as well as your friends and family, are part of it. So if you are part of something, you should and need to **be aware of what you have and where it comes from!**

Your world comes from THIS world where WE are, who speak to you. We used to be with you on this side, you (= *me, BR*) have now gone to the physical world but have managed to learn to retune your link to us, so that the link between the two worlds has not disappeared. Ask yourself what you know about the beginning of this Earth, now you have one solid answer. Solid because you could not have thought out all this! And **the Knowledge is given to you by us,** because your active Mind wanted to learn from us.

So we thought we would help you understand what you always wondered about. You can of course reject it, or discard it, or argue. We have no objection. But it would be a pity not to take any notice when you are given free help to understand what can be quite difficult to grasp coming from a non-scientific background.

Make those who want to hear it understand that milestones after milestones have been reached by Mankind. But the origin is **not** an Adam and Eve sitting under a tree, eating apples! Nor is it bits of particles exploding into others! It has to do with Souls wanting an adventure, as many others have been had in a different type of world!

There are thousands and millions of worlds, whether solid as the Earth or ethereal like ours here; they are of the Mind, or of the Feeling of Touch, or Emotion... So much can be done simply with the Thought Power that we all have!

All could be ignored and not attempted, but the thirst for more essays, more 'what if we tried this?' attitude, **will always lead to more being created.** Why? For Joy is in the doing and the trying and also the failing, because by failing you or anyone finds out how to do better and differently.

112

So as you learn, do not be afraid of making mistakes! Since we had to try and fail too, as the Earth and its inhabitants were being created, why can't you do that too - try and fail? It's normal, it's all in the line of Creation, Experimenting and Experiencing!

SUN

The sun that shines on the Earth seems to be just a ball of fire, simply sheer radiation from a mass of atoms, which have no other objective and aim than to radiate light and heat. You can't imagine it could be a 'persona' who would want to do just that, can you?! Yet **a 'Being' of Light CHOSE to send its Creative Power**, its constant attention towards the continually burning mass of atoms it created for itself, **so that this side of Creativity is of use to others**!

This 'Being' does **not** have to be '**in** the sun' itself. It only needs to know it was, is and will be useful and doing some good to those in need of that light. This was fixed even prior to the beginning of the Earth because it had to be thought out in advance, before things could be put into place to 'get going'.

All those aspects involved in the creation of the Earth, its planets and the conditions needed to sustain Life (as we chose to create it then and as it is still being created), **all those features stem from a 'big decision' made way back in 'Time'** !

Except that the vision of 'beginning' is totally different seen from here. **Mankind imagines it started one day, 'Boom!' and all stemmed from that! The Truth is different!**

The start was slow and progressive, where there was a build-up of facts, of ideas and of experiments made with 'mistakes', inaccuracies, dead ends or no results at times, because all had to be created step by step, for better and improved results.

113

When they decided to 'put their heads together' (this is a figure of speech, of course!), the Minds met and considered many **various options**, which would **be tried out on Earth by Beings who chose to be the pioneers. They would try them out, then would come back quickly enough to say: "This works, that does not."**

So, what we were saying about the **sun** is that this shoot from the 'Original', Eternal Mind Box, has chosen to be, probably among other things, **a light of intense heat, to help those around it create themselves and improve, grow and live their chosen path.**

But no doubt the 'Being' who chose to do that (I use the past tense to help you grasp better) has other things to do too. **It cannot be limited to just glowing as a light for the Earth etc!** This is just part of what that 'Being', that Mind, chooses to use its power for all. It has to do with helping in the particular Experiment of creating the Earth, with possibilities and experiences different from what one can do in our World of Mind and Light.

Everything is an Experiment. Everything is Creation and Creativity!

****

Chapter 11

ANIMALS: THEIR IDENTITY & REASONS

SENSITIVE BEINGS, WITH DIFFERENT GOALS

'Animals' are not a different 'species' like Humans consider them. They are **other Spirit Beings who chose to be born and decided to encounter the challenge of Matter on the Earth,** in a non-identical context as Souls 'driving' bodies of various shapes. If they had not chosen to be 'Animals' as a particular path, they **would have been something else**, should they have wanted to be on the Earth. If it was in another world or realm, they'd be something totally different!

The idea of coming as 'Animals' germinated when some 'Beings of Thought' wanted to express themselves in that flesh Matter in a different way from what Mankind was going to do and look like. They wanted ideas of speed or smoothness, fluidity, acrobatics, all sorts of possibilities to be available and **expressed in a manner which is unlike what Humans can do.**

It was better that way, rather than making or trying to make 'Humans' do those things as well, or at least some of them doing it! So, 'Animals' are the **Thoughts of speed or lightness** etc. **expressed as Beings** who can do some of those things or feats mentioned before.

ANIMALS' SENSES

'Animals' overall have a very **heightened sense of smell and sight** as well as **hearing.** All the more since their own **sensitivity** to anything happening to them is very high. Therefore, there is a **great need for a better perception and understanding of their feelings, physically, emotionally and mentally.** This is of primordial importance when one wants to understand those Beings who have come to Earth as 'Animals'!

If they are not understood, they'll never be free from the traumas imposed on them by Mankind, the slavery, the tortures and all those horrid treatments which should never have happened or happen.

ONE LAW: "DO NOT HURT ANY BEING"

Millions of Spirit Beings 'disguised' as 'Animals' bravely endure Humans' **wilful** cruelty. Why? To shame People and open their eyes!

Making 'Animals' suffer is AGAINST the Law of the Universe: "Do not harm **ANY** Being". *(Battery rearing/Slaughtering/Cooking and Eating live creatures: Crab, lobster, seashells etc. /Hunting/Shooting/Fishing and all so-called 'sports' using 'Animals'/Trapping and Fur Industry/Vivisection, etc.).*

Humans involved in those crimes will pay a heavy price and their **Minds and Souls will be tortured with remorse when** they, at last, listen to their conscience and Inner Selves! That will be their 'Hell'...

Those Spirit Beings (as 'Animals') courageously choose to be such slaves to Humans, in order **to make Mankind aware of horrors it imposes on them.** Such an ultimate sacrifice, which they try to bravely suffer for the 'cause' they are fighting for, is not easily accepted or borne up when they become physical Beings actually enduring it! YET, sadly, they **will not be unable** to feel physical pain, trauma and shock, though we all do what we can to reduce this. We give them the inner strength needed, we back them up with our love and support so that those brave Beings can see through the path they have so heroically and determinedly chosen!

As the 'Animal' (i.e. Special Spirit Being) **endeavours to show to his torturers that they are doing wrong,** he will 'gain points' or, rather, Knowledge itself, but it is mainly for Mankind in general that 'he' does it. It is his very generous contribution, in the hope of changing things for the better.

116

If many 'Animals' suffer in specific conditions, there will be other Earthly Beings, as kind and spiritual Humans, who will revolt and fight and campaign against it, so that the selfish people causing the agony, the horror and the cruelty could hopefully eventually learn and realise what they are doing.

All the ideas you may have to stop this from happening would get nowhere as long as Humanity, as a whole, has not understood what is **the** basic and fundamental Law: **"Thou shall not kill any Being"**. End of story!

The whole of Humanity must grasp this, once more! Because people used to know that and think along those lines when they first appeared on Earth! This is how it used to be when we created the Earth Experiment, from our world into yours.

Sadly, the sadistic torment and killing is done merely to satisfy self-centred physical desires, or to arrogantly use and torture such defenceless Beings to test distorted, erroneous or closed-minded ideas on health treatment, or man-made rigid and pointless 'traditions'. Those repugnant views have overcome the calls from the Inner Selves saying: "NO! It's not right. It's against what we were meant to do, we are all one large team of travellers in this new physical world."

So you may wonder: Is there a 'guiding personality' to help each 'Animal', whatever its kind or size? Yes, there is. Perhaps a rather different type of communication, as you will **not** have Human Beings talking and sending words in their heads, say. But the Knowledge is Inner Knowledge from both sides and this is what matters - that the Knowledge is absorbed and acted upon, as soon as it is received or reactivated.

All for the safety of the individual, no one is left to his own device without back-up of some kind, as we explained earlier.

People have to accept that **'Animals' are Spirit Beings.** They chose to be a certain kind of 'Animal'/'Bird'/ 'Fish' etc. for a particular reason of their own choice. But, as said before, apart from the experience to be 'experienced', there is always a more **profound motive** for their going to that world of Matter, as they could have chosen other places to go to, other things to do.

If they chose to be a particular 'Animal', there will be some important underlying reason which your Soul won't know but theirs will!

HUMANS WERE NEVER MEANT TO EAT ANIMALS

The fact that originally Man was only eating fruit and plants, then some started killing 'Animals' and each other for the pleasure of the taste of the flesh, or for the pleasure of being superior to another Being, THAT is definitely wrong, against the law of Justice and of "no harm done to others"! *(Note - So 'true' vegetarians & vegans must be more spiritual? BR).*

We could underline the fact that Mankind 'grew' on Earth, as they learnt to do more in that body of flesh. They also developed interest in certain things they had not thought of in the first place, when choosing to go there. For example, life as a hunter had **never** been planned! **Why should anyone want to go and kill another Being** who, like you, chose to be a physical Being, coming from the Spirit Realm?

But this probably developed, sadly, because the men and women (not all did) who saw **some** of the 'Animals' eating others, decided it would be 'fun to have a go'... possibly to eat as a change from the vegetation they ate?! Unfortunately, they did not know the underlying and **unselfish reason for carnivores and prey to do so** *(More on this on next pages)*. It means some Humans thought they'd try it too for selfish reasons!

BR- Could it be they saw it just as an experiment?

118

It may have been considered as an experiment in their eyes but it **certainly was not planned in the first place**, since all came from our World of Light, just to explore the possibility of being in the flesh, **to help each other,** not to be killed or hurt! Since some Humans thought they could act like that, others copied! Because no one stopped them, they told themselves it was ok.

As they came back here, **it was pointed out that no one would condone such practice** of hurting others in the same situation as them (i.e. being Creatures of Flesh on a material Earth). But the source of power is always the Thought Power and they selfishly used their Thought Power to do harmful things to others.

Looking around them they saw what could be done, they saw that once you **are** in the Flesh, you can use your physical senses and enjoy them, if you give yourself time to explore them and give in to them. So **sounds, sights, tastes and textures were more and more developed and investigated**! Unfortunately, if you let the senses take over, who would know what could or would happen? As all **these things were experiments,** remember no one had really tried that one... and no one had expected it to happen!

However, if you wanted to stay on a higher level of Thought, you did use the Earth body **but** you tried to stay well linked to your origins, which were the Spirit World of Light.

BR- Why weren't they shown in the World of Light that they were on the wrong track?

They were. But can you imagine having to tell people who have travelled to an exciting new world where they enjoyed what they did, that they were wrong to do it? You know how difficult it is to convince people who have set their Minds on something! Yet they knew the Law .That's what must have happened, they'd set their Minds on such things and others copied! Moreover, they had the freedom of having Free Will!

119

FLESH TAKE-OVER

BR- But surely they first came from Spirit World where it was known it was wrong to go specifically to try eating 'Animals'?

Sadly, pleasures of the Flesh became a far more important subject and goal than you would think! It was something that had not been explored deeply before. Because it was new, there had not been any so-called 'rules' set about it. Though the Universal Law still stood firm. So the **killers will have to judge themselves for using their Free Will wrongly!**

As people started developing a taste for all this, the Earth population grew, because instead of wanting to come back here and stay for more spiritual knowledge or other experiments, they wanted to go back there for more Earthly 'fun' and 'tries', trying to be as many different people as they could, because it became indeed an exciting adventure! The pleasures of vision, hearing, touching, food, sex, association with others, experimenting together, became an incredible scope they had not anticipated. More decided to go and stay and go back again!

As the rule of Creativity was "You go and do your best to explore and find out what can be done", they indeed 'explored' and 'found out', but it turned out to be in **exaggerated ways** and **that led to downfalls!**

It did not have to be like that, because people could have remained more focused on their inner link and played with the Earth as a side experiment! Instead, the experience became: Focus on the physical world senses and experiences... and maybe look up to the Other World if they remembered where they came from! That's what happened in the end anyway. At first it was not so bad, but as things developed and time passed, **the links between the two worlds became rather blurred in the Minds** of those who were so intent on coming to Earth!

BR- (feeling ashamed) - Since I live here, am I one of them?

Look at yourself, silly! You are talking to me, to us. You are not to feel embarrassed! You have **not** lost the link! On the contrary, you wanted to remind people of their origins and **that's why you have come to Earth**, didn't you know? So, do not be daft thinking you should be ashamed. People who knew that Man is 'Spirit' first, before choosing to come on Earth, were ahead of the others, always! But **those who chose to forget** that fact created havoc in the end, because ruling the Earth as Man of Flesh, instead of as a Spirit in a Man's flesh body, made all the difference.

So, Mankind chose to go that way, in a deeper direction towards the flesh pleasures and activities. A great majority chose that, rather than acting on Earth as planned, to try experimenting with the Power of Mind over Matter. **This gave the whole experiment a new, unexpected twist** as said before- and a twist which became a nasty one, because **Mankind started suffering from it.**

Humanity had no idea that stepping into such flesh activities would cause troubles. Because **the problems it brought itself were caused by the rift between its spiritual origin and its physical creation**. *(Note: More in ch.33 on tug-of-war between Soul and Flesh causing health trouble. BR).*

The Soul was meant to play with the Matter of a physical body, by willing it into a chosen shape, to feel its way around the world and discover new sensations and new possibilities of creating things around the Self... by still using that Mind Power it had as a Spirit.

If Humans had stuck to that plan and programme, they would have invented even more things, used more tools etc.

121

WHY SOME ANIMALS ARE CARNIVORES

It became more apparent when some 'Animals' **chose** the special way of living and **'dying' to help each other**: **"If I want to leave my body** (= to 'die') **I'll let you eat me**, **so that you are fed. If I don't want to leave that body,** I won't let you eat me and **I'll let you know.** You must pick up my signals and not attack or hurt me." That's simple enough. The idea being: **"You'll eat me when I am ready to leave for my own reasons.** If I am not ready then I'll run away safely".

But this fear is not the same as the deep seated fear that eats Mankind away. **Mankind has umpteen kinds of fear,** from health worries to family, relationships, jobs, survival with food and having a home, wars etc...

ANIMALS LIVE FOR 'NOW'

We cannot say 'Animals' fear all that! Yes, they fear being attacked when the opponent is within their range of vision or knowledge. They may know there is a dog or other dangerous 'Animal' around, they may sense it or smell it. But this is a proper reaction of survival, you may call it the instinct of survival because they want to stay alive since they came here. Or they have little ones to look after and protect.

Yet an 'Animal' does not fear losing its home in a month or a year's time. It does not look ahead and fear. **It lives for now and does what is right for now.** They may plan, in a way, like building a nest for the future brood, but it is in fact what 'feels right now'. Then, the next step will be its next 'now' and so on.

So it is not the kind of worries Mankind had learnt to build within itself and its life, its society and people! **It has become 'normal' for most Human Beings to live in fear** of their superiors (authorities, governments), diseases said to float around, dangers from some 'Animals' or countries or even cosmic fallouts etc! Who wants to dread having radiation constantly bombarding you or fallout from a meteor etc? This was all man-made gradually over the centuries and millennia!

'Animals' do not fear the next tide or tsunami. It's not in their psyche. They will know within themselves when one is on its way, but then they will act accordingly if they can at the right moment. Not fearing it for months ahead!

WHAT HAPPENS TO MURDERED ANIMALS?

BR- Let's say, during the 'Avian Flu' abroad (2005), millions of birds being murdered, gassed etc. How did 'Animals' feel on arrival?

Once they pass over they feel free again and have no worry. That is because we knew they were coming so **their Souls were prepared** for the passage over.

BR- How do you do that?

There are groups of dedicated helpers preparing such poor 'Animals' to the sudden shock of finding themselves going from one world into another, without any warning. So we prepared them. We do what can be done for **anyone** who needs that kind of help. We come close to them as a loving light, a caring person or whatever the individual needs to think is coming to help him/her/it.

(Note - My 'departed' parents and grandparents often do this 'Souls Rescue' work too - as reported in 'I'm Not Dead: I'm Alive Without a Body' - NDAWB).

Then **we show them glimpses of where they'll be coming to,** so that it is not a shock, but a new place they are already a little accustomed to by the time they arrive here.

(See NDAWB Book 1: People are helped too: Mum said she had been shown Spirit World and its Light in her Earthly sleep but only remembered it once passed over).

So all is well with them. Those birds will be roaming new pastures etc. and won't feel upset at having been killed out of their previous body.

You know we say and said: "Do not 'have your cat put to sleep' simply because he is very ill. The cat knows he is dying. He may choose to have a slow 'slipping out' for many reasons!" We do not know all their reasons. So we need to **respect their free will,** you see! They are Spirits like all of us! *(BR's Note - This is a big bone of contention between my guide and me! I can't bear seeing 'Animals' in pain).*

If some 'Animals' have to come over suddenly because of such 'emergencies' caused by Mankind, then we come in force and give the creatures the support they need, by showing them where they'll be going in a minute, or a day, or a week, or whatever you'd call it.

If we did not, they could feel quite lost and would probably imagine they still are in cages or being battered, or gassed, or have their throat cut etc! So **we need to free them from the risk of trapping their Minds and emotions in the trauma of the death** or before death. If we cannot free them in time, there is more work to be done to get them out of their mental nightmare.

DO ANIMALS HAVE GUIDES?

BR- Do 'Animals' get a 'guiding voice' helping them while on Earth?

The Being who chooses to go as an 'Animal' (and there were and are many choices of course) is not an 'Animal' as it starts its journey. **It is a Being of Light and Mind, a creative Mind** who chose to **design** a special and specific 'suit of armour' for the life on that Earth it is going to.

That 'armour' may be a cat or a dog, a lizard or a lion, a bird or fish etc... and that's not the whole list! So we see it as a brave Being selecting that particular life as a big challenge most of the time. It's not that it will necessarily be difficult; some are not 'difficult', but the learning will have to be **appropriate to the creature it has chosen to appear as** physically.

124

As no Being has ever been 'sent' or allowed to go on any trip without any 'backup guidance', we can assure you they all have the reassurance of some **Knowledge instilled in them** if they have problems. Some of you may call that 'instinct' but it is not quite correct.

The 'Animal' may rely on its own senses or may also tune in instinctively or involuntarily to the inner sense that is brought by the Collective Mind and Knowledge accumulated over aeons by those who have been such an 'Animal' and who have left their imprint in the Knowledge or 'Facts Box'. This is collective Knowledge that has been experienced over the aeons of coming to Earth and brought together for anyone going back there, to learn from and to get inspiration from. They will be able to dip into it whenever danger or need crops up.

The 'instinct' talked about is that ability to pop part of or its whole Mind towards or into that area of Knowledge, to pick any information necessary to their survival and well-being. That Source has always been available to all who have lived on the Earth, as only from here can they see ahead, not when at ground level. Seeing ahead is every creature's desire, to ensure their own protection and survival as well as their offspring's.

This is built-in within any Being, but Mankind feels it has to rely on a go-between, a 'guide' linking the 'Facts box' and themselves and able to do the 'dipping in' for information! In fact, you can all have a look into it, if only you tried more often to relax well and be attuned to that high vibration containing all information you may wish to have.

So first of all, the Knowledge they have is **from their own Higher Being, their Inner and Higher Self.** It is fundamental that you all have it. Humans too. Your Inner Being tells you when you are not staying on the right path for yourself and talks to you as if you were another person, i.e. it gives you guidance. The problem is you Humans don't always listen to the inner voice and thoughts coming from beyond your own thinking.

ANIMALS' INNER KNOWLEDGE

'Animals' do not reject their Inner Knowledge. They always adhere to what is sent and felt and known innately. So that's no problem, they know what to do. We are talking about guidance for their own safety and aptitude to survive in difficult or dangerous conditions. They may not always survive, but that does not mean they were not listening to their Inner Self and guidance. It is probably because they'd chosen not to stay any longer on that path and in that body.

The 'guiding voice' of their own Self and Inner Knowledge is sufficient to keep them safe and help them stay alive. But the Knowledge is Inner Knowledge from both sides and this is what matters - that the Knowledge is absorbed and acted upon as soon as it is received or reactivated. All for the safety of the individual. No one is left to his own device, without backup of some kind, as we explained earlier. All creatures have support from this world, a Mind which helps them and sustains them whilst they are in the world of flesh.

This is to say of course they have 'someone' to help them! It is not necessarily a 'person' as you see a person, because whoever the 'Animal'/creature on Earth is, it is not a 'person' in the flesh. So the 'personality' in our world can be either another of its kind (e.g. a cat) or a superior Being who has never been form or shape and has knowledge of that sort of environment through his own learning. It will be what you'd call a 'higher Being', in the sense he will have a lot of Knowledge regarding the way a pure Spirit thinks when here, but also may have to think when faced with the world of flesh.

126

The Earthly 'Animal' does not need a personality 'talking' to it. But there could be another 'Animal', say a cat, who has been in the Spirit World for a long time and has acquired the knowledge necessary to be a cat when on Earth and has now a friendship or link of affection or other with the one you have on Earth. That cat here may very well stay near yours and inspire him for various happenings in his life, for example, danger looming round that bend or bush. But it is mostly another kind of guidance the Earthly 'Animal' will be relying upon - its own ability to sense beyond human expectation of what a cat can do, to sense beyond what Humans can comprehend.

This sensing comes from **a heightened awareness** of its surroundings and its Earthly world. It will sense far beyond eyesight and hearing! It will know deeply within what is and will be going on soon. This is due to its ability, as mentioned before, to dip into the larger scale of information available which has accumulated over aeons.

It can also sense all vibrations produced by other Beings and mostly by the Earth itself as a vibrating Energy body and world. That ability has always been **labelled as 'uncanny'** by Humans but is only natural in 'Animals'. It's an ability Humans are born with, but they do not use as much or at all, as their Mind focuses more and more on the outside physical world instead of what is vastly available 'within', i.e. in the invisible world which has no bounds or limitations. All is there for the taking, all is available, but none or hardly any make the effort!

ANIMALS' GOALS & CONSCIOUSNESS

There are great differences and yet similarities too between Humans and 'Animals' who are both Spirits 'in disguise'. The difference is a question of **degree of consciousness**, of how much he, say a cat, has put his Mind into being a cat on Earth.

127

If he really wanted to be a cat, then he will have focused all his Energy being one, creating his body and acting like one in every way. This means when you have a cat very interested in his life as an Earth Being, he'll be enjoying his food, loving his new body, making the most of his creature's comforts and pleasures. He won't mind where he is if he gets what he has come for or aimed at.

If it was for a 'less intense physically' reason, this cat will find itself less focused intently on his new life as an Earthly Being. He will be interested in it but not quite as much as some others. It is all a matter of **intensity, not focus**. He may be **more interested in relationships** with other cats, or with other 'Animals', or even with Humans, to fulfil what he wanted to achieve.

Having an 'emotional-type' of relationship is a dissimilar experience whenever you have a different kind of body, of flesh or other. If he is less intensely focused on his body, he'll be sleepy and eat only because it has to be done to keep alive, but it won't be the main focus.

BR- A friend (Jack) finds it hard to accept that everything living has consciousness. He keeps asking why, say, a worm would choose that body and whether it has consciousness, or as much as a large 'Animal' or Human? He also asks: What was it before and after the Earth trip?

A so-called 'worm' chose to come to Earth to do a good job as it does in the world of Nature, to enhance the ground and feed on what it needs to find. So it will be of no consequence to any of you to worry why or how it came!

But since it is on some people's Minds to query the existence and ins and outs of worms, we'll say this: Worms are like any other small or big creatures - Beings from the World of Light that you call 'Spirit World'! If they did not come to your world, you'd be lacking good contributors to enhance the soil of your Earth!

128

But it is not just that. They have thoughts at their own level. **They have a Mind of course, as all creatures possess a Mind which is simply the creative tool of the Spirit Being within.** So the 'worm' that you see there is not necessarily a 'worm' in our world. It could be a charming Light of Energy which desires to help others (as other Beings do here) and also, of course, wishes to experience the World of Matter.

All creatures choose their size and body shapes. So why not have worms? We wonder where the problem is.

BR- It's not me, it's Jack asking!

He wants to know more about worms' intentions? They have no ill intentions towards Mankind or other Beings, which is a good point and a good representation of our Spiritual World, as we do not harm others here!

Their consciousness exists of course. They know where they are, they react to things happening to them. They have **chosen** to be small, because the task and help they provide show that it is impossible to do it as well if they were larger Beings!

But is a worm less important than a Human? It had not learnt the technology of going to the Moon or building machines, but **it had designed itself a body** that can dig the soil and digest it and make its own body a useful little machine that no gardener would want to do without! It provides efficient help at low cost (That's what Humans like, isn't it?!). As to what they are as **'Spirit Beings', they are a Light with an Urge.**

It may not be their aim to always be a worm on Earth. Each may have another 'idea' or urge at some point. They may decide to go and experiment in other dimensions at some other levels of Creativity. It is not because something is small that it is less efficient than or is inferior to Mankind, who thinks it can do everything so imagines it is 'superior'!

129

What is the point of calculating mathematical equations when the soil needs leaves recycled for compost to feed the trees and other plants? We see with great sadness that some people still have a closed mind, rigidly focused on the Mankind point of view, without allowing themselves to think further and wider and be open to **all** possibilities!

There is no one at the centre of the World of Matter. Developing your intellect does **not** make you superior to anyone else! In the same way as developing your muscles or being beautiful for a while does not make you superior to anyone else! In fact the more attention is given to the physical aspect, the less it is of any use, if it is not done for helping others on the Earth as an ultimate aim!

So where do we go from there? There is no doubt whatsoever that **a worm is a very intelligent and clever Being** which can regrow part of its own body when it had been traumatised. Can Mankind, with all its intellect and machines, do that? NO! As it does not need too many emotions for its purpose, a worm will probably have a limited range of them to be able to focus on its job and its existence, which is needed for the purpose it came for.

It will feel pain if cut because it has nerves and will react to any painful, or not, changes. It cannot scream or cry loudly but it will ache and suffer. It has that built-in system and mechanism to regrow its body and that is what makes a worm superior to many other 'Animals' as well as Humans. But it does not need to build machines or learn languages.

So what is your point of comparison? How can a Human judge whether a worm is superior or inferior to your pathetic murderous so-called civilisation?

A worm has what all living Beings have: Life in it. And Life is the Power and Energy of the 'Spirit' World, which means the lowly and little worm in your garden is a lovely spiritual Being, who wilfully chose to come to Earth to experience the world of the physical in **this** particular type of Matter! Any problem with that?

It is on a par with all other Beings of flesh because, like them, it is on a journey of discovery and experiments in the World of Matter, having come from the World of Mind and Spirit? Where is the problem? We cannot see any. So why do some of you have a problem? It is a mystery to us!

ANIMALS HAVE HEALING POWERS

They are definitely special Souls who can do so much good on Earth and even here, because they heal people and other Beings by **simply being there**, especially pets. They have a particularly strong power in as much as they love to be loved if possible and give out one hundred times more than they receive. This is why they are so great. They **can empathise** with people and other Beings and **have a built-in mechanism to magnify their own power!** They don't even know they are doing it!

BR- But aren't all Spirits 'Spirit stuff'? Aren't they equal?

Yes, all are **Spirits,** i.e. **Energy from the 'Universal and Eternal Energy Pond'.** But these Spirits as 'Animals' have a quality within themselves which allows them to **magnify what they are and how they give it out.** That's why an 'Animal' as a pet is a soothing, loving creature who makes people feel better.

If it has been hurt, it will feel it even more, because it is so sensitive to feelings in any direction. It **can suffer more emotionally than a person** because of that extreme, intense sensitivity and power of love and compassion built in itself.

It is not usually known but we thought you may like to learn this, so that you understand even better those you love on Earth, this time round. You (*me, BR*) are surrounded by the love of your cats, both the ones near you now and the ones who have been with you before, because you have loved them so much. You cannot realise how much it has helped them progress to a heightened sense of love and compassion. Their Soul was good, of course and was a healing Soul, each one of them. But by coming to Earth to help you too, they **increased their awareness** of the touch, the physical contact and therefore **the exchange of vibrations between Beings at a closer range on Earth.**

That has helped them understand the need for closeness and the need to give out even more. You would give to them without thinking, you loved them full range, that's it. So they loved you back full range.They are around you whenever you think of them, of course, but even if you don't, because they sense your vibrations and they like it! They enjoy being close to your 'loving cat vibrations', the love one gives only when one has that sort of love for them.

Make your senses more aware and you will feel them close. Sensitivity has to be worked on, my dear. A sensitivity which needs heightening needs to be worked on by simply feeling around oneself, letting outside influences come close.

As 'Animals' are on the high vibration range they need to be felt in a quite strongly different way. You see, the feel of material impressions is reflected on the skin, the five senses in fact - whereas the **sensitivity required** for outside range vibrations has **more to do with your inner senses** than your outer physical senses.

EMOTIONS GAUGE

BR- Don't emotions come from the Spirit within?

The Spirit within you is indeed the driving force but **the scale of these emotions varies very much according to what you are** on Earth, say.

If you have a snail 'loving' another snail, is it going to be as emotionally involved as a cat towards another a cat or its

132

owner? The snail is more likely to have physical attraction and urges rather than real emotions.

The crux of all emotions is how one reacts towards them. The emotions one feels are a kind of gauge of how much consciousness is involved in the proceedings of being in a flesh (or other!) body.

So, **if the emotions are strong, then the consciousness is higher, as the degree of self-realisation and self-observation is higher and stronger** than if there was not any.

An elephant is a large 'Animal' with a lot of intelligent thoughts with analytical and emotional aspects. She must use her wits all the time and has lots of emotions churning inside. She feels pain physically, of course, but she **feels pain even more when her emotions are tampered with**! She has a great attachment for the ones she is with, for the keeper if she has one, for the little ones she has, or whatever. It is **always a great bond towards those she knows and loves and cares for.**

It is important to know that, because people often overlook the emotional aspect of the life of 'Animals' in general. **All 'Animals' have emotions at various degrees** and that is what people must be aware of. When an 'Animal' has a strong bond with a Human, it has very strong feelings for that person. Anything done to an 'Animal' will have repercussions on its health, both Mind and bodily health, like it does in Humans and other creatures.

So Mankind needs to remember that the 'little something swimming here and there', or the big 'whatever' running hither and thither, or any beautiful (to us) Being who has chosen to come to Earth as an 'Animal', **has the right** to feel what it wishes and the right to express its feelings as well.

That is what is lacking in all the rearing of 'Animals', in any kind of intensive money-orientated way. If that activity exists, then it must always be done with the **'Animals'' emotional health taken in consideration** too.

STRICTER WORLD LAWS NEEDED

BR- Some rearing is done a little better nowadays.

Yes, but not all countries do it! Not all 'Animals' are helped either, even in your present country. So where are the laws which protect them?

You need **laws to cover the whole world,** in many countries and many homes and numerous ways of using 'Animals'. That is what we are trying to put across. It **must** be pushed more. It has to be made known to those who ignore that basic fact. Of course, health, physical comfort and **normal behaviour** for each 'Anima'l is paramount, but there is the hidden side which is not always by far looked after and seen to.

You have to help make the world understand the physical welfare will respond more easily to a **good mental and emotional welfare.** Make 'Animals' happy and they'll be healthy. If you are trying to make money out of them, well at least make them be happier and you won't lose money or won't have to treat **the physical problems resulting from an unhappy mind and crushed emotions.** That's all.

NOT 'ANIMALS' FOREVER

BR- So to sum up: 'Animals' had not always been 'Animals'? At 'the start' it was more 'ideas' of shapes/speed/flying etc. which took hold of the imagination of the 'Creative Urge' and they eventually took shape somehow? Some came to 'Earth', other Spirit Beings decided it was a good idea to experiment, so carried on becoming various 'Animals' and creating a 'way of thinking like an 'Animal'?

Let us say, you've got the gist of it anyway. Saying the 'way of thinking of an 'Animal" is not quite correct because that 'Animal' way of thinking may only be related to that particular species for so long.

When Beings who incarnated as 'Animals' evolve to such a 'high' level once back here, they gradually won't focus on what they've been 'before' physically. Humans do the same, eventually! But there is no rush. So 'departed' **loved pets will be reunited** with their Human owners when they all come over!

When all progress and evolve, they'll become again High Energies with a great Creative Force within themselves, a Power provided by their thoughts or Inner Urges. The Inner Urge is always there, suppressed at times possibly, but always there within the 'inner sanctum' of that Energy which the Being is, in fact.

The basic, fundamental Energy of a Being of any kind or shape will not ever disappear! So that base will remain what it is: A Thought Power itself, a Creative Energy, which cannot and will not remain still or stagnant. It will automatically want to fire away more of itself into Creativity, always abundant Creativity! This is an endless 'fireworks display' (to use words you may grasp and visualize better).

The 'lost' attitude, as an 'Animal', say, is **not really 'lost'**. It has enhanced and enriched, improved, altered or added to the original Power. This Power has now more facets and skills and Inner Knowledge and anything else it has absorbed and been through over its experiences on Earth or elsewhere. As there is no end to this Creativity, you see why eternity exists! It has to be to help fulfil all these myriads of myriads of never ending possibilities!

****

135

Chapter 12

WHY HUMANS CAN'T COPY CARNIVORES

'Animals' are Beings who chose to be 'Animals' for one reason or another. Not all 'Animals' eat each other. The prey who chose to be eaten don't mind as such, since **they intend to leave their bodies anyway,** their body will feed a hungry fellow creature. Though no doubt the pain they may encounter will be part of their development as a Soul.

An 'Animal' has no more or no less Spirit in itself than a Human. **It is a Spirit Being dressed as an 'Animal' body shape'.** But the Soul who chose to be an **'Animal' has a path it decided upon a long 'time' ago** and this is something which is more difficult to understand. The Soul mentioned will have accepted the eventual, possible pain as part of its path.

BR- Why?

It is a mystery to those who don't live it, it is not a mystery to those who chose it. An elephant may not be eaten by another one, but it may accidentally eat small insects on the leaves it eats. This is not part of the law of herbivores, but it does happen. So why does the insect accept to end its Earthly days, by being swallowed by an elephant it probably does not even know the existence of? It is part of the constant creation, recreation and flexibility of the laws of Creation.

INTENTION MATTERS

It is not what happens which matters, it is more WHY it happens, with the intention more at the forefront than the action.

If the elephant had **intentionally** tortured and eaten the insect in order to kill it, **its own Soul would need to learn a lesson on cruelty!** But the beast only had a meal on which an

136

insect died, so that's clear. *(Note: Food for thought for those who order lobster, crab, mussels etc. **knowing** these are cooked alive? BR.)*

Carnivores eat meat because this is one of their aspects of living on Earth. If the prey had not wanted to be eaten, they would have changed the rules at the 'beginning' of things on that planet. *(See Ch. 11)*

But the fact that **Man was only eating fruit and plants,** then some started killing 'Animals' and each other for the pleasure of the taste of the flesh, or for the pleasure of being superior to another Being, **THAT is definitely wrong, against the law of Justice and of "NO wilful harm done to others"**! *(Note: So sincere vegetarians and vegans must be more spiritual?)*

BR- Many people will find it hard to accept the prey chooses to be eaten.

The mighty choice of having Free Will meant that no one could interfere with what was desired. It is not possible to see what everyone chooses individually and why it is part of their life plan. Nobody forces them to choose a death that is more painful than can be imagined!

The Law of being kind has always been so, from the beginning of all creation. That was the way for all Beings to know what boundaries to look for. Yet it was not so restrictive since Mankind and 'Animalkind' had a hugely wide range of possible activities. It is important to see it was fair as it was chosen by all, since no one wanted to be hurt themselves. Needless to say, we cannot be responsible for anything that has been decided for all, aeons ago! We can only pass the message!

The prey has always been a subject of contention by all who love 'Animals' of any kind. If the prey did not want to 'die', we've already told you they would not be in the vicinity or reach of the one who kills them.

137

BR- Are you one hundred per cent sure this is correct?

There is no way we would tell you something which is not **one thousand per cent** certain! The way Beings go out of the physical world and back to their original state of Beings is by 'dying' one way or the other. Their way is not always known in advance (how they will 'go') but when they are ready to leave, that is how and why they feel the need to go 'here' or 'there' to 'attract' the accident, the murder or whatever to let themselves be killed to free them.

BR- Why don't they just leave the flesh by willing themselves out of it (without the need for a killer) and leave the body within the vicinity of those who'll eat their flesh?

We know that can be done as well, of course and many people do - they just 'pass over' in the night, for example. But those who are killed are perhaps looking for an excuse to go in the eye of their families, or a 'dramatic' reason for going because (who knows?) they may have a dramatic personality.

BORN TO TEACH MANKIND

BR- Currently in Ukraine (Eastern Europe), stray dogs are poisoned or buried alive etc. Didn't they know when they were born they'd be 'polluting' and dirtying towns or perhaps bringing the danger of rabies?

The laws of each country are different as you know. So if a law says "To discard nuisance dogs, we'll do this", then that law is cruel and wrong!

BR- Why were those dogs born then?

Because they chose to be born! That is the problem with Free Will. People and 'Animals' can do whatever they want. Then they can't complain that they had been forced.

So those Spirit Beings who were born as dogs there do have the responsibility of causing lots of problems indeed. But Mankind should have learnt to respond in a less cruel way than those nasty methods.

Who caused the trouble? Those dogs choosing to come... but it is not as clear cut as it seems. If Mankind's laws allowed them to be killed humanely it would be better than torture or a slow death. If the laws could go around the problem by having them neutered, it would already be better!

BR- Yes – but it's not always possible cost wise and manpower wise.

When the whole or the overall majority of Mankind has learnt not to hurt others, then it will be a turning point. When such cases look as if they do not need to exist and turn Mankind into decision makers opting not to be cruel, then the law of the countries may be changed successfully. It could be why those brave Spirit Beings chose to be born there, say, as those poor dogs, to push that particular group of Humans to learn to make decisions which comply with the Universal Law of Compassion.

We find it hard to give an answer for every case, because it has to do with Free Will on your physical side and Free Will on our side. Some of this was set a' long time ago'.

We cannot budge from the teaching of: **Mankind has to learn to be kinder**! Mankind has not learnt to respect wildlife and other species, even races of its own. Humanity needs to be shown the right way, to be made aware of the cruelty of their actions by those who have understood and rebel against such actions! Mankind can only learn by being pushed against the wall by public opinion, which is led by caring and compassionate Beings who have specifically come to Earth to show them the right way.

As the odd case may not be sufficient most of the time, this is why so many thousands and even millions of Beings have indeed actually chosen to come to Earth and be the victims of such cruel acts. They may have been a few at the beginning but no one was paying attention!

So the huge impact made by **large numbers of sufferers turned out the only way Mankind opens its eyes,** eventually!

It has been proved that Mankind overall is a very slow learner, because of the greed and the cruelty bred by those who live for money and profit! So the gentle approach is no longer sufficient. It has to be a mighty blow or shock to open the eyes of those who want to fight it and push the perpetrators to stop committing those crimes - or at least reduce, improve and eventually find a way of not being so abominably cruel .

BR- So some 'Animals' choose to be born as farm 'Animals'?

When an 'Animal' is born, its Soul chooses to come as an 'Animal' and if **it has chosen to be born now** (in your century), **it will be to help people live, to give them a chance to open their eyes** to what is going on on Earth and to make the choice. Those 'Animals' would be evolved Beings who sacrifice themselves to help Man progress!

It gives people the chance to make the choice wilfully. If all there was to eat was grass, people would not **progress by making a choice**, they would be forced into eating grass instead of cows, pigs, chickens etc. and that's where the difference is in the long run, within the scale of progress of the Souls!

BR- I wish Spirits did not go into those 'Animals' bodies!

They have to do what they feel is right, if it falls into line with the laws of Physics, Chemistry etc. If an 'Animal' is born, it's because its body has the Life spark put into it by the Spirit Being.

BR- Why aren't they still-born, say, in intensive farming?

Still-born could be a solution but they don't always want to be. **Many choose that way to make people realise the horror of what Mankind is doing** and to be 'heroes and victims', so that the heart of those who care is revolted by the crude practice and eventually it will happen!

140

It will happen not just because there are **no** 'Animals' left to eat, but because Mankind at last chose to go back to what was Humans' **original plan: Eat Plants but do not kill other Beings of flesh,** because that is unnatural.

A Soul does not always know everything, it depends on its 'previous' other experiences and facets. If it had not learnt it is wrong to injure others just to eat, it will have to learn it, compare, judge and **make its own decision. Nothing is ever imposed.**

All is presented and evident, but nothing has cast iron rules. That way Souls cannot say: "You've imposed it on me"! It's much better to be able to say: "I chose to do this because I've learnt and realised it is wrong" than "I've done it because I am obliged to do it."

An experiment, by its own definition, implies possibilities in all directions, of failure or success, of attempts or a decision to withdraw etc. So the experiment of the Earth Creation means all involved, from Plants to People, passing by every kind of creature you can think of, accept to try what is there with its constant possibility of changing at any time. That is **what Creativity is about - possibly changing this as you go along.** So, do not moan or berate the fact that some choose to do something which may not look right to you or even the law of Spirit. **They are WRONG to cause harm if they KNOW it should not be done. If they don't know, then they'll need to learn and they will judge themselves eventually** - but it is all in the learning and the experiencing...That's what Life in this physical world is about!

DO ANIMALS ANALYSE THEIR LIVES?

BR- Do Carnivorous 'Animals', once back in the 'Spirit World,' analyse their actions against the Universal Law of no killing? Do their Souls regret to have killed even though the prey may want to leave their flesh that way?

It is not so much that they would be exempt than them thinking it is ok, as the prey have agreed beforehand, even while still in this world. We do not have the nitty-gritty of every single case, but overall 'Animals' who kill will have done so because they were hungry or had young ones to feed and the prey had appeared at the right moment, as mentioned earlier.

BR- Do they judge themselves against the Law?

The Law of Compassion is not against anybody! **The Law is for everybody, to protect them!** If the prey chose not to be protected then that is their choice! **They do NOT have to be protected if they do not want to be!**

The lioness will not punish herself by sending herself to an Inner Hell for having killed an antelope, because the antelope wanted to go anyway. The lioness is not a guilty party in this case. She only did what she had to do as a lion, since that species had agreed with any other that are eaten, that they will help each other.

If you want to know whether all 'Animals' analyse their lives after leaving the flesh, we'll say you can rest assured that all Beings look back and assess what they've learnt or not, what they need to gain knowledge of or not. They do look back and see what improvements may be made, but it may **not be in the same way as Humans do!** Because Humans examine their lives with their Minds and analyse facts, whereas 'Animals', whether endowed of higher or lower Consciousness, will know instinctively what was 'wrong' or not.

Except that there was not so much anything 'done wrong' within Animalkind, because they live for the moment. They do not premeditate evil deeds; they act as feels right at

142

the time for the 'right' reasons according to the situations. So it will be totally different from what Mankind would face doing it!

It is not important to worry whether 'Animals' or Plants bother to analyse themselves! Or whether they are 'right' or 'wrong' as what really matters is what this, our book, is trying to put across to Mankind: **"Wake up and STOP doing harm to each other and to the Earth you live on!"** Humanity needs to improve itself and stop the bloodshed, the torture and the starvation of millions!

It is not 'Animals' who cause problems to the Earth, it is Mankind.

This is what you have to explain to the crowds you'll talk to! Having extra details about the Creation was to help you all understand where you come from, not to engender great discussions on the nitty-gritty of who chose what, as far as other species were concerned. You have Mankind to cope with... **THAT** is big enough a problem indeed!

****

Chapter 13

UNDERSTANDING PLANTS

As the Earth world began to take shape in a physical sense, the nourishment it was also to provide was accumulated into it. That's why the 'Plants' which were to live there decided to become 'Plants'.

PLANTS' CHOICE & INNER KNOWLEDGE

Plants are 'Spirits'- but not quite the same Spirit personalities as Humans now are. They are living, sensing Spirits; they had and have the Will that everything living has, i.e. the choice to choose or reject whatever path they are on, or is offered to them.

A Plant does not have to live if it does not want to!

A Plant is a **living** creature and 'per se' is a Spiritual Being, **choosing** to be in a physical 'plant shape', but it cannot produce People or 'Animals'. It can only produce Plants and according to whatever type it is, will have fruit, flower etc. But **the Plant Inner Being is a source of Light and Knowledge.** It has a certain type of Knowledge **which other Beings have not**. They know about the weather more than People or 'Animals' do. They know about the seasons or what is to come; they sense it well in advance of it happening, so they know more than some Being!

BUT they have a different attitude to other spiritual Beings, because their view is of a linear nature, i.e. when a Plant chooses to come to Earth, it is for the simple purpose to be a Plant, so it has no feelings or sentimentality.

144

PLANTS DON'T MIND BEING EATEN

A Plant lives its life for itself so that it grows and dies. However, as they were created to help Beings coming to Earth, they **did not mind being eaten** or of other use, because that fitted within their pattern of life as they knew and know it. Those 'Spirits' wanted to be of help, simply because they were told a Plant could be useful to feed Humans and 'Animals'. So they expressed the 'thought' that if their life could be of use, that made no difference to them because they'd be a Plant anyway, so it was ok. They desired the adventure on Earth too; **they had the chance to be a Plant elsewhere** if they had wanted to.

Mankind wished to join the lot, Plants and 'Animals'. Those who decided to be 'Humans' chose the shape of 'Humans.' 'Animals' who wanted to be there too, chose to be that. And Plants started it all, by being around before them, so that the scene was set, the stage and scenario were complete for them to arrive!

PLANTS DON'T FEEL PAIN

*BR- What about hurting Plants? Critics say to vegetarians: "You **kill** carrots and cabbages!"*

Being a Plant - carrot, cabbage or whatever - is no different from being a Human or an 'Animal' in as much as they are travellers to the Earth plane too! BUT the difference, if any, is in what they have come for and how they react to it; their **sensations are limited** by the senses they have or do not have.

When Plants feed their body through or from the Earth, it is not a 'pleasurable sensation' to be likened to eating or drinking for, say, a Human. So, the necessity to feed from the minerals of the Earth does not count as a sensation per se. On the other hand, the warmth of the sun, the rain on them, the wind, the cold or heat, also their mobility or lack of mobility

145

rather, all that registers clearly in their spectrum of experiences. It is something **that** particular spiritual Soul or entity has chosen to experience.

If the Plant is hacked repeatedly 'to death', so to speak, it will feel sensations, indeed it cannot **not** feel something when its state of being is changed. But it is **not** the kind of 'pain' you would understand as a flesh Being; the **pain is not a pain, it is more like a sudden change,** or shock maybe at times. That 'jolt' will register too but it is not a real Human/Animal-like pain, because **the receptors receiving it have NO BRAIN to record the emotional distress or the hurt** or pain like it would in an 'Animal' or Human.

BR- What about Cleve Backster's experiments (*1) recording how burnt plants reacted?

The answer to this, my dear, is: **Plants have no nervous system**, unlike other flesh Beings, so they CANNOT feel what you Humans call 'pain'. As said before, they register changes and they can indeed **pick up** other changes from fellow plants if linked up to them or in close proximity, because **their Energy field will be receptive to the reactions** of the latter. But the 'jolt' caused by pulling a carrot, or cutting a cabbage, or picking an apple etc. will not be a pain! Therefore, the plant has no objection to being eaten by either Humans, 'Animals'. They exist and they **stop existing in a Plant body, to remain an Energy Being as before**.

WHAT IS CONSCIOUSNESS?

BR- Has a Plant any consciousness? When is there consciousness?

A Being of Flesh has usually some kind of consciousness at various degrees or levels. This is another long subject we may have to discuss in more detail.

BR- Doesn't being a 'Spirit' mean having some consciousness?

146

Consciousness is a state of awareness of what is going on within oneself, as well as without. That means an analysis, a comparison can be made at any moment about each experience experienced. Since a Plant just feels the actual moment or impact, but does not remember it as such, or **does not suffer mentally** from it, we cannot classify it as consciousness.

Beings with consciousness have created and built their body to suit their plans and goals. Plants have too but in a different it's difficult to explain. We'll try: What is a Plant? Stalks, roots, leaves, trunk etc. What makes a Plant to your eyes is the outer casing. The inside life is intricate indeed, with a different anatomy from a Human, say, but even **more differences in the workings of the Energies driving it.**

The basic Energy filling it with 'Life' is the same as reigns in our world and in yours - the Energy of Life, of Creativity etc. But the Soul which wants to be **a Plant is still learning to control or handle a body** of some kind. Before that, it had been a Soul as an Energy in our world and that means **it had not reached the same level of intricacies relating to Soul searching**, goal searching, affinity with others etc. It just is an Energy, enjoying being an Energy and 'wishing' to be a bit more at each step of its development.

BR- Doesn't 'wishing' imply consciousness?
An Energy has within itself capacity to choose its directions. Any Energy is like a wind which can change direction, it can be 'this' or 'that'.

NOT ALWAYS A PLANT

BR- If it is a 'Plant' on Earth, what is it when in the 'Spirit World?

Plans are made by Minds. Plants, or Energies you know now as 'Plants', do not make plans as such, of course, but 'wishing' is still inside them by their very nature. We say

147

'wish' because Creativity is within everything and everyone in Creation! If you want, **replace the word 'wish' with 'Urge'**. An Urge is less thought about, it is more followed or resisted.

The very fact of 'being' means you are a creative Being; it may not be on the same scale as others, but you have that Creative Urge inside you. Therefore, the **built-in, inherent Urge of Creativity**, of change and progression, or at least extending the experience(s), is within all, including potential Plants! That Urge is what allows a Plant to be a Plant, because the **Energy Urge is to be fixed, useful, ornamental or open to elements** etc. That's what makes a Plant a Plant!

So the Energy we see here chooses, or possibly is guided to choose, a body on Earth which offers all these criteria and that's how you see a 'Plant' on Earth, because it has followed its inner Urge, obeys the laws of Nature on Earth and is, of course, a fellow traveller helping others. This is because its inner Being is Spirit Energy which encompasses all said before - inner Kindness and inner Creativity or creative Urge.

That's **why a Plant's consciousness is not as developed as an 'Animal''s yet**. But if the Urge grows for more experience, the experiences will appear. Thus the Spirit within will acquire more Knowledge, as far as **awareness** of outside influences and eventually of itself reacting to these influences, which will lead to awareness of itself, as such, **as a separate Being.**

****

*(1) Cleve Backster - *Primary Perception: Bio communication with plants, living foods, and human cells* (2003) White Rose Millennium Press.

Chapter 14

HOW INCARNATION OCCURS

(BR) You once told me briefly that when Spirit Beings plan to incarnate into a Human body, they train on a 'course' to manipulate the flesh. I had never heard of that before you revealed it. Is it prior to every incarnation? Or just for first timers, or those who have forgotten what they learnt on previous 'courses'?

The purpose of coming to Earth is, among many other things, to learn to manipulate Matter of **that** particular kind, with the Mind of an Energy Being (or 'Spirit' Being as you call us). That is purpose nº.1. There are other reasons attached to it - goals that the individuals wish to achieve or at least tackle and solve as best as they can.

If it was all straight forward there would not be much challenge and experimentation, would there?! So there is always an element of 'testing', because the objective has not yet been achieved since it is chosen as a goal. Therefore, there is the 'doubt' or rather the question: "Will I succeed or fail or forget my aim altogether and do something else as I go along, because I will get distracted from my original idea?"

All rests with the Will of each owner of the body of flesh and new traveller to the Earth world!

The 'course' you mention is what we told you very briefly about. It is no compulsory activity. But if you want to drive a vehicle properly, you have to or should practise what is needed to handle it properly! There are Beings who have chosen not to bother with this, but **that's where they go wrong** and cannot manipulate their body of flesh correctly!

ATTENDING A COURSE

When a Being decides to go and study something in the world of Matter, 'he' has to attend a kind of **course to learn to project himself into a flesh body which 'he' creates to suit his purposes.**

Make the world understand that the process to become a Human is quite tricky and delicate - you don't 'just' become a Being in a human flesh body, just like that! You have to process the systems **in your Soul**, to fit in the criteria.

It is not just a question of deciding you want to become a 'human body' as well as being a Spiritual Being. It is so much more complex! It has to do with **adapting your vibrations**, our vibrations, to the Flesh which will be 'transporting' you, so to speak. It is **your Mind which will direct your flesh body** in all its gestures, all its actions and activities in the world of Matter.

So, the Mind (being the tool of that particular Soul) **has to be taught how to fit in** this type of thinking, since the way to think in our world is quite different as you go along and progress. It is not just a question of thinking: "All right, I am a Human now". It is something which takes 'time' to **prepare over the period preceding the departure to the Earth.**

So there are loads of people here who have been on Earth and understand the process, and also lots of scientifically-minded Beings, (as you would call them) who have **the know-how to reduce and alter the vibrations in the Mind** of those wishing to travel to the Earth. (*BR- Note: It's the first time I've ever heard of those details! Astonishing!*).

Once they have started the process of adaptation, it has to carry on and be fulfilled; it cannot be half done and left at that! Otherwise the personality won't know whether it is of the Spirit World or of the Earth (material) world.

One has to think in a different way when one is on Earth, it's not a question of 'just' changing outlook as to what

150

one will be doing for the rest of the time there. It is a question of **thinking in a different way.**

The magnetic vibrations of your Being have to be synchronised with those of the material world. That means we have to look at what is 'You' now in our world and what it will need to be vibrating at when it is in the Earth world.

ALIGNMENT OF YOUR VIBRATIONS = GOOD HEALTH

Every single Being has its own attunement, its own 'pitch', its own resonance. That's why if you find at what 'pitch' you function, you can re-establish your health more quickly when it goes out of synchronisation, you understand?

You only need to re-balance and realign the vibrations which need it. Once that is done you are all right and can be 'normal' again.

Should you let the alignment go out of true and be uneven, then you won't be functioning properly. You can test and check that with most of your so-called complementary medicines. That's what they are all about, whether one theory or the other, one therapy or the other. You cannot have balance if you are out of balance, can you?!

Therefore, we work at balancing the energies of the Spiritual Being, so that it can **be in tune with the Energies of the world it is going to**, in your case the Earth material world. This is what scientists and other evolved Beings here have to do to help any future travellers.

It can **also be going to some other worlds** you have no knowledge of yet, but it will be the same - having to 'fine tune' the balance of mental, emotional and physical levels.

It is not an easy task, as every Being has its own radiation, its own magnetic field and its own pattern! But it's obviously feasible, otherwise no one would be on this Earth you all seem to want to go to!

HOW TO DESIGN A FLESH BODY

So let's say it's a 'Man' wishing to do this. He'll actually be a Man in body, not necessarily a Man in Spirit World at the starting point. The personality wishing to be a Human Man starts with thinking about what he needs to learn and experience in the Flesh. He needs to know how to **project those thoughts into the formation of a Flesh body.** For that, he must learn it, especially if it is the 'first time' he is doing so.

An example: If he wishes to be a large, fat man for one reason or other, **he needs to visualise such a large body on Earth, so that the flesh formation follows the present thought patterns creating it.** If he wanted to be thin and skinny, he'd have to do the same of course. So, all is in the way he is thinking, as **the picture he projects** in his Mind of what he'll want to be **will find an outlet into the flesh** formation of that body, do you see what I mean?

LOOKS REFLECT SOUL'S AIMS

Once he knows what shape he needs or wants, he'll have to add lots of little details to make it look as he wishes. The reason being **the 'look' it will have will reflect the personality and desires** and attributes of that particular person to be created.

A tall man has the advantage to look over and above others. He may want to dominate or lead. A smaller man may not want to be a leader or domineering; he may want to work at a level closer to the level of others to reach them better. Everything is a lesson, a practice, an experiment, a reflection of what's behind the Flesh and within the Mind of the owner of the physical body. As you see someone tall and handsome, or small and 'ugly', or tall and 'ugly', remember they all have their **self-set pattern** to experience situations which have nothing to do with you or others! They want to learn for their own reasons.

152

BR- But don't we also inherit physical traits from our parents?

Yes, physical details are also partly to do with the **genes chosen to be inherited.** If you had chosen blonde parents, you'd probably have been blonde, but you chose those you had, because **they had qualities you wanted to inherit or learn from** and because the situations you were brought up in showed you many things and facets of life, which were useful to your upbringing and to your knowledge later in life.

As you grew up, you learnt to discard what your Soul judges not right, or to take in what your Soul judges to be good. All was not perfect in what you were shown or taught, but **you knew within yourself** when something did not agree with the Inner Knowledge, even though at the time you were not aware of your Inner Knowledge. All of these put together create the personality needed to live that particular life and of course also the body of flesh!

DAMAGED BODIES

Being born with a **damaged body** does **not** necessarily mean an injured or damaged Mind, as you may think from what was said earlier! But he may have wanted that body so that the injury or damage reflects either something which happened to him 'before' in a separate life, or will happen in this life, or **to give himself a handicap to overcome, or to teach others some learning point.** An unhealthy or sick body means the Soul within wishes to experience that state, for its own reasons, like everything else endured.

Those who chose a particular body which may hurt them during most of that life **have their reasons**. They chose very bravely to put up with that impediment or handicap because, like exams one puts up with but works for, it is an **essential part of their trip** on Earth.

153

A disabled body has a lot to cope with usually, but **the Soul within knows** it is a reflection of its attitude, or way of thinking at the time.

BR- What about a serious injury during one's lifetime?

An injury later in life has been brought on by something happening earlier, usually. If the injury was not self-inflicted but happened unexpectedly, it is often caused by a weakening of the flesh body where the counterpart exists in the spiritual body: an **injury in the flesh is a weakness in the Spirit body**. And the reason for it is always because of the clash within, a tear, **an inner upset**, a trauma. All of these are accentuated if the lifestyle or physical life leads more easily to troubles of that kind.

SUDDEN ACCIDENTS

An injury is **not always a reflection of a trauma** if the cause is a sudden accident, caused by others of course. But in the deeper levels of the Soul, there could have been **a hidden inner** desire to be hurt, injured, incapacitated, so that the Flesh responded accordingly to that wish, when the opportunity occurred!

An example: A man falls off a tree and breaks both his legs. He may not 'want' to be injured as a family man and bread-winner and it will possibly cause him and his family hardship! But inside him there may have been the desire of not having to work anymore! And even though it was not possible for him to do so for good monetary and familial reasons, his **Inner Self** felt very strongly that need for rest and freedom, and it resulted in that fall! **The body followed the inclination of the Mind, of the Soul.** All the intricate details are always complex and usually very entangled, but seen from here it is usually quite clear!

An extensive inner search seeking to understand oneself is one of the most useful endeavours one can make! Because it is by knowing yourself that you'll be able to understand your life, your purpose, your results (or lack of) and anything else happening around you, as **YOU are the cause and the creator of what happens in your life!**

You make it happen by wanting and not wanting things to be, by wishing or hating, by reacting to others or ignoring them. It is like a big web of feelings and emotions constantly twirling around and inside each individual being.

So this is the crux of the matter. **Matter is made**, in this case of Earthly life, **to reflect the inner desires and needs of the Soul in charge of that particular flesh body**. And when the needs clash with the life built by the personality, there will be some kind of trauma one way or the other!

If all is well, it is because things are as they should be, unless of course some hidden problem is slowly brewing up and may reveal itself later on! All cases are complex and complicated to understand. Interwoven among these facts are others due to lessons to learn, lessons not learnt before and many other such factors!

INNER SEARCH FOR CAUSES

Since one needs to know oneself, it is **essential to go deeply within oneself, to search for the causes and the lessons brought on by everything happening.**

It is within yourself that the Truth of your life resides, no one else is to be blamed because **you** chose a path and lead it with Inner Knowledge, knowing why you went there and did this.

It is all in the inner make-up of the individual personality. All are true to themselves and all are there to learn, experience, avoid, or fail (if need be) on their pathway... but all will be helped eventually to find their way again, whether in their Earthly life or in this one, when they come back home again.

155

BR- Why were there monsters such as Hitler, or Dr Harold Shipman (who murdered old ladies for their money)?

A murderer had not come to Earth to murder anyone! He came to Earth to learn whatever else he wanted to practise. BUT if he was weak and materialistically minded, instead of rising above it, **he let himself be driven** by his 'animal instincts' and his worldly ways of thinking, then he'd go down a path which will lead to all sorts of horrid events.

On the other hand, about the likes of Hitler (and other mass destroying dictators), such a man is so involved in his idea of either grandeur or ruling over the population, that he leads no real inner life and follows what he has been blinded with or blinded himself with.

He has **no excuse because the Inner Guidance is always there**, if only he looked for or listened to it. An Inner Guidance is the route finder, the inner navigator, the built-in tracker which anyone can turn to at any time if he wishes to listen to the signals given by this hidden helper... but not everyone listens and many fail!

You can all do what you want since you have free will, but you need to also try to be sensible. If you choose not to be wise, you will find it will lead you to more problems than you anticipated.

The suggestion to all wanting to incarnate is to think hard and well about which type of body you want to 'live in' and 'manipulate' for a while as it will be the expression of your personality for **that** particular lifetime. That is up to you, the owner and designer of your own vehicle!

You have to be reasonable in many respects, but you can be guided if you wish to be. You can always have help, suggestions and extra knowledge at any time. NO help is ever refused or impossible to have. But the majority of people are happy to follow this, so we are not saying it is a problem.

DON'T IGNORE ADVICE!

On the other hand, there are Beings who decide they'll do what they want at any time and do not listen to suggestions, because they want to implement their own ideas, even if they have not thought out further down the line of causes and effects and results. This is when people end up with problems!

We can say that at every incarnation, it is advisable to listen to advice from those who have more knowledge than you, because the type of body or gender you choose, the place where you'll be born to live, the type of surroundings and family you'll have, all this is of some importance or can even be very important.

If you do not know how to use a 'male' body because you have never had one before or never been on Earth, you cannot always **react correctly** if you are not aware of what makes a male body act differently from a 'female' one. It is a different vehicle!

As the Mind has such a strong influence and creativity on the flesh parts, you have to be advised that it will be primordial to know what will happen in circumstances where the male apparatus may react unlike a female one!

Also, the fact that **emotions** have such a powerful effect is not to be ignored! How can you ignore something which actually **creates imbalance and therefore diseases in a vehicle** you want to use through a lifetime on Earth? It is, therefore, advisable each time to have a refresher course or a starter's course, to be made aware of what could go wrong, or what needs to be done to behave according to the personality you wish to be and project in that particular lifetime.

There are plenty of ways to practise and get used to it. Like visualising so strongly the 'person' you want to become this time round that you see him/her appear in front of you. Yet you can feel his/her emotions and thoughts because they are your emotions and thoughts.

So, if you visualise the personality and see in your Mind the main points of your goal, the examples of situations you'd like to meet in that life (to help you carry out your experiments and be more enlightened after it), then you'll be able to feel his emotions and see how you'd react as, say, a man in that kind of situation.

You could feel very lonely if you did not know your new body. A bit like being thrown in a new car or any vehicle (say a tank!) you have never driven before. So this is why you need to be able to have some contact with it beforehand, to learn the 'manoeuvres' (to put it simply). We recommend people should have some practice! That has always been done best by visualising (as this is what we always done here anyway!) and **creating a 'mock-up' model of what you plan to use**. That is the prototype of the real body you are going to create.

That prototype is not fixed and rigid. It is a creation of **your** Mind, to see whether you are happy with the basic points you wish to project as a personality - and a body from which you'll learn - or which will help you experiment or achieve as best as you can, the goals you have chosen for that lifetime.

What colour hair or eyes you choose is not that important. That is less significant than the fitness of the body, its height and strength, its beauty or not, as seen by Humans and the **resistance to illness, which will depend both on the strength of your character and your Mind power, your emotions and on the way you will look after that vehicle, or not!**

There are so many subliminal aspects which will influence the resulting 'outer/ surface' results in the flesh! You cannot guess what happens in this world. It is so complicated to explain in detail! We are only trying to give you a quick overview. That 'prototype' is the blueprint of what you want to be like. As it is polished and designed, **you** put all your thoughts and desires into its final construction. It is a mini acorn in the making of the great oak tree that you will 'blossom out' as eventually.

So the blueprint has all the emotional energies built-in, as they will trigger the reactions and their activation into the flesh replica. (This is a very simple description to give you an idea of what happens. Understand there is much more to it than that!). **That Energy blueprint and template is the future YOU**, as it embodies all the emotions and thoughts of the new personality which has a goal, an aim for that new life as a new human Being.

WHEN A SPIRIT BEING LINKS TO THE EMBRYO

It may not be changed once the thought of existing in that mother has taken place, been sent and reached its destination. The mother's body will have received the seed of flesh with the sexual act, **but until the thought of 'being in existence', of wanting to exist, has been implanted in the 'flesh seed' to give it Life, there will be nobody**. An egg can create a flesh form of an embryo, but cannot give it Life until the Thought Power with its desire attached to it (desire 'to be', to live in the flesh) has actually been sent by the personality who wants to live there and then. **That is when it happens to give it its Life Force** with its Will to live in a new body.

Unless the Will diminishes and leaves the flesh embryo or foetus, the creation of the future baby will take place according to the laws of Nature, but **should the Will to live in that body disappear completely,** the fetus or baby will not become whole or not live as planned and that will be the end of that incarnation.

When we say the thinking of the future personality is in that Energy blueprint/template, of course we don't mean all the thoughts he'll have in that life ahead (how could one foresee that?!), but the basic way of thinking of that personality, his character, his emotional type. (Is he the quiet type or the anxious, excitable one, etc?).

159

NO IMPOSED PREDETERMINATION

It's important to see that we don't mean any kind of 'predestination', except in the fact that there is Free Will in the choice of the shape of the body, its state of health at first arrival, its aptitude to cope well with physical life, also the way it reacts well to its 'driver', the Mind of the 'Spirit Being', who wishes to experiment with a new life on the Earth.

Any kind of 'predetermination' may only be created by the Being himself, for example, he may decide to only have a short life, by human standards, to fit in with his original plan. Not everyone wants to live a long time on Earth when he can be freer and happier in our realm (or possibly in other places)!

He may even change his mind on that, as he goes along during that life. He may realise he may want to stay longer than he had originally thought he would, because he may feel, for example, that he is needed, or he wants to remain to see through a new project and experiment he's tackled, possibly in addition to his original plan? Who knows?! Only the Being in question would know why.

But no one is 'forced' or 'sent' to do anything that he does not want to do or be. He is in charge of his flesh body, which is the vehicle for his Mind, i.e. the tool of his Higher Being.

BR- The blueprint is sent into the seed of the egg/sperm mixture, with the thought of "wanting to exist". Since one creates one's own body, who created that egg and the sperm for that? There is also obviously a genetic influence from both parents on the new flesh being - and some parents could create other foetuses of very different persons.

The blueprint/template we mentioned **is the template of that particular** personality, who will have, say, blond hair/blue eyes/will be tall/a famous physicist with a bad temper and a stammer/a love of sailing and swimming/who may want children later on, but is not that bothered, as his main aim is to be a 'parent to Mankind', to teach them about, say, the origin and possible use of microwaves in space?/Or prevention of earthquakes?/by first doing lots of research which will take his time and be his passion. Right?

Those main points are in the blueprint/template and sent to the mother's egg, which has a receptive area for all that. Let's explain more clearly: When the sexual act takes place and succeeds, the form resulting from it is a mixture of cells that will be dividing and forming an embryo then a 'fetus' etc. But the LIFE of the 'embryo' is not given and determined until the blueprint and its Will to live in that form, there, is received by this embryo's cells. So there is **no future baby until that is achieved.**

As soon as the Will to live (i.e. giving Life to the embryo's cells and body of the new personality) has triggered things into motion, for all the above to happen, **then** you'll have Life in it and a Will to form itself as a new Being of flesh.

EGG CHOSEN AND PREPARED

But the day the mother decided to have that sexual act, the cells of the egg were 'prepared' very quickly indeed to receive the new blueprint which was due to come. It could not be sent beforehand until the egg was ready to exist and ready to receive all that information, without which it could not perform its job. We repeat: A baby cannot be formed to live if the blueprint has not be sent and received.

The body of the mother creates eggs, but not every egg is deemed suitable by the future personality, i.e. the Being in our world wanting to project himself as a new Human for a while. He will wait for the 'right time' in the life of that person and his life there to take place.All those little details are worked out to help him make the most of his trip, a bit like an astronaut being sent to planets, but not until the position of the

161

sun or the moon etc. is correct for the success of the trip. So he will go when his advisers have worked out the right moment for that space trip. Your future Human cannot do all that on his own. He needs to have **help from more knowledgeable Beings here in our world**, who have experience in those matters.

BR- Is that part of a 'training course' that some are silly enough to ignore? Or is everyone always advised?

The ones ignoring this would have to do it at their own peril! That would be extremely thoughtless and feckless! This is essential for the correct result to fit a particular life plan. So anyone 'stupid' enough to ignore this will have mishaps, will not succeed in creating life in a new Being of flesh, or may do it at a time very 'unsuitable' for the whole family.

There are indeed Beings who have carried out their plan without paying attention to the correct moment for the egg to be produced, of the right consistency or receptivity. All those little details cannot be worked out by someone who is not qualified and knowledgeable in that particular field. So yes, there are people who have done so! But the results have not always been good... and then they complain they have a 'bad' life! But whose fault is it?

It is a new/unexpected experience, so that's something in their 'favour', but is it the one they were hoping for? Well no, not always.

Yet since Creativity knows no boundary, nothing can really be labelled a 'bad experience,' since it is an experience - but perhaps of a different type to the one originally planned. In this case, there might be two consequences: Either the new Being realises his huge mistake (and thus has learnt from it!) and decides to **remove early his Will to live** in that body and that environment. Or he **sticks with it bravely** and sees it as an unexpected hurdle and even direction and carries on valiantly in this new path, to see where it will lead him! But he will no doubt have learnt it would or could have been better to seek and listen to advice before setting off!

BR- What about that sperm? It's one in millions.

As said before, **the gender of the new personality is decided by the future Being, who is a 'Spirit Being'/Energy Being** and chooses to be male or female. But the action of the sperm helps that to happen, as far as it gives the type of chromosomes provided correctly into the cell of the new creature. So this 'right' type is not fixed by the sperm (who does not really think or fix anything), but by the future creature/personality who will have wanted the right receptive egg and the right sperm to be guided to succeed in the fertilisation.

The power of Mind and Thought is the only tool we have here. The Mind of the Energy Being who wants to project himself on Earth **projects the intense wish and desire** to be a male/female. That attracts the sperm with the suitable type of chromosome accordingly.

It is not as complicated in the end as you may think. Only a question of sending the correct but **intense** Thought Energy in that direction at the 'right time' - before and while the sexual act takes place, to **make sure all is well orchestrated to suit the needs of the new person**. All in all a fairly well organised orchestration, wouldn't you say?!

INFERTILITY

BR- What about infertile parents wishing for a child, yet having none?

Everything resides in the fact that 'children' are future Beings coming to Earth to live a particular life of experiments in using or learning to use Mind over Matter.

Those who want a child as a baby and 'doll' to pamper are not always the best parents for some Beings who wish for strong parents with higher motives to have a child. That's point one.

163

Secondly, no one is born who has not already 'discussed' the situation 'way back in time', you would say. Understand **it had been organised in our world, or even in a 'previous' incarnation** when it may have been talked about first. It was then confirmed when they came here (in Spirit World), where they set up the system of chronological order to exist on Earth (so that parents are older than their child!).

You all choose the parents who will provide you with some genes which will physically help you have the colour/ shape/height/etc. you wish to have in your new body, but you also may want to match personalities. If you want an outgoing excitable personality you are more likely suited with similar parents. You may also choose parents for their knowledge or the learning they want to acquire and provide you with, so that you are brought up in a suitable environment for your plan.

Or you may chose a poor family (which itself is learning the experience of struggling with poverty, like you) but you will rise from that, to study hard and become, say, a pioneer in fighting children's poverty or illnesses, or doing social work for the deprived classes. So that you will have learnt what it is like in order to provide better facilities and fulfil needs etc.

Therefore, with parents who have no child and want one, it could be it was their own lesson and experiment. They may have wanted to know what it is like to experience that unquenched thirst and desire. Or, possibly, they may have created children in a 'previous life' but not taken care of them when they had them - and they had not appreciated the wonder of creating new lives. So now they experience the opposite and that makes their own Spirit/Higher Self more knowledgeable. There are **many possible reasons**, but all in accordance with the laws of Nature and our World.

If the body of, say, the mother is not able to bear a child, then there won't be one - but **that was known to the**

mother's Higher Self when she created her own vehicle when coming to Earth! As part of her own experimentation, no doubt.

UNWANTED PREGNANCY

The number of people wanting a child and not having one, is not as high as the number of people having a child and not having planned or wanted one.

If some of you think this statement is an 'inconsistency' it is not one really. It is to do with the fact that, even though there are discussions beforehand in our realm (before anyone goes to the Earth in the 'right chronological order'), it is always possible for the family member, say, the mother, once on Earth, not to have planned to have a child at this time of her life or career! It may be that she has forgotten the life plan organised (that's not unlikely, as most people 'forget') or that she's changed her mind, or got distracted by more interesting options in her life and has taken a 'side road'.

But if **the 'child' wanted to come at that time, because of his own reasons,** then he will! Of course, it could also be, as said before, that they had not organised the 'blueprint despatch' as they should have, i.e. they did it without any superior advice and guidance.

FAMILY MEMBERS' ORDER OF BIRTH

It's all in agreement with the blueprints and plans that have been organised among yourselves when you were all still here (in our World) and you all planned the Big Trip, the Experiment to the world of Earthly Matter - as there are other Matters, but that's another topic! So you all sent thoughts around about wanting to go on Earth and learn/practise/offer help : "Who would like to join me in this trip with the view to doing xyz?"

Whoever has been with you before and **you have affinity with** may help in some cases. Other times you may

165

want to **swap roles** - one who was your 'father', now will be a mother or child to you, or you will be theirs. Or it may just be Beings with whom you get on well, or who are (or not) on the same wavelength as you and there is some significance in your paths crossing on Earth for some reason that you will all weigh up.

JUGGLING TO FIT IN GOALS

All along, you and every other individual concerned have Free Will and freedom of choice. When all the main details are worked out, the **trip is organised** for that particular group of future personalities, so that their individual purposes and goals for going are taken care of, whether happy or tougher as some may be.

But no one is abandoned, as all along there are bands of us, the helpers and loving, caring friends from here, who will be watching over all of you individuals. We'll be **trying our best to inspire you and remind you of your life plan** if need be. Yet we may have to cringe if ever you stubbornly refuse to follow the reminders! We cannot stop you from doing what you want once there. We can only remind you that you wanted us, the guiding friendly voice, to be keeping an eye on you.

But if you steadfastly refuse to do so, there is not much we can do, as **none of us is allowed to infringe on your Free Will**. All Beings have Free Will. This was set and agreed upon as the Earth Experiment was set up 'aeons' ago. All wanted freedom of expression and experimentation. All have it. No one can block that.

Only the ones who persistently act against the only guiding 'rule' given **will feel the weight of their own conscience and Higher Self** when they return here: "Why have you flaunted the law of not hurting any other Being travelling along like you and why didn't you try and help those you saw in trouble when you could have done so?" Then **their own Inner Hell will start** and that will have been their own doing!

166

BABIES IN THE WOMB

Simple facts of life are not always known. Just look at the birth of a child, who will be a grown-up Human, of course. Has anyone wondered what the baby in the womb thinks of his position, his situation? He is in a strong situation, he is a Human in the making. He has just left the world of Spirit he was in, perhaps for a very long time; and now he encases his spiritual Energy in a body of flesh, which will have to be his vehicle for possibly a long while! What does he think of it, as he lies there being created bigger and strong enough to come out and face the world of Matter?! We know he is a Spirit - but no one on Earth seems to remember he is a 'Spirit in a vehicle of flesh'!

Well, we can tell you the experience can be a torture or a delight, depending on the aims and the goals that particular Soul had set itself before setting off on that trip. So, the torture could be part of the **built-in fears** the baby, or child, or adult will have in their life. They come for something to learn or experience but are dreading it at the same time! That is how some youngsters are 'tortured within', without even knowing it.

If people could learn to send healing thoughts to babies in the womb, it would help them emerge more safely and also in a saner state of mind. If the baby needs calming before he is born into the physical world, he'll benefit from the healing vibrations sent to him.

BR- Couldn't Spirit World do it before he is born?

The healing thoughts are to come from those who are going to receive him into the physical world, because they have to be on the same vibrational level as the personality's new Energy level.

Once one is in a flesh body, or part of a flesh body, the Energy levels, the vibrations of the flesh, have a great influence on the way that personality will react. The fact of being into a 'casing of flesh', so to speak, makes a great difference to the way people react. It has a greater influence then on one's way of thinking. So, the baby needs to be told within himself that he can be healed, that he does not need to suffer and dread what is coming, if it is in that 'position', that way of thinking.

BR- But we can't know what he is thinking!

The fact you don't know whether he is thinking that way or not means you all need to send healing thoughts to babies 'on the go', in the making, to send them strength, determination and encouragement! They have to make a big trip, a hard one for some, as they dive into a new world... once more possibly! They may be looking forward to it of course, but it is more likely they are dreading a lot of it. Why?

Because having to leave the world of Spirit (as you call it), in order to 'dive into' a restricting body of flesh (which no doubt, will come with all its problems!) instead of staying in our wonderful World of Mind and Light is a big, big step to take!

All of you should feel sorry for babies who are being born - sorry, not happy! That's what we wanted to tell you: that everyone rejoices at the birth of a new Soul in the world is very nice... but you don't **see it from its point of view**! It/she/he **may** be very miserable to have had to make the trip!

That's what should be set up, a healing minute or whatever for babies coming into the world, for their Souls to settle down, their Minds to have more peace within, as they make their way through nine months of pregnancy and the years of babyhood. To be a baby is very hard work, when you have been a free Spirit, a grown-up Soul, a knowledgeable personality who has chosen to go back to Earth for whatever purpose.

A Soul making that trip has indeed a lot of courage no doubt (may be mad too, I'd say with a smile!), but indeed very brave to have left the world it was in, our world, to go to your present one and face many unknown factors.

168

So will you try to let people think about it? Those who have to be the parents will need healing too, they have a big responsibility and many are not always up to it, even though they've created the little one. It takes a lot of courage and dedication and often basic knowledge of Man's Mind to handle the upbringing of a child and future adult!

All in all, healing has its value on all levels and scores. You all need to give healing to babies, future ones or those who have arrived - and their family because that is what the world of Humans is made of - children and parents. The world cannot be made of unhappy Souls who dread what they are going to live in.

BR- Is it the majority? Some seem to be happy.

Many children are happy indeed but I am talking of the many millions who have chosen to come, knowing they'll probably have a life tougher than most. It makes it even worse for them in the long run, because they arrive dreading what they may be in for!

BR- May I ask a question? Why are poor people born, say, in Africa?

It has been said that a pupil who asks questions is one who is interested, so do not be afraid of asking questions. You wonder why they are born? Because they want to learn something, experience the fact they are poor or starving, to understand better those who are also poor and starving, to help them in turn. If they did not, there would be no one knowing what it is like!

BR- So one can't break the vicious circle?!

The vicious circle started when Mankind did not make everyone equal, back in time. It started long ago and still exists! Mankind had forgotten that the trip to Earth was supposed to be an enjoyable experiment, in harmony with fellow travellers. It has turned into a battle or competition between who can be stronger or better than the others. That was NOT the original aim!

So, to come back to what we were saying. The little one being born dreading his trip on Earth has to be helped by sending him (or her) all the possible loving, healing thoughts to fortify him in his endeavours. If you don't, if no one does, then he is really on his own, you see, and that could make his adventure much worse than it needs to be.

BR- I had never thought of it like that. Is it the same for 'Animals' then'? We would be at it all day long, sending healing thoughts!

Bravery is more what 'Animals' are coming for. They usually come to experience physical life, of course, but also the link with Mankind in some cases, or the freedom of having a flesh body but not linked to Mankind, as in wild 'Animals'. So, in the latter case, it is all a question of being brave enough to risk being on one's own, to face the world of flesh with all its demands: the demands of the body of flesh versus the adversity caused by the elements and wilderness. They have to be brave and need bravery in their hearts to face the world.

Many will die young, simply because they cannot cope too long in that world and would rather come back to us here. Others will last longer but will still need courage to face the world.

All are Souls from our world, on a journey for themselves usually and who, whether 'Animals' or Humans, need badly the help provided by healing, living thoughts.

BR- But that means millions of them needing my healing thoughts!

My dear, you don't have to heal them all now! You can simply help by sending thoughts now and then, but most of all also teach people to think that way too! The rest of the world could and should do the same.

That would be the ultimate aim, eventually...

****

Chapter 15

INCARNATION: FIRST BABIES

BR- Incarnation: What about the 'first childbearing and birth'?

There is the problem of being unable to project yourself whole. The body could not be projected whole as **it was planned to be developed from child to adult size.**

So, though the first prototypes **may** have been built as 'adult' and tested as 'adult', without going through the procedure of child bearing and birthing, it was essential that the proper process be followed afterwards, otherwise they would not know how well it worked! There was a 'batch' of people who fancied trying the 'proper procedure', while others were more interested in the smaller details of how each part of the body worked.

TESTING MATING & BIRTH

The process of being born on Earth had to be tested too. For that there were people who were checking it here first, then tried it on Earth when they arrived there. They had, of course, to wait for 'nine months' to see whether the whole procedure worked, but what is 'nine months' indeed? Nothing seen from here. So, as the whole of the population was rather limited at the beginning, they had no problem with being the few who were there, trying out other ideas on the planet, while they waited for the birth of that first idea of 'himself' as a baby who chose to be one of the first 'offspring'- as there were several who tested the system.

It was a 'matter-of-fact invention', if you see what we mean. The sperm was injected in the woman as an experiment. They did not need the complicated idea of relationship and so on. It was to make sure a 'baby' could safely and correctly be reproduced by the physical means of a sexual act.

When we talk of sexual act, we are discussing between man and woman, not amongst 'Animals' - as 'Animals' also tried it, then they had their reproductions checked too. But let's consider Humans for now.

So the males who did it as a matter-of-fact did not particularly care or not care about the females. They may have tried it many times amongst themselves for all we know! Basically, the knowledge we got is: it had to be tested for all to know it worked.

BODIES: AN EXCITING INVENTION

BR- So the idea must have been of filling the Earth with a population then?

You need to grasp how excited 'people' and others were to think they'd be able to **create this new 'invention'**. It meant there were many hundreds of Beings and more, no doubt, who wished to have a go at participating in the full scale operation, from **designing bodies** (ideas of what is to be done on Earth, hence bodies to match the goals) to actually going there themselves!

The whole thing took some 'millions' of years to be worked out, no doubt. The entire concept had to be projected 'one bit at a time', all in different parts and pieces. As there must have been so many myriads of trials, it's impossible to give a list of details! But we can tell you for sure, there were a great deal of **interested Beings from here who dedicated themselves to this new venture**! They chose to be the testers, therefore to go and be at the receiving end, which means some made the decision to stay here until their 'parents' were ready to 'produce' over there.

It may have first happened without babies and birth, when they first projected ideas into shapes of various sizes and

172

number of parts, but when it was gradually settled to Beings with two arms and two legs, then it became more interesting for those wanting to go, to wait to be a new 'baby', a new little Being becoming a big Being.

That was no doubt quite an exciting event for all concerned, as that had not been done that way so far on the Earth!

MYRIADS OF POSSIBILITIES

You see, those are part of many possibilities. Some were not leading to anything and may have been aborted half-way. If a Being did not want to stay as a foetus/baby and changed his Mind, he only needed to pull out! But the overall activity was indeed bringing more Beings from our world for a **temporary Experiment in Creativity**, by the means of a male and female and an egg plus sperm mixture. **This** was the invention they thought exciting and very clever!

OAK IN AN ACORN

It could have been done otherwise, but the whole concept was from small to very big, from seed or egg to full-size adult; and from the whole adult being designed, encompassed and contained in the tiny miniature that the body of the mother (in this case) would bear and bring to fruition.

That's not the only time there was anything like that done, as a seed is the miniature and replica of the future tree or plant to be. So we can see the **idea of minute to mighty big**, making the Earth world a wonderful miracle, bearing and producing all those new Beings in a gigantic variety of possibilities. And **there are still some new ones to be 'invented'** and thought out. This is not a completed experiment! It is still going on but you Humans can't really see it from where you are, because you are in the middle of it!

NEW BODIES CURRENTLY BEING INVENTED

We can see it if we look hard enough. Lots of new Plants inventing themselves and 'Animals' trying new ways of existing! And People who have not so much the idea of changing their shape than **resisting the onslaught of illness** (viruses etc.), i.e. preparing bodies which will be much stronger. Why? Because the Minds of those now wishing to come to your world will be very strong and very determined to **make themselves immune** to verbal and emotional attacks! Why? So that they can carry out their work and plans: to instil in what is left of the Earth population, very strong and renewed ideas of what should be done to live happily in this wonderful physical world!

RESTORING THE EARTH

The Experiment is not given up upon. Some want to 'escape' to other planets by 'being born' there (we are talking of Beings in our world choosing to do that) but **some want to see the Earth Experiment through**, so it is re-established as it should be! It has been knocked off its balance and pedestal in a way, because the harm and damage done by the 'bad' population have made great indents in what should have been left in a good state for others to enjoy.

So we'll say those coming now (and **you** are part of them and so are your open-minded close friends) have decided to be 'troops and armies' of volunteers to go and re-establish and restore what should have been there in the first place. The leeway for testing and experiment is still there; plenty of opportunities for ideas and inventions, but the aims and goals must be based and **not infringing upon the Law of no harm to other travellers**!

BRING BACK THE WONDERS

That's why those like you, who fight for the good of your world, have chosen to go and restore what was rightfully there - and others will choose to do the same over long periods of your 'time', no doubt!

Pull out and crush any bad deeds and activities. Repair or replace what can be and **re-seed the Minds of those Earthly travellers** to make the surroundings and the life offered there, the exciting and wonderful experience Life on Earth was and is meant to be - all together enjoying the new way of using your Minds, ideas and thoughts. How? Using them to improve or extend abilities or enjoyment **without doing any harm,** whether to the Earth itself or any of its inhabitants, who, after all, are ALL 'Spirit Beings' - Beings from our World of Mind and Light.

May we all succeed soon is our wish to you all.

****

Chapter 16

FEELING IN THE WRONG BODY

BR- People who feel they are born in the wrong body: Is it a life plan or a wrong choice or...?

There is a strong need for such a question. Too many people feel they are not right in their own body. In a way, those individuals have not exactly 'made the wrong choice' because they have actually designed their body with their Creative Mind, remember! **They** have had a hand in it! Those Beings just felt they wanted to try something very different, as the choice had been too much 'either male or female'. They thought it would be more interesting to have a bit of each! But the trouble is they did **not look into it** properly, as they'd need to adapt the ways of thinking and feeling and **the reactions this will cause onto the flesh.** This is what needs to be explained.

If a designer of a body thinks he can make himself a male body but adjust the inner workings (the ways of thinking and feeling) to a female one in that body, it **will not work**, as the body is the reflection of the Mind and inner thinking personality. So if he builds a female body but thinks like a male, the female body will not be a true reflection of his thinking and attitude as a male. Therefore, there will be some hiccups! The efforts put into it are not really worthwhile because in the end it will bring or lead to a dead end in that particular avenue, won't it?

GUIDANCE

BR- Wouldn't they have been warned about it?

Of course they would, but the Law of Free Will prevents all guidance from infringing on the Will of the Being!

The idea of choosing to do this is not really approved here, I can tell you that! It is rather daft, as we know the body of flesh is definitely driven by a personality from our world who takes charge of it. If he designs for himself a body looking like a woman, but he wants to be a man, why does he do it?

If it is for the 'fun' of swapping, it can only lead him to more trouble, as said before, because it will not work as soon as he tries designing and 'constructing' it, knowing there will be a hiccup and change needed sooner or later!

UNSTABLE STRUCTURE

There is a **need for stability in any construction** and building, whether physically as on Earth (with stone etc), or in our world as they design and build a body of flesh. It cannot be juggled with, because the components won't be steady and securely 'fastened' as an image. If they build an exterior as a woman it might just about be feasible physically but the workings won't react as a woman - she'll feel male, she'll think like a male and she won't react physically like a woman does!

If the body is not meant to be the one of a woman, it will not behave like one. There'll be 'male' ideas, urges, temptations and likings leading it. It is important to get this right.

If people had all the same urges, life would be very different and no co-creation would occur. So it is essential to have a gender of each to populate the Earth but, having said that, now that the Earth is overpopulated, it is not so much a need or a problem.

Nevertheless, the creation of an ambiguous Being, who does not know whether 'he' is male or female, will create all sorts of problems for 'him'. It is better if one can stick to one gender, so as to focus on the life one has chosen.

EXPERIMENT OR MISTAKE?

But if someone made the mistake to consciously create, say, a female body 'for fun' but wanted to be a male to have an experience of a different kind, it could not be 'blocked', as such, because **it could still be classified as an experiment** and 'experience in Creativity', which means if the Being tried this against all advice, 'he' will not be prevented even though advised against it (if he tried to ask for some!).

If 'he' proceeds, he will have given himself (and whoever tried to help him with the physical creation of the female body) many a headache, so to speak! Even if he aborts the attempt at the last minute, he will still have caused himself complications, because **the remaining thoughts of a 'dual creation' will still be floating about and may be picked by someone else** who may think it is feasible! As to wanting to 'step in' such a body, he will be confused himself in the end. The workings of the flesh won't be the same.

BR- Would he go on a 'course'?

There is a greater likelihood he would not be attending a course for it, as the advice would have been given many a time in various ways.

LIFE PLAN?

BR- So it is the wrong body then?

As far as Life Plan and goals are concerned, it would be a far too complicated plan with definitely lots of hiccups, problems, confusion and heartache. But if that is what he really **wanted to experience, as a painful experience**, then he'll be following it to the end! He may not live long on Earth if he can't cope with it, or he may survive it and have his fair share of problems! But who is to say it is really 'wrong'?

No one can criticise Creativity, as it is meant to constantly be an experiment that has its pitfalls, failures and

178

successes. The success of being able to 'swap bodies' at the cost of further painful surgery (or whatever one does on Earth for it) will be an achievement which 'he' could have spared himself if 'he' had been born as a female or a male in the first place. We cannot say it is wrong. It is just **not advisable** if one can't quite see what it will lead to. Some have succeeded and some have blazed the trail for more to copy it.

BR- Do you see a difference between: totally 'born in the wrong body', needing surgery - and being homosexual (= simply attracted and happier with one of the same gender)?

Those who chose the other sex is the 'normal', more run of the mill/usual thing, but **those who have an attraction to the same gender have let one side of their personality as a whole Being dominate** so they will have a feminine tendency tinting the male personality (and vice-versa), perhaps because in 'previous time' he was a woman? Or he may have chosen this as a life plan (or part of) to make a point that there should not be any discrimination amongst travellers on the same Earth.

As the only rule is 'Do not harm others', **if he does not actually harm any other Being, if he matches his tendencies with another Being who feels the same, where is the harm? None.** It's only when the dominant feeling and urges are allowed to go beyond personal life, or lead to harming any others (like affecting vulnerable children who have no choice in the matter), that it has become wrong, because harming, hurting, killing are not part of the plan of Creativity. Those are banned and never even considered!

So, to sum up: Having a body of flesh which has not been thought out properly, or been rushed or decided upon for the wrong reasons, will lead to failure of that vehicle, one way or the other, even before it is born!

Choosing a body which does not match the personality's way of thinking and desires will lead to many problems.

179

If those problems are actually planned/designed/wanted by the personality driving the vehicle, then so be it! 'He' is the only one who will suffer from it, if anything.

It is not against the one Law of not harming others. So...!

****

Chapter 17

COMA: WHAT HAPPENED?

BR. Could you explain about people in a coma for years?

If we told you they are in 'no man's' land' it may upset a lot of people. Yet it is true. They have chosen to be in 'suspended animation'.

A person who, say, had an accident and stopped living as a Human on Earth - just staying as a body alive but not reacting as a personality - is a very traumatic experience for those around 'him' and even for himself. This is because he is no longer aware of anything, as such, since his Mind and Soul chose to be in 'no man's land' for a while.

Such people chose it, so **their Minds create it**. They see themselves as nothing, in a way, yet it's not quite correct. They do not actually think they are 'nothing', they just stop thinking for a while. They have taken a break from anything and everything. They have suspended all activities, possibly because their Minds were overworked, or overburdened, or even confused with their lives overall. It's hard to know why a person does it; it's their own Mind creating it.

DEEP-SEATED REASON

The accident or incident which caused the rupture of a normal life, was **not** 'unplanned'! It will have been **subconsciously craved for,** to give the person a breathing space, a moment of non-committal, a suspension of activities. It was no doubt **needed by the Mind and Soul, even if others cannot see it like that!** No one can really see within anyone's Soul and thinking, so he will have taken the opportunity to escape, to refresh his batteries and take a breather. That's what it's for.

RECOVERY?

Since his body had not died, it may be possible **to bring him back** to normal activities, **if his Soul and his Mind accept to do so.** If the brain has been so damaged that the man won't be able to function, then it is very unlikely he will recover or come out of his blank state. He will just slip out of the whole body and will be at rest where he was meant to be in the first place - the World of Mind and Light.

He may have wanted to know that experience, or his family and friends may have chosen to be part of that sad 'experiment' too. All are their own, private decisions.

Any attempts to bring him back **will fail if the Soul has decided to leave the body** under the guidance and directions of his Higher Self. But it may be possible to **bring him back, if the solution has been found by the Soul,** if he has regained his inner balance and appreciated or gained from the mental break, the self-imposed suspension. **He will then react to memories or calls from those around him** who encourage him to wake-up. But that's always a personal decision, only taken by the person involved as he lies there in his bed, or wherever. It is not to be worried about as such.

All that can be done from your side on Earth is to **send him a lot of Healing**, to give his Soul and therefore Mind, the calm needed to make the right decision for him. Also do send some Healing to the family and close ones who may be suffering from that unsettling state of affairs.

All Healing given works, as it always has an effect on the inner personality before you can possibly see any results physically on the flesh. If he slips out and 'dies' as Healing as been given, that shows that the **Healing energies gave the personality the strength and courage to make the right decision for himself,** for his plans in that particular life.

****

Chapter 18

EUTHANASIA

BR- I know we must not kill but could you explain to Mankind the Spirit World's views on euthanasia? As it is terribly difficult for his family when a patient in great pain begs them to help him die.

You have already been told that no one should take anyone's life away, as it is not theirs to deal with. You should not kill or help kill anyone.

What to do when the person begs you and you see he is in great pain and could do with escaping from that body soon? The reason he is still in that body is because **he has let himself be in that body!** He is in charge of his body. It is his vehicle on Earth as a Spirit Being. He has chosen that body to take him through his life, for his own purpose. So you are not to interfere with it, as you are interfering with his project, his Life Plan on Earth.

If he was that desperate to leave, then he would leave, my dear! His Soul would simply step out of the vehicle of flesh and the body would be left behind. The body is only his representation. Why hasn't he gone yet, in spite of the pain? Because he as his Higher Self/High Spirit - the 'Real Him' - **does not want to go yet!**

WHY IS DEPARTURE DELAYED?

Perhaps his Higher/Real Self may want to be there a little longer to see loved ones a bit more, in spite of the pain or fear of what is to come?

Maybe he wants to experience the slow passing out of the flesh, instead of being propelled out of it like a cannon ball?

183

Or he may want to take his time, so everybody has been able to come to terms with the fact that he is leaving and must leave. That vision of him suffering, or in a bad state, will probably give strength to the ones left behind, to feel happy that he is soon going, they will accept it was the best thing for him. So they may need adjusting to the idea at that slow speed.

If he is in pain, he can be given painkillers or be 'knocked out' by doctors. If he had healing provided by those he loves, or whoever can give healing, he **will** definitely be helped to ease out gently and have the courage to let go at last, **once his own Soul and Spirit are ready.**

'TESTING THE WATERS'

He needs to have accustomed himself to the Other Side he is going to land on, anytime, so he'll be making little trips (to our World) in his Mind and during his sleep. He will get there in 'short stays' in order to become used to his future whereabouts. That's why we say: "Don't rush someone into leaving his body if he is not quite ready for it emotionally and spiritually".

This body may want to get away from the disease or trouble it is in; but **the Soul is the driver who decides** when he is to arrive at his destination and does not need the battered vehicle any longer.

So, the euthanasia idea is of no help to those who are being kicked out of their body before the Soul and Spirit are ready to depart. It is to do with their Life Plan and the state of Mind of the Spirit Being who has been driving the flesh vehicle. A very difficult situation indeed for those watching, but the best is to give wholehearted love, healing, compassion, support and encouragement to the Soul of the patient.

TALK TO THE SOUL

Talk to his Soul in your Mind and Heart. Send thoughts to his guide and loved ones in our World, so that he receives all the Energy he needs to have the strength to make the final decision, when his own Soul is ready for it. It has to be his Soul's decision to leave the body naturally, not being forced.

He'll just need to remove his Will from the 'driving seat' and the liberation will be achieved. So simple!

Let the Soul embrace the idea it is ready and has had enough. The Soul and the Higher Self. Not the thoughts of the Human because, if he is sent too early, he may well regret not to have had that little extra time to suss out and sort out where he is going.

It may even be part of his Life Plan to feel that little extra pain or upset, so that it gives him courage and determination to leave the flesh - as well as, possibly, to want to experience what pain is like... so he'll enjoy being free from it as soon as he comes over! That will help him not regret not being on Earth. **He'll be glad to have escaped in his own time.**

****

Chapter 19

KILLER ALWAYS WRONG

BR- The Universal law is: "No one dies whose Higher Self did not want to leave the flesh body". Spirit Masters also reveal that: "No bullet kills anyone whose Higher Self did not want to leave the flesh."

Yet nobody has the right to kill others and deprive them of the life they have chosen to live on Earth.

So in theory even if a murderer/bomber plants a bomb, he won't kill you (if your Higher Self is not ready) and will only kill those whose Higher Self is ready.

So it looks then as if the criminal is not 'depriving' people, not 'interfering with their plan or their right to live'?

No need to look for holes in the Law! There is one simple rule: "Do not harm any other Being". If the harm is **done wilfully**, the killer will have to 'pay' for this, in the sense that he will be faced **with his crime against the Law** when he comes over and **analyses his own life** and actions.

But if you think a person wanted to be killed by a bomb instead of dying in his bed or of a disease, then that's fine, it may be so... BUT the lesson to learn out of this is from the point of view of the murderer: he tried and wanted to harm another person! Whether that Being was willing to die, or intended to, has nothing to do with the fact that **the killer had not listened to his Inner Voice, his Inner Self** and he ignored completely the Law of the Universe about letting all Beings have their own trip in the Experiment and not to interfere with it.

His crime may not 'interfere with a plan' by killing the man who may have possibly died anyway, but the killer is not allowed to try to kill and certainly not allowed to injure, hurt and cause pain. After all, the victim may have left the body in a more peaceful way.

It is **the fact that the killer made himself be a killer which is wrong** and it will have to be rectified by himself eventually.

PACT BEFORE BIRTH?

If the victim has **chosen** to be injured, attacked or 'to die', that was and is his prerogative. If he had asked the (future) attacker **(before they were born)** to behave like that, it's between them. *(Note- See Rob Schwartz - 'Your Soul's Plan'*)*

So if they made a **'pact'** before birth (may seem strange but could be, who knows?), then the 'evil deed' may have a reason which will 'exonerate' the attacker/killer but that is just in extreme cases! **And they will sort it out between themselves when they come over.**

Remember, there are no 'judges on thrones', just 'actors'- those who acted - analysing what they did rightly or wrongly. If a victim chose to die to make a point, or if his death helps bring a criminal to justice on Earth, again the victim has chosen that method. But that does NOT mean the criminal was right to do what he did... and he will have to find that out himself! How? When he comes over and looks at himself in the mirror of his Higher Self, who will **not** have approved of any violence towards others for own purposes.

****

(* Robert Schwartz - www.yoursoulsplan.com)

187

Chapter 20

SUICIDE BOMBERS' EXPECTATIONS

BR- Since we usually see what we believe in strongly, would a suicide bomber, once he has 'sacrificed himself' in order to kill others, find himself where he was led to believe he'd go: "A happy place full of fun and plenty of pretty girls to pamper him"?

ACTING AGAINST HIGHER SELF

You are right to think he will imagine he'll go to a lovely place filled with lovely girls and other pleasures. UNFORTUNATELY for him, it will not **happen** that way, because **he has acted against the wishes of his Higher Self**, the 'Real Him'.

If he had acted according to his Higher Soul's wishes, he would have those pleasures for a while... but he would soon realise they are temporary and self-induced! He would not even be able to react to them as he would on Earth, because the senses of the flesh would NOT be there... so he would **not** feel or taste what he would feel or taste in the flesh!

As we said, the Higher Self/the Total Being Self would not be happy and would not agree with what he has done, since he has taken Life! So the result is likely to be very foggy instead of pure and clear.

BR- But the Mind creates and is the tool of the current Soul (who is a bomber for now), so why couldn't he see all this 'fun', at least for a little while?

As the Mind creates, that man's Mind is still linked to the Superior Part of His Whole Being (a **facet of which** is the **criminal** that you speak of). So the Higher Mind will impinge and intrude on the results of the criminal's Mind.

Minds are not just 'tools' to pick up and use and drop. Minds of individuals are part of their Whole, Higher Beings. They are not little utensils in a corner, detached from the reality that they are a Whole, after all. It is the very essence of their Being which has that faculty to make things happen to them.

If criminals make things happen in their imagination which are not suited to their evil actions, i.e. which basically they do not deserve, they will have problems! Because their actions went against their Higher Soul and against the Basic and fundamental Law of the Universe: **"You will not harm or kill any other Being - and you will help anyone you can, during your travels to that (Earthly) sphere"**, so they cannot create anything 'good' for them!

They produced 'bad', unkind acts against the only Law there is, therefore, the criminals cannot reap 'rewards' from it. This is the basic, fundamental and direct result from their own way of thinking - you think nastily, you receive the boomerang effect of it. **You cannot produce light and joy out of hatred and crime.**

Taking **any** life is against the original aim of the Creation of this world. (We have already explained to you about carnivorous 'Animals' [*see ch.12*] so that is a different topic and **not** what we are discussing here). We are discussing the fact that anyone who has hurt or killed wilfully, on purpose, cannot possibly 'reap rewards'. Why? Because his own Higher Self, his own Real Self will be revolted by the acts that the Lower Soul has committed! Committed against his conscience, which **will** have tried to dissuade him from doing wrong and doing harm.

EMANATING DARK THOUGHTS

The harm done will always reflect itself in the thinking of the perpetrator. That means any **harm done on purpose**, with strong intentions, will be mirrored in whatever thoughts he sends. **He will be sending dark, hateful, gloomy projections around himsel**f. So he cannot expect to see sunshine, beauty, joy... and pretty girls! No 'pretty girls' would want to approach such a darkened Soul, whether on Earth or in this World!

We have tried to explain as best as we could. Do you think you have understood the dilemma he has put himself in? He is a 'lost' Soul as long as he does not realise what horrendous harm he has caused. When he does, he will be so full of remorse and regrets (eventually, we hope!) that he will not think of pretty girls and wonderful happenings to please him and his non-existent senses! He will be **filled with burning regrets and gnawing remorse** at the sight of what havoc he has caused.

MEETING HIS VICTIMS

He may even somehow meet those he murdered at the same time as himself... That will not be cause for joy and enjoyment! **THAT** will be the beginning of his **own inner hell, within his own Mind!** He will not need to be 'sent' anywhere. He will have built his own blazing hell and hole in his own Mind and Soul. It will take him 'time', more than likely, to try and surface from that, only no doubt to want to make amends somehow to those whose lives he's destroyed and shattered!

ONLY ONE JUDGE

We cannot think of any worse fate than feeling guilty and eaten up by remorse. Each personality judges himself individually - not someone on a jury bench, or a big judge in a wig, or one on a throne, or any other kind of deity!

There is only ONE judge: YOU! So the criminal will be the most severe magistrate one could imagine - himself! And **that** is sheer Hell in itself!

Chapter 21

REINCARNATION FOR HUMANS

MULTIFACETED DIAMOND

You are not just who you think you are, you are not just this current personality. You are a huge multifaceted 'rock' made of the 'stuff' called Spirit! Think of it as a rough rock of carbon, which is what diamond is made of. For a diamond to be turned into a sparkling jewel, it needs to be hammered and chiselled, so that each polished facet shines and glitters.

Likewise, the 'REAL YOU' (your Higher Self) is a Spirit Being (= 'rock of carbon'). During each life, all experiences, experiments and ups and downs chisel out and create a facet of you, shining with the particular knowledge acquired during **that** life.

The more lives are lived and experienced, the more knowledge is gained, carving even more glittering facets. These create a huge **sparkling multifaceted 'diamond' - the Real You/your Higher Self.**

Progress is extending your experiences and knowledge in many directions and levels. You are constantly creating your Self and polishing its multi-facets. Humans have **chosen** to carry out myriads of experiments within Earthly physical life.

FULFILLING A NEED

The 'Spirit World' to you is **the first stage after life on the Earth** you are on, simply because you came from here, to make the decision to go to the Earth to carry out your experiments there. That usually takes you all into a kind of cycle, merely because there are so many things you could be, or want to be, or feel you should be, or try! It has to be experienced to be understood. If one has not finished the cycle, one is not 'punished' or anything like that, as Free Will is always the dominant factor here!

But if you start something and you feel you have not quite achieved it or completed it, you would be left with a feeling of something lacking, whereas if you use all the opportunities offered, then you feel you've achieved something. So, **that's why one feels one needs to reincarnate,** i.e. go back into the 'flesh' as a **different** Earth Being.

Whoever wishes to conduct experiments is welcome. All who try things out have lots to learn and live for, on both sides of this divide. Not to be 'punished' by some deity, but to be helped to expand their knowledge.

You and everyone else are made of a Mind with an almighty Power. **You cannot escape from being a Being of Mind and Thought**. Once you have understood that, you cannot escape from wanting to play with that creature you are! You are a creature (in the sense of Creativity and Creation) who can 'create yourself' as you wish and that's what makes it so exciting, like **a play where you decide to be a different character at each turn.**

Reincarnation must always be useful. We do not go to the Earth to do 'nothing'. We must always live **for** something. Therefore, it means one must not waste one's time with idiocies, because that's not really what we incarnate on the Earth for!

Getting on board a flesh body, then starting to waste one's time with stupid trivia, or totally useless or dangerous things, could mean the result will be that **the Soul will no longer want to stay in that flesh body** and will decide to leave it! So making the effort to come on Earth may as well be worth it!

TEMPORARY AMNESIA

BR- Once back in Spirit World, why do people often not seem to recall they were 'Spirits' before birth, who knew how to use their Mind Power?

All those who have been to Earth come back here and **remember eventually**. It all depends on how much they have forgotten when on Earth.

BR- Why have they?

Many people choose to blank all memories of previous lives on Earth, elsewhere, or in the 'Spirit World', simply because **they prefer to think of one thing at a time**. But once the shock of transition in either direction is over, or the lesson/experiment is over, they will begin to remember where they were when they first started that first step, why they did it, how they did it, who or what they were.

All that is not very important in the long run, as it is only a small matter of adaptation again, that's all: like someone falling asleep and waking up feeling a bit 'out of place', or so it seems to him. That's quite normal, most people do.

WHY GO BACK?

The most interesting points are not so much the life we had or who we were, but more **WHY we had chosen it,** then **HOW we coped with it,** what good we did, or perhaps less good... as that is what matters in the end - why did we go there and was it worth going? After that, we all have to come back here, so we may as well make a trip which was useful!

We make journeys into the 'past' in order to get to know and 'appreciate' ourselves better, but also to value what our other lives taught us. **This is why we go and live on the Earth,** to learn things that help the progress of our Higher Self, the 'Real You', who is made up of many personalities who lived and will live elsewhere than here, in our beautiful World of Love and Light.

EXAMPLE OF LIFE REVIEWS

(BR- My mother's experiences in the Spirit World regarding possible reincarnation - whereas on Earth she could not grasp 'past lives' and rebirth. The following is an extract from: 'I'm Not Dead: I'm Alive without a Body').

"I look into what I can do with my thoughts, whether travelling in 'Time' as I have often done, or creating things, or analysing myself more and more to discover what kind of person I really am!

The most difficult thing to grasp is to forget I am not just (for example) **your** Mum, that Suzanne who was born a long time ago and 'died' not so long ago... but I am another 'person' in a way, as there are heaps of **various facets to my personality** if I study them!

I do wonder how we can get round to accepting oneself as one personality made of several facets. We have to constantly remember we 'are' not only from the last life we've just had, but from another one... and many others too! It can become complicated! I reckon one must do it in little pieces, small 'mouthfuls'. I think of the four of you as 'my children', but there must have been other 'times' when I was not that and you were not 'mine'!

We do not have only one life on Earth! Otherwise it would be very **boring, hardly useful and quite limited!**

On the other hand by having lots of lives, over centuries, we learn loads of very useful things and we discover other points of view.

We do not feel we are just 'one person of only one gender', we learn to understand others' way of thinking. But all that takes a lot of time, probably centuries and it doesn't stay in your head, you 'forget' it from one life to the other... Yet the Soul and your Spirit Being remember a little or a lot. So **you begin to accumulate this knowledge gradually and to improve yourself**... and that's what matters, I am told here.

194

BR- Have you discovered some of your own facets?

The life I examined first was the recent one with you, because it was important I understood why I had come to Earth and had the four of you. Now I know why! You were my 'raison d'être' (my reason to be) and my life. The rest was simply revolving around that. I wanted to be your mum, my life was you. **My choice had been to be a mother as I had not been one** like this before.

But there were other lives too; this is what I am beginning to examine a little, from time to time. I don't have to do it all the time, it's only when I think about it or get interested in it.

BR- Did you discover you were one particular person? What job?

Overall, **I have been a man** several times before. So I no longer wanted to be a man, because I did not know what it was like to be a woman as a mother! But one of my lives when I had been a woman before was childless, that's why I wanted to be a mum (this time round), to understand and learn what one feels when one has children one loves...

Little details are not precise. My 'visions' and glimpses of those lives are only short visions, impressions and brief memories rather than long detailed films. We are **not interested in fine points but in the main feelings** which have shaped that personality, that life. After living it, we always find ourselves back here, to analyse it sooner or later and ponder on how we could improve what we have or have not learnt!

It's more impressions and getting some comprehension rather than lists of facts, dates, genders and jobs, do you understand? So I'll have to delve into it gradually, several times, to understand it all better. After all, it's of no importance **who** I was: what matters is mainly **how** I lived before and how I reacted or felt. So there is still a lot to discover about all this!

Yet there is always the possibility of returning to Earth though one is not 'obliged' at all - only **if** one wishes to do so.

There is no reason why I would go back myself, considering you are still over there and you won't have the time to wait for me. I would have to be a baby once more and grow up, meanwhile you'll be getting older! It would be very silly to do that.

Moreover, I don't see why I would want to go back to Earth when I feel so good here, having fun learning all kinds of things without any problems or disease or worries. Personally I do not want to go anywhere! I only want to wait for you (when you are ready!) while occupying myself usefully.

After seeing all those little pieces of 'old or previous' lives, I understood there is only one thing to do in each life: **Do your best all the time!** That way there will never be any regrets and you won't risk feeling obliged to return in order to repair stupid mistakes or learn better.

All that is needed is to **listen to your conscience** and tell yourself that if you cannot do some good, at least you must avoid doing any harm to whoever. After that, the main thing is to improve yourself in every possible way and I am not talking of money in this case! Money is very useful and allows you to be comfortable but you must not live **for** that... as after all, where is it, once you've passed over to where I am, hey?!"

SEEING OTHER FACETS

BR- How is Mum (in Spirit World) helped to see her previous facets? She was also told that they 'still exist'. Could you explain please?

The notion of 'Time' will confuse your Mind as long as you try to make everything fit in like it would on Earth. We need to take you out of that and into extra dimensions, where there is not such a notion.

You need to understand that the equivalent of being

'here now' and 'there now' is possible! That means being ubiquitous, omnipresent, not only in space but in so-called 'Time' to you, but not 'Time' to those who live 'omnipresence', because they would not have the same 'Time' reference as you.

We have to see things differently since we do not have the use of a sun to fix minutes, hours and even years.

You need to grasp that the vision of someone in the so-called 'past' does not necessarily mean you need to fleet through 'Time'. It **can be done by going within oneself and SENSING the various personalities, without feeling the notion of Time.** It's more like watching a film of oneself at a younger age, when you look at your cameras and recording devices.

As you look at things from the Earthly point of view, you'll find it difficult to grasp the whole concept. Let's look at it differently: The little girl who is now you, say, has been a man 'before' by your time standards, but the Higher Self of that man is the same Higher Self as yours and the same Higher Self as the other personalities that have been and still are forming the Whole 'Real You'. So, **these personalities have the common linking point of a joint Higher Self** and **that** is where the common ground is.

But the individual reaction to various 'deaths' is not quite the same thing. It lies within the fact that, say, when one personality 'dies' of a horrific accident, the accident will have reverberated throughout the whole Being of the Higher Self, so they will all feel it and may all remember it. Or may not! According to whatever you've felt coming from 'previous' lives (as you'd say), you will react with various memories at times. So it is not so surprising. But the 'longevity' of each one somehow does not affect the others.

BR- But after a 'death', that life is finished, gone?

The fact that it's been lived may have an effect if there was something traumatic, say, but if the Soul or personality in

197

question (e.g. male) is 'not gone', as such, it is because **the rest of the Higher Self will have absorbed it** and it will be part of it.

The 'male' **influence** will fill up the recess of every one of the other personalities which are part of the Higher Self. It will itself be influenced by many other aspects which come from the other 'facets', so it will live in each one of its facets, whether they are 'gone', finished' as an Earth life or not. Therefore **they will still 'live' in the rest of the Higher Self.** It is alive because the others are alive anyway as an eternal 'Spirit Being'; but also because the influence still permeates everyone of them, as said before.

NO 'WALK INTO' DEAD BODIES!

BR- What can you tell me about the claims of 'walk-ins' into bodies, mentioned by Deb DeBari, one of the USA mediums quoted in R. Schwartz's book? I met people who were worried after reading that paragraph.

As we listen to your Mind and your query, we want to say you must be given an answer to this important question. It is vital to understand such points of view thoroughly, so as to be able to discuss the possibilities (or lack of) with people wondering the same thing too.

It is essential for Mankind to know how to differentiate between man-made stories, distorted truths, real but badly understood facts, or total nonsense and complete lies! This is what we are here for. We want you to know the Truth; you want to know the Truth! So we'll tell you this: (*Notice how he purposefully took his time building up to getting round to answering! BR).*

The idea of anyone walking out of his body has been an idea 'eternally known' since everyone does so who 'dies', i.e. leaves the flesh body! No one can stay in it as it will decay sooner or later. It is impossible to stay 'alive' in a flesh body for eternity, as the flesh is **not** meant to survive that long! **It is a temporary abode**. All the more, since you know that the Soul of the personality, the personality itself, does not wish to stay on Earth forever! That's because, after all, it is just a 'school', a place for experimenting, not to live forever in it, because it would be too much hassle in the end! It was **not** designed for this!

There is also the fact that **each individual has chosen and therefore designed, with his Mind and Spirit,** the kind of vehicle he needs for that particular 'life' he wants to experience on Earth. He wants **that body** to achieve **that** particular experiment, whether the body is a good looking or healthy one or not, depending on what 'he' (the person using it) wants it for!

So, we are back to asking: Why on Earth (or in heaven, or elsewhere!) would any Being imagine he would want to jump into a second-hand, half or three-quarters worn-out flesh body that he has not designed himself for his own purpose?! It is not what is feasible or done, because the physical body of a Soul (i.e. of a personality) is designed to match the thoughts, feelings, desires, sadness, joys, ups and downs, of that personality. **How could the flesh body reflect and be part of someone new, who'd never been there at the start of its formation and creation?**

It is a practical impossibility because the vibrations one sends to create one's own flesh vehicle are especially honed in to match, to the tiniest detail, the very vibrations the Spirit personality is made of. The lack of knowledge expressed in that 'statement' (by that 'medium' who you mention in your question) is all the more obvious that the follow-up is the other person's 'walks out'! Walks out where? To 'die'.

So, **if a personality leaves their flesh body for good, they remove their vibrations** to fulfil their 'career' elsewhere; they will leave the flesh vehicle and no doubt come to our

World of Mind and Light. Then what happens is that **the 'template having come out'** (so to speak) of the flesh body frame and constituents, the flesh body will gradually but surely collapse and rot! No other Being **whose vibrations are totally different and who had nothing whatsoever to do with the original creation of that body in the first place** can just 'walk in'! It would be ABSURD!

BR- They claim it is to avoid being a baby, just to know adulthood!

Like lies or distortions or idiotic remarks made on Earth, people have an ability to be gullible and believe the slightest 'guru' or leader they meet! Those people professing to link up to such 'high (supposedly) masters' would have to prove it very hard! That is because NO **real Masters** (or whatever you Humans wish to call any evolved Beings wanting to pass on knowledge over to Earthly Beings) **would lower themselves to play the part of an ignorant Being , not knowing the fundamentals of the creation of Mankind and its individual components!**

No real Masters would say Mankind can pop in and out of its body and leave it there for someone else to pop into it, like in a secondhand car salesroom! This is ludicrously ridiculous or ridiculously ludicrous, or both, if not a total sham!

The important fact to point out is that NO body of ANY Being alive on Earth (as we are talking of Earthly Beings only anyway) has ever been made, or will ever be made, by anyone else than **its own maker, who is its own 'inhabitant'**, so to speak, or 'driver' if you wish to call it that. The body is inherently the reflection and **replica of what that Soul and personality wants to represent itself as**, experience and use it for!

There is **no way** that same shape and mass of vibrations (which are absolutely **unique and individual to every single**

200

Being!) would be of any use (if ever they could get in it!!) to other Beings from our world, who would have different plans, aims, thoughts and vibrations anyway! No one is similar to another Being. Not even twins! They still have their respective individualities. So you can be reassured that **no one** can technically, morally, 'vibrationally', or spiritually 'walk-into' someone else's carcass and take it from there!!

You could argue that everything in Creation is an experiment and that someone may want to decide to experience this strange swap! The 'idea' may be good to someone ugly leaving such a body and deciding to 'walk-into' a newer, younger, much prettier flesh body... but it is just an 'idea'. That would no doubt feel lovely to such a person, **IF** it was technically possible! But then, why not have the idea of walking into a fish so you don't have to learn to swim, or a cat to be furry and cuddled, or a bird to fly without using an aeroplane?!! These ideas are no more ridiculous than the pretence that a man can walk out of his body and walk into another one whose owner has just left.

So to sum up what has already been explained: No Being coming from our world would ever be able to 'drive' a flesh body constructed by another Being. That's because the mass of heaps of atoms and vibrations a body is made of, is to be linked to the vibrations of the original owner and designer: the Spiritual Being wishing to use it for its journey (whether short or long) on Earth.

Hence the answer to the question: NO, no 'walk-ins'! No 'walk-outs'... except for leaving the flesh to disappear at its own rate, while the Real Being of Light flies back to where it comes from - our World of Light and Love.

That fact really needs to be spread, because there is nothing worse than stupid erroneous remarks spread out as so-called 'profound/knowledgeable truths' and swallowed by people unaware of the subterfuge. A great shame!

(This discourse was dictated energetically by my Spirit Inspirers/'Evolved Masters'(!): in one block, at full flow, as quickly as my fingers could write the words down. Their comments certainly do NOT criticise Rob Schwartz himself or his own admirable work and dedication in trying to demonstrate that we all chose our Life Plan. www . yoursoulsplan . com)

****

Chapter 22

ANIMALS & REINCARNATION

BR- You have access to 'Facts Box/Akashic records', so could you get lots of facts which I definitely need and want about 'Animals'' and reincarnation?

We have indeed access to far greater knowledge than you could think of, as that is where we obtain it from. We always tell you the truth as we see it from our 'elevated' point of view, compared to yours.

As we told you before, to obtain 'advanced' information, we ask, as we reach further and deeper into the Realms of Knowledge, reaching the layers of more and more refined vibrations that contain much more subtle insights than you could envision. So we get to them, find the answer to your queries and gladly bring it back, both for ourselves if need be and for you too, of course.

COMING BACK TO EARTH?

BR. Can 'Animals' reincarnate as a different 'Animal'?

All that is needed to understand this is to grasp rule n°.1, which is: **Nothing is 'forbidden',** as such, in Creativity, **except anything impinging on the Law of NO killing**

An 'Animal' has a particular type of Soul. He has chosen to be an 'Animal' as a Being of flesh on Earth. That means he may choose to come back again as an 'Animal'. Not always the same type necessarily. So, nothing is 'impossible', as such. BUT, indeed... there are many things which would be either illogical or very pointless and **no incarnation is pointless!** All have a purpose and a reason for being. No incarnation is gone into 'just for the fun or it' or for the difference, it has to have more purposeful aims!

So we would not see a cat becoming an elephant or a fish 'for the hell of it'. It would have to be really, really **useful to the Soul** to become that, if chosen. You could say: "Well, it's a new experience", but the 'experience' is not quite enough for a Spirit Being to undergo the **transformation and training needed** to be such a different Being, just like it would be silly for a Human to try and be a fish or an alligator, or a bird, or a horse. We know it might look tempting from where you are, to 'have a go' at being another such Being. But it is not what is advisable or sensibly feasible, since all Souls on Earth have a purpose for being there and it is **not just to 'enjoy the flesh body'.**

They may indeed learn and practise to manipulate the physical Matter of the body, but that is not all they are there for. You won't always know why others have chosen to come amongst you! You won't and neither shall we. It is a private matter for a Soul to be what it is, where it is.

BR- So has it ever happened that a cat became a dog, a panther or a tiger? Could a little bird come back as a larger bird or fowl?

We'll try and straighten the facts for you. The 'possibility' of a cat becoming a dog, say, is only a theory, as it would be a different way of thinking in a way. It's not quite the same as being another cat. A dog cannot climb trees, cats can! That's just an example. So it could be that a dog wishes he could climb trees, but is it good enough a reason for his Spirit to **undergo the long training** and absorption of facts and many ways of thinking etc, as well as the manipulation of a different flesh body? No, it is not quite what Higher Selves have in mind when they 'send' sections of themselves into other incarnations! The fact remains, it is not 'forbidden', as nothing is forbidden, but... it is not likely to happen, let's say!

As for birds: well, the same applies. All we could say in the same way as a wild cat may want to become a pet, that may be possible if the physiology is not too different, but the psychology side may take some training, as it will be a very different way of thinking as you can guess! So it is not impossible and possibly more likely than being a dog... But...!

BODY: A DISGUISE FOR A PURPOSE

People have to accept that **'Animals' are Spirit Beings.** They chose to be a particular kind of 'Animal', Bird, Fish and so on for a particular reason of their own choice but, as said before, apart from the experience to be 'experienced', there is always a more **profound motive** for their going to that world of Matter, as they could have chosen other places to go to, other things to do.

If they chose to be a certain 'Animal', there will be some important underlying reason which your Soul won't know but theirs will! If that cat had a real need to be a panther or a tiger, if there was an urgent need for the good of Mankind or Animalkind, it will be one, after much preparation no doubt! If it could be a 'bird' it might even like to do that, BUT it would require **such** a **huge amount of training** and adapted psychology that it may not be worth the effort! And, of course, there would have to be an extremely good reason and goal, as stated before!

All 'fish' and other creatures have the same pattern, or 'problem', if you like. They cannot just jump from one shell to another flesh body. It has to be well planned for a good motive. But it does not mean it is 'creatively impossible'. That's the point. There are no definite fixed limits to either ways of coming back, **if** they chose to come back. After all, life is happier here!

As already mentioned, they usually go back to Earth for a purpose. They could return there because they wish to help or teach Humans. They may have a plan to get Humans to react more 'humanly' towards 'Animals', or it could be they need to feel the love of Humans for them. Or the worst scenario, the need to feel what it is like to be hurt or hated, because that feeling needs to be felt to be understood; that is **part of the learning** process of Life, Love and Death. All is useful. No one wants the worst aspects, but they are part and parcel of the lessons on Earth. If one only knew the good parts of what has been created by Mankind, one would not know the other sides, i.e. the fact that **Mankind has spoilt its chances** to be happy for a long time, by constantly reverting to its silly ways, to its obsession with material and physical pleasures and by forgetting its true spiritual origins!

Creatively, anything can be manipulated and visualised and made to happen, BUT to sustain it, it must have the Inner Self's need, will and wishes to follow that path all the way, for a useful purpose, either for itself or for the good of the rest of the Creation.

BR- Just in case someone asked me this: What about, say, a cod reincarnating as a fairly similar fish, e.g. a haddock?

It's well-known that the fish in the sea have a totally different attitude to the world from other creatures who live on top of the ground. It is obvious that you have an overview of the world from your point of view, which is totally unlike what sea creatures see and can do!

As explained before, if a Spirit Being from our world chooses to be a certain type of fish, for his own reasons, it will become that fish. Then, if it suits 'him' and he wishes to come back to Earth (as a fish again, necessarily, as it would be too big a difference to become anything above water!), it will just be a question of deciding **why it does it,** of course.

As we've said earlier: All 'fish' and all 'birds', all Beings have their own agendas. They **know deeply** within themselves why they have come as they are and what it achieves, if anything. Some will achieve it for themselves, others will do it for the good of others. As the 'cod' is not far from being a fairly similar fish, it could well be they choose to change to that, BUT would there be a good enough reason, apart from the joy of creativity? Well, we are not sure because it's not so important.What **is** important is to **grasp the NEED for reincarnation,** rather than seeing it as 'fun' - yet not much fun is left in this Earthly world since Mankind chose to impose its unkind ways and spread fear.

DIFFERENT OUTLOOK

BR- How do 'Animals' in Spirit World evolve after Earth life?

Those you Humans call **'Animals' are a very different type of Energy Souls**. They have all the qualities of a Spirit Being, in the same way as 'Humans' will have. But...the big 'BUT' is when a future 'Earth Animal' comes back here, it will have a different outlook on things, because it will have experienced events and emotions very **unlike the experiences felt by a Human**. So, it would not be possible for it to see/sense/feel the same as a Human who has had a lifetime of happenings. What takes place in an Animal's Mind is different from a Human Mind, because they don't think or feel in the same way.

Little 'Animals', like worms or insects, will not be on the same mental/ intellectual/ emotional levels as, say, an elephant or a wild boar or anything else. They all have different experiences and outlooks, which means once they are back here, at first they come as what they thought they were (on Earth), but eventually **they will move away from the 'feel' of the flesh shape and happening**. They'll exist again as a Soul, as 'Spirit', wanting a body for an experience of a new kind in a different body. This is why they have to go **back to a sort of 'melting pot' of Energy,** of Consciousness, from where they can readjust their thinking, so to speak, to decide what they wish to do next.

If there was not that Consciousness 'melting down', that gathering of Energy with the vibrations of experiences brought back from whatever they've been through, it would not be possible for them to progress very far!

POOL OF SHARED KNOWLEDGE

Basic Knowledge is always what is needed in all cases. Any Being wanting to know anything in any field whatsoever has to learn the basics in that field. So, if any Being/Soul/Spirit/wishes to become an 'xyz', it will have to learn first, experience first what life as a 'xyz' is. It will need to be in the egg or the pouch or whatever and go through the process of becoming a Being in that kind of flesh body. If it did not follow the pattern, it would not become that bird/fish or whatever. When it has done it once, it knows what it feels/looks like.

Once it knows that, it brings back this feeling and knowledge and experience with itself to this world, where **it can share it with others** by blending its thoughts into a kind of big **pool of 'Thought - Knowledge - Experience'.** This is where **others can dip their Minds into** and think: "This is what it could look like or feel to be a bird/fish/elephant etc". But they have not lived it really themselves. They might become interested in this type of life in the flesh, so they might decide to go through the process of being born something else. They have to start from the beginning, of course, they have to go into an egg or a pouch etc. But it will have been taught how to do it by first learning the outlines via the **Pool of Knowledge.**

BEWARE OF MAN-MADE DISTORTED VIEWS!

The whole topic of reincarnation has always fascinated, intrigued and confused Mankind. One more 'worry'! 'Animals' do not worry about the Afterlife or reincarnation! Their Soul and Higher Self know what's what! They don't need to discuss it with their peers! So, Mankind has gradually built up various ideas about it, against it, even for it, though far too often they have **not reached far enough into the Knowledge and have not got to the fundamental facts**... Instead they have attached their own human ideas to it! Thus conflict of understanding!

Many think (in some religions) that a Human would reincarnate as a cow or other Animal. **That is not so!** And the rats down the sewers are not ex-convicts or criminals who are still being 'punished' by some deity! No. Wrong again! All that is not right and we've explained why it would be most unlikely to happen! Therefore, we'll end with saying: Trust what you hear from us and you'll see you won't go wrong. We do not try to con you and we do not impose our own individual, ex-human ideas. **We are here to teach the Truth obtained from even higher levels of Understanding and Knowledge.**

****

PART 2

WEIRD AND WONDERFUL

"Fixed ideas are rocks on our path" -
W.D Judge

Chapter 23

LEY LINES & CROP CIRCLES

BR- Could you explain what we call 'ley lines' please?

Lines that are within and 'without'/outside, external to the supposedly 'solid' (to your eyes) body of the Earth. There again, there are no real boundaries, as all 'lines' merge with each other. A line is a kind of boundary, isn't it? So we'll say lines to please your ears, but we are really **talking of Energy Fields, rather than lines**, as fields spread out far more and can blend much more than 'lines' do. So we are discussing fields. You know what we said before about areas blending with each other. Then that's the same thing. All fields blend, overlap, overcome or 'under support' each other. Always in a useful way, so that whatever system we are talking about can function and remain operational.

You have to realise that 'lines' that are felt on the Earth are not simply lines on the surface of the Earth. They are just part of the **particular field of emanations** that a sensitive person *(like a dowser)* may feel and reacts to. His or her own field of Energy is reacting to, noticing and blending with, a particular area of a field which is spreading itself there.

When we say 'spreading', we mean in the sense of pulsating, vibrating. It could be 'on the spot' so to speak, without necessarily going too far, but is a constant Energy which can be picked up if well received. The blending of Energies is inevitable. They all blend somehow one way or the other and with other outer 'batches' of other Energies.

CREATING A 'SOLID LOOK'

But the ones we are talking about are specific to the Earth body, so they need to stay within and close to its structure, **to maintain the appearance of 'solidity' to those living there** and to those who want to manipulate the so-called 'solid' items on it. Though those fields stay close to it, they still can emanate somewhat, so there will still be some blending with any other Energies coming or being close. Therefore, if you have a sensitive person who can sense those packs of Energies which are close to the physical world of the Earth, it means 'he' is very much in tune with his world. He has senses blending with and matching what is around them.

This is exactly how Mankind and Animalkind used to be when the **first pioneers** came to join others, to play with the experimentation of living in a physical world! They all **had the ability to blend not only with each other's Energy field, but with their surroundings** too. This is therefore an asset! But sadly most of Mankind nowadays seems to have lost that aptitude. They are ignorant of the fact that all Energies blend and support each other.

LEY LINES GRID

We know 'ley lines' exist, because **we can see them**. They form a **gigantic 'grid'** with intersections of blending, enveloping and underlapping those various Energies which are there to hold up the structure of the material world.

They weave a pattern of support, like a cloth has a weave of threads to make it look like a solid piece of fabric, but in reality it is made of hundreds of 'lines' of cotton interwoven to make it **look** 'solid'. We have, therefore, a weaving of very powerful Energies which are all at various vibrational rates, so that the whole remains constantly at that rate. We need to make the whole structure visible and touchable physically! But in effect, **it is fake, since it is not solid.**

213

Only the human eye and other senses experience it as 'solid', because **Humans have set their senses' vibrational rate at that same level to be able to live in a 'solid' hologram!** This allows them to feel and think they live in something solid but which is, in fact, hollow and flimsy as a 'gas' or a 'light' would be, to use words you understand.

So, you have got the weaving of a grid made of lots of various Energies, vibrating at constant rates which create what **you** see as a physical world. Anyone able to sense them has their senses well developed, beyond the ordinary human reception nowadays. But those 'lines' have great power! **They maintain Life in the body of the Earth**. Life in the sense of creative and conscious Energy.

EARTH ENERGIES REACT TO EVIL DEEDS

The Earth has receptivity to what happens on it and around it. **The Earth 'knows' what goes on because it has those 'Energy sensors', since all Energies blend and merge.** Therefore, it will receive and react to other Energies going on nearby.

As Humans, 'Animals' and Plants suffer, the Earth Energy will feel it and react to it, because **all** are pure Energies blending with each other! All 'shake' at the same time, sooner or later. All 'scream' at the same time, in unison, sooner or later. It's just a question of Energies reacting in a 'domino effect', triggering one that triggers another!

So if you want to **save your Earthly world** from more catastrophes, **stop creating negative and disturbing energies on its surface** where you live! Because the trauma of it all will react more deeply down right to its heart, its core and the reaction will be the 'shaking', the grumbling, the tears of a wounded creature. **The Earth is a sensitive spiritual creature** which has a heart and core of Energy, reacting to other surrounding Energies. Do you follow me?

POWERFUL CROSSING POINTS

We'll now talk more of the surface 'ley lines'. We are discussing the 'no boundaries' between Energies once more. All blend. As they cross and meet, you will therefore have a 'doubling up' of the power.

People who can sense the whole thing will no doubt realise that. **Use the 'cross over' of Energies to be healed, to be re-energised, to build some structures on, as they will constantly be maintained in a sustainable way.** (Just like you can take water coming out of the rocks in a mountain).

You cannot go wrong using natural Energies that way for the purpose of good. You cannot do well if you do not know they are there, or ignore them and carry on creating havoc on your Earth... as it will react to tell you that it is hurt all the way down; it will react to its traumatised state!

CENTRE POINTS

It is of the utmost importance to be able to **sense those crossings of Energies,** as **there** reside the centre points from which other Energies can come into - such as being doorways to provide an entrance or an exit to overflows and incoming batches and flows which wish to be present, to provide additional support to what is already there. It **is essential for you Humans to sense them**; the older populations (of 'ancient times') could do so very easily as a matter of fact!

This is important, because there are so many flows that you can **learn** to distinguish between them, if you know how to read your own sensitivity. And when you know how to do it, you'll find you'll 'pick' the flow of Love, the flow of Creativity, the flow of Strength, the flow of Sustainability, the flow of Diversity, the flow of High Energies, the flow of low Energies. All that is so mingled and intermingled that it is very difficult to separate, of course, but **that** is the basis of what is coming or going or merging. You can try sorting it out, but it will be like trying to unravel ten balls of superfine mesh, entangled and woven, yet disentangled if you look at them with the right aptitude.

BR- Did you say aptitude or attitude?

Aptitude, indeed. You need to have the aptitude, the ability to do so. Not many have it. It is imperative to have an awareness of those particular **crossing points, because the level of Energy there is far superior and totally different from elsewhere!** As you pick them, you can **re-energise yourself, enhance your abilities, place buildings on them.** You can use **any** of those abilities **on any** of those points - they are all valid! A point can do all that, it is not specialised in one direction.

SKETCH

My pen started sketching very vigorously overlapping and increasingly expanding 'figures of 8' shapes, linked to more '8' shapes filling the page wildly. They were connected to a kind of 'tunnel like vortex', wide at the start but gradually getting narrower as it got towards the bottom of the page - and suddenly that last tiny 'whirl' was linked with a line shooting back to the centre of the original 8 shapes sketch, stopping, like a full stop, at what looks like a junction of lines. Then I heard my communicator:

While we draw, please keep staring at the paper, so that we can see what we are doing, ok?

BR - Sorry. I was not sure whether I should do that or just relax. Do you want to do it again?

You can start again if you like, but we are quite pleased with what we did!

I turn to another blank page. At once, the pen drew energetically a brief sketch n°.2, similar to looking into the 'eye' of a hurricane or a vortex - lots of circular concentric lines, leading to a centre 'point'.

Then the pen shot at an angle, tracing a straight line to the top of the page where it wrote the words: - deep 'tunnel' - look into the 'sky' around - *(Inverted 'commas' included; perhaps meant 'space'?) Dictation restarted:*

Lots of deep tunnel-like passages into deeper avenues and other openings leading to deeper, thicker, faster ranges of vibration at high frequencies! We are so intensely looking at the smallest of the smallest levels that you could never reach with your instruments. We feel you have to look within the range of the level of 'sub-atoms and beyond'. Not for ways you can measure with instruments, but for ways you can **measure with your sensitivity**, which stems from your own Inner Being as a sensitive Light, not a thinking Mind using a brain!

All fields and areas meet up and blend and fill each other, overlapping and superimposed on each other and all others! It is not possible to say there are real boundaries because they are like a mesh of vibrating fields!

How can you see lines of boundaries? It's too difficult to observe as far as we are concerned. We can only sense the whole programme, constantly pulsating at such a fast rate that no one could determine which is what, so to speak. So if you want to give it lines and labels, that's fine, but **we can only see overlapping and blending of multi-coloured vibrations at rates you'd never guess can exist.**

If this is how it appears on Earth, that's all right, but what we see is fine too as this is how it appears to us! Two different view points for the same thing!

BR- Thanks. Can you explain your drawing of 8s in more detail, especially that line going to the centre?

All the lines meant they were all linked. Nothing is separate. The 888s are so because each one comes back to where it started and yet there are more expansions than you can imagine. All is one, one is all - as always told. Everything is one and all others expand from it and them in different directions, because it is a **new generation of Thought possibilities, of Energies trying out something different**, of 'sub-Energies' trying to become 'top Energies'.

This is to do with the **constant Urge to better oneself**, whether Energies at a basic level, or a consciousness which has developed itself well. All are needed. All the structures and infrastructures and super-structures and multi-dimensional structures are just part of **ONE big, gigantic super-immense field of energising Energies, who have the power to re-create themselves... and therefore produce more creative Energies!**

READJUSTING TRAUMATISED GRID

BR- Can one pass from one field to another, or move them?

You can indeed move the areas. It is not done physically, it is done totally with **blending your own Energy field** (which you are all made of, of course!) with the field of the particular area you are focusing on. So you blend it and you guide it towards the point **you feel is right** for it. You need not ask or 'pray' or whatever! You just simply need to feel the right or wrong place to put it.

It has not been moved on purpose by some exterior 'Being' or whatever! It has been gradually moved by the internal extension of the grid we mentioned before. If the grid is traumatised and activated or deactivated, there will naturally be reactions and the reactions will be such that the Energy field/line will be shaken, distorted, pushed out of its original and previous emplacement.

UFO BLOBS

This is what happens when you have those 'UFO visible Energy blobs' coming to reactivate them in the right place ; you think you see a '**UFO blob**' crossing a field and making lines or patterns on the ground. It is not a 'personality', it is **a Field of Thought, though they are sent from superior fields and dimensions of Thought Power, who come to readjust the dislocation** of those poor little Earth lines ('ley lines', you call them).

They need readjusting because the grid forming the Earth would be all truncated and distorted... and you'd find your Earth would otherwise become a totally different shape and all on it and in it would have to change and not be as they are! Too complex to try to describe the alteration endured by this. We can tell you more on the 'UFO patterns' if you wish.

CROP CIRCLES

A lot could be said about so-called crop circles, but it is not easy to explain! We'll try as best as we can understand it ourselves. It's a question of **Energies that have Knowledge,** Energies of intelligent 'Entities', we'll need to say, as they are **not** human. When we deal with things like that, how can we explain with human words when it is difficult to grasp even in our world?

From what we understand, it has to do with Energies of the Earth combined and used by ' Beings' who cannot be labelled as 'Beings' as you think of them, but more Thinking Intelligences, **planning Entities of Thought and Energy.** They can do things without having a solid 'body' themselves. They can create tools, objects, accessories, thus making themselves seen doing things, if you see what I mean. It is to do with creating 'power places', **power points to re-energise the Earth,** to rebalance it as there has been and still is too much imbalance. Those patterns have the power to rebalance certain parts of the Earth, possibly at weak points, or at points where there are links with the Earth's own Energy.

When we talk of power points, we mean very large areas, not just 'dots'. So, there are areas which need reinforcing or through which one can **inject extra power and balance**, because what Mankind has been doing imbalances the whole system.

Those 'Intelligent Energies' know that and do their best to rebalance the whole thing. It is not easy and they are trying hard. It is a question of going to places where they feel and are aware it is leaking and to rebuild that power as well as they can... without overcharging the area so as not to blow it up!

BR- Why damage crops? Why not do it on plain fields, moors etc? Why such patterns?

The moors will have been used too but you may not notice it there, as there are no visible signs of their presence, unless seen from the air. Why such different patterns? It would appear that **the shapes have a power of equilibrium** in themselves. They seem to be very balanced if you look at them. We think that is what it is all about.

When the Earth was created, those Intelligences were at work then too! They had a say in it, because they were 'superior', as you would say. They had Superior Knowledge which could be used to put into place such an experiment. So, it makes sense they come back now and then, to redress and rebalance if they can the work of art they created in the first place, as part of their experiment.

BR- Why do it physically rather than sending their thoughts?

If they only used their intelligent thoughts, they would not be able to manipulate things as easily as they are doing by coming closer. They send thoughts but the **thoughts are materialised into balls of Energy producing results**. This is why it is not a Being, or Beings, that you witness, but the **result** of their thoughts, of their Energy, their thinking Energy. You see how difficult it is to explain, because they are not 'people' or 'Beings' as such.

BR- Why do they reduce those patterns to such a small area each time, considering how large the Earth is?

As the balls hover and '**burn in**' the **power towards the centre of the planet**, the place they have been above has marks indeed. It seems it is not necessary to go deeply in, or else it is not so visible if they do so. It looks as if they are happy to stay above it. We don't have detailed knowledge regarding this for the time being, but we will try to understand and learn more for you to be told.

BR- How do you receive it then?

The Knowledge becomes inner knowing when we think of the subject. Every question regarding this triggers an extra delving deeper, an extra prodding and searching for more answers to 'float' back to our own consciousness. That is why **we can** find out but it may take several 'goes'! We need to think and ask ourselves about something and the **access to Knowledge opens itself** according to the query and the thought and **desire** put into it. So we'll ask and think more and let you know when we have more.

So far the appearance of 'crop circles' is understood as coming from 'Beings' (but not really!) of high intelligence such as those who have created the Earth. We are all one, remember. We are all part of one mighty ball of Thinking (therefore creating) Energy. As we all think, we all not only create ourselves but create around ourselves.

That is what you are all doing unwittingly on Earth too! So, we are a part of those who are keeping an eye on the Earth creation, but we are not so close as to knowing all the details. This is why it comes in 'bits'. As you ask questions, it brings more answers.

BR– Surely there must have been mediums asking questions many times before?

It is like individual 'wires' of Knowledge responding to the enquirer.

221

BR- Ah! Like our telephone line linked to an individual call, or the Internet. All answers are there but we need to click and search individually.

Precisely. We need to do that too here. So we'll make more enquiries and let you know what we can to help you (and ourselves!) understand all this.

EXPLOSION IN FOREST

BR- What happened in Russia, in that forest near the Tunguska River in 1908? It destroyed lots of trees.

The forest you mention was well known to our world – we saw it happen, some of us anyway. There was a very strange incident which we've witnessed by looking at its 'replay' in the Memory/Facts Box.

It was a huge meteoric explosion. An absolute ball of fire which eventually hit the Earth at that time and place. It did not destroy everything completely but it did leave a huge mark of its happening as it struck the world of the Earth. It had been hurtling through Space for aeons and suddenly encountered this part of the Earth on its passage.

It is lucky not many or any Humans were killed or injured, we are not too sure. There might have been none. But there certainly were little 'Animals' who passed over quickly that way! It was gigantic. But the fact it hit a remote area was a 'blessing,' as you'd say, as no one was burnt alive apart from the trees. Yet they did not really all burn, did they? They did not completely disappear.

It was a strange happening but it did mark your Earth. We have no more detail on that, except that it was not a man-made or 'alien space ship' attacking or falling. It was a natural disaster which fortunately had its limits. That's what we can tell you about it. Surprisingly, we do not see more than that. So there can't have been many repercussions from it.

BR- I think I read 'Animals' there grew abnormally big afterwards, possibly due to radiation?

If it is so, then it may not be unexpected because as you know, rocks from meteors etc. do have minerals and also radiation which will contaminate the areas they arrive to. So we will not be surprised to have this occurring – but as it was only a temporary situation for a definite span of time, it won't have registered dramatically in what we are seeing.

EFFECT OF COSMOS

BR- Please talk about the effect of the Moon and Sun on the Energy lines?

My dear, you know very well that the influence of the Moon and the Sun and all stars and planets of that particular part of the Universe that you 'kind of know' about, has no limits as far as blending of emanations and Energies is concerned!! **Of course** they are part of your whole Energy field! The creation of the Earth planet was not a single object being created! It had to be balanced, maintained in place, 'cajoled' into doing what it had to do regularly, to maintain what had been decided by us all, to be Life on Earth... and to have Beings of flesh Matter conducting experiments to see what it is like to live in a flesh body of one kind or other - even though deep within each one and behind and beyond the flesh, resides the consciousness of a superior Being who had that goal from the start!

Therefore, **the Earth had to be placed so that there was (and is) a constant and regular equilibrium**, which could not fail to do its work. That way the 'planet' you are on did not suddenly disintegrate with you all on it... and scatter its ashes and crumbs all over that Space it used to be in at one time! All the **asteroids, stars, planets and other bodies are there for a particular purpose**! They did not 'just appear' because a star sneezed or some exploded! (*See ch.9*).

You cannot ever grasp the 'gigantism' of the experiment and its construction! It is one of the most wonderful master pieces we have realised - because it has so many facets in its building and implications in its running! We cannot believe Humans still imagine it has 'just happened out of an explosion', or some unique Being of no-existence created it and washed its hands of it!

In our 'superior levels' here, we are all **continually overseeing the maintenance of the constant Energy needed to fuel the whole contraption of that part of the Universe** that you call 'your' Universe - but which, in fact, is a **little** corner for experimentation of a new kind of Matter we had devised, as the whole concept fascinated many millions of superior Minds, wanting to constantly create, invent and have fun with new possibilities!

We can talk forever about this, but there will be many times when the words in your Mind will fail picking what we would love to be able to express: not because **you** have no vocabulary, but because **human languages have no vocabulary** to explain all those happenings.

So yes, the Moon and the Sun have a great influence on **anything** which is part of the Earth body and its inhabitants, as well as over other planets, 'stars' etc. All are one, one is all - haven't we said that before? *(I feel him smile and wink)*. If only you could see the world you are on, the way we see it from here - weaves and patterns of lit-up, crossing-over, sparkling energies, like illuminations of festivities (such as you have) but even better! Pulsating, vibrating, colourful, wonderful! And none of you know it! What a pity! You have a world of Light which you trample on and treat as if it is Darkness, or else you try to turn into Darkness! That's what ignorance of Reality does to you all! Well, nearly all of you - present company excepted!

224

All explanations are given with love; we are here to help you understand what needs to be understood, even though the limitations of the human way of thinking have often put a cork on the extent which can be absorbed and comprehended!

We are pleased you are asking such interesting questions to help you understand what is not visible to the majority of Humans, but is very visible to us all here! Make your day useful by spreading this information to those who want to learn from it. We are always pleased to have an audience!

****

Chapter 24

ADAPTING TO UNIVERSES

Last time we spoke, we told you there are many universes which can be tapped into if one wishes to go there. There are indeed hoards of possibilities, that's why the number is endless. It would not make sense to choose to be a Being fleeting from one to the other, because it would probably never adapt to any. On the other hand, if one chooses one particular place or level to go to, one can concentrate on **that type** of Matter or vibration range, in order to perfect its use and one's behaviour and handling of it. Therefore, it is always advised to concentrate on one type, one area of 'work' of experiments and then develop those necessary skills there.

PLAN THE TRIP

An example: If the level of vibrations required was to do with the Earth, say (then you'll understand better no doubt), the Being could choose to be a Human or an 'Animal', or a Plant, or whatever else it may choose, of course. But it has to do with **preparing oneself for the trip,** as we told you before.

So, if we prepare a Being for a trip as a Human, he'll have to think as a Human in a flesh body. If a Being felt he wanted to go as an 'Animal', he would have had to choose which kind of 'Animal' he wanted to be, then he would have to adapt his thinking and mental behaviour to that particular type of 'Animal'.

It is just **not** a question of 'jumping into a flesh body' and thinking he'll be able to cope with it, as we said before. So, the truth to consider behind all that, is that all Beings have to weigh the pros and cons of the trip they are going to make, understand why they want go 'as that Being' and finally make

226

the necessary adjustments for that trip, in many different ways and levels! They may even be asked to practise a little in our world before they make the big jump into the other one!

BACK-UP TEAM

Another point is that the Soul choosing to be one 'creature' or the other is not going on its own. She/he/it has 'his' followers - those who will stay with 'him', in our world while 'he' goes to have a go at the new life elsewhere. That too has to be organised ever so carefully. This task cannot be imagined or understood unless one is here. We have so much to take into account, so much responsibility towards our 'protégés'. We cannot risk jeopardising their trip and their experiments.

This is all very well if it is to do with the Earth, as we have been to the Earth too, so we know what to expect more or less. But if they wish to go to other places or levels, which have not been tested or lived in by any of us who have lived on Earth, then **they have to be guided by other Beings who have the experience of those particular areas or levels of thoughts and behaviour**. That calls for totally different types of personalities from the ones you personally are used to, my dear. This is where you reach what you could call 'science fiction' in your films. We have no films here, we have only Reality. This is where new ways of thinking and accepting new ideas come into play.

DIFFERENT WAY OF THINKING

The level of thought or thinking of Beings who have **not** been on the Earth will be **different from your own way of thinking**. Another point will be the **intensity of the Power of Thought** could be or would be very different. You don't seem to be aware how much power you have, compared to other places where they use it far more!

Power is the key word and tool. Power of Mind, Power of Action, Power of Creative Thought - all that is one. As they think, they create, like we do here, but there will be different ways of creating whatever they may want to create. The slow way is to think slowly, bit by bit. The fast way is to see something or some action all done, ready, prepared for use.

So, the Being who goes there knows why he wants to go to that particular level of Thought Power. It would probably be why he chose it instead of a different one, where the focus may be less intense in that direction, but more focused on the Inner Self, the **levels within, which are and have worlds of their own.** Beings of all kinds exist 'physically' or even in a 'mental way', if you can guess or envisage that! In other words, all possibilities are open to those wanting to try anything, as anything is possible!

VORTEXES OF POSSIBILITIES

All possibilities exist as potential, powerful vortexes or centres of Energies which are ready and willing to be put into action, even before someone comes within their vicinity. The mere thought of doing 'such and such' would start the ball rolling in that particular direction! The creature or creative Being which would be involved would have triggered it into action, by figuring out its own existence within that particular 'time frame' or more exactly 'action frame'. That's where the Power starts exerting its influence and those who have not experienced it before will be surprised at first, but delighted afterwards. An example may be more fruitful to you - a little insect in your world does not know what it is capable of doing until it starts doing xyz. It has to learn its way through handling little objects or twigs or leaves.

A bigger insect, which has already been a little one but grew up, has now more experience in what he is doing and he'll cope even better. But when he sees another little insect, it thinks it's silly not to be able to do things well.

228

BELIEVE YOU CAN

It's essentially a matter of convincing oneself one can do it before assuming one cannot. It is not impossible for a 'young one' (insect or other) to do things older or more experienced beings can do. It is just a **question of believing it can do it** and not mistrust its own abilities. If trust in oneself was paramount in whatever one did, there would be far more achieved everywhere, in any world or dimension!

It is the usual reaction of thinking: "I can't (yet)" which holds back any Being, whether 'Animal', Person or others from 'elsewhere'. They all have the faculty to think one way or the other.

BR- Is thinking the same everywhere, whatever 'the place'?

As you 'think', the power comes out of yourself, your own Thought Power. That in itself is such a creative force which you really have no idea about. It's so intense, it can do anything... yet it is not used enough within your own Earthly world!

As to 'other places', as you call them, there are so many diverse ways of expressing that **Inner Power**, which is **a constant Urge to express itself into some kind of reality**, whatever that may mean, wherever! It's an Inner Urge to have more, better, different, intense and yet be calculating if need be. It cannot create without Intelligence behind and within it. It has to be controlled too, to be successful in its creativity.

INTELLIGENT INNER URGE

You cannot create 'things', let's say, which would be destructive to the Self creating it. So it has to have within it **a built-in Intelligence which directs** the construction, the creation, the gathering together of the necessary components to make it a viable success.

That Intelligence is not added to it from somewhere else, it comes part and parcel of that Inner Urge and self-creating power. The creative power is a multifaceted action pack if need be. An action pack - a pack of **actions that feel the need and urge to be created**. Yes, to be created, as the idea of 'them' is emerging or even just germinating in some corner of the **'Thinking Urge' to create**, or the Urge to think... which is in itself an Urge to create! Create, that is the key to creation, obviously! But that implies the deepest **Urge to 'BE!** Be whatever 'being' can or may mean, wherever.

This is what is so difficult and nearly impossible to put across to those who read these words, because of the intensity of this **inner desire to have an outlet** as, or into, any kind of 'structure'; it is an endless representation of itself, or a succession of representations, as they develop into more developments. This is indeed mind-boggling! But that needs to be known, in order to understand **the world you 'know' is nothing compared to what could be known,** if one could overview all the universes and dimensions that could ever exist! A totally impossible task, of course!

But understanding or at least accepting they do exist will make a dent into the **narrow-minded conception** of what Creation or Creativity is and means. My job here is to try to put across the explanation from a point of view above and beyond the ones that may be seen or heard, or thought about by Earthly Beings who have not even come out of their shells yet - but they think they can judge and work out a cosmos of tiny dimensions within their instruments, yet which is in reality far bigger and forever unfathomable to them!

MULTI-UNIVERSES

One must accept there are Beings all over the multi-universes:
- of physical or non-physical Matter,
- of Minds that have nothing to do with your own way of thinking,
- of Thought Power expressed in so many unspeakable ways, because there are no words for it !

So, when it is accepted or glimpsed at, that there are far, **far more ways to exist than having a flesh body and a little Mind** reduced to only thinking of materialistic thoughts then the door to REAL understanding starts creaking open gingerly!

OPEN MIND TO NEW KNOWLEGE

It is not a criticism of Mankind as such - we have been part of it! It is a mind-opening exercise to try to encourage some people at least to think further than what they are used to doing. If they think: "Oh! There must be also something beyond all this, there can be things we'll have to understand and experience", then they do open their inner door to Knowledge. It can be poured a little at a time, like with a dropper, into their gradually more receptive Minds, which will hopefully soak up the new information as it seeps into the cracks made in the old ways of thinking.

That's a slow operation but one really worth working on to improve Humanity and its general attitude to what it does not know or refuses to even consider. We have your interest at heart, all of you, so we'd only give you what you can take in as you go along.

****

Chapter 25

OTHER WORLDS

BR- You mentioned 'other dimensions' which are levels of Mind. What about other worlds of existence?

Of course there are some! Do you think your world is the only one?! All areas of vibrations and sensitivity have 'Life'. All create something that can create more. All can sense and multiply. **That's** what we call 'existence': Being able to perceive one exists and sense the Urge to multiply oneself, to the extent that the multiplication has gone so far that you completely lose the feel and the 'likeness' of the 'original' Thought starting it on its way to create more and more. All 'Life' is like that.

Therefore, **'existence' is the fact that you can create more out of other Thoughts which multiply themselves!**

If you mean: Are there other Beings as such, like or dissimilar to your own flesh Beings, we'd say: There are Beings but there are lots of various types of Beings!

All cannot be like you, as the Earth place **was chosen and designed to be the recipient of this particular type of Matter** you all are made of and reside in. Life has all possibilities of Creativity within itself; it has not got limitations and boundaries, but it has inner guidelines.

If you look for different types of 'Matters', of course there are loads! But you would not know or understand if we tried to describe them, since there are no words in your languages to express what we see **made of 'material' totally unknown to you**!

Let's start with the world you know. You are made of carbon Matter (as the main matrix) and its subordinates, but we won't go into great detail since there is no point telling you what can easily be found in your books etc. But we can tell you there are other worlds of 'solid' **matter of a different kind** indeed, which has nothing to do with the Matter you know of in your world!

The Matter you know is **not** the same as what you'd find in some far away planets or stars which have not even been discovered yet (if they ever are or will be!). You cannot conceive something you have never seen, so we'll have to try to give you some approximate descriptions.

FLUID WORLD

That world which you could consider the 'nearest' to your type of Matter is one well away from your side of the Universe you know. It is made of more 'fluidic' type of consistency, but it is not solid to the touch as yours seems to be. **The fluidity is,** again, **created by the Minds of those who invented their surroundings.**

There is a great need for Mankind to understand those concepts as they are very different from the Matter Humans are used to - Humans think there is nothing else. We can delve into the 'Knowledge Box' of gathered facts and find out what is asked.

This world of Fluidity is not what you know or think of as 'water' but a texture which looks and feels a bit like that, but has more a mercury-like consistency, solid yet fluid, moulding itself to other things when close to them. So the **feeling of freedom and fluidity is what is experienced as a delight** for the 'Beings' there, who too have a Mind of their own as their Mind is a Creative Force like everywhere else!

Their world is not a ball of fire in the sky or an 'Earth - like bundle', it is a 'plasma-like' world with no boundaries as such. Very difficult to explain since you don't know what that experience is like. The lack of boundaries may puzzle you, as you'll no doubt imagine the 'fluid' to flow out into nowhere in the vastness of space. But it is not in the 'space' you know of, as that space of **yours** is among physical Matter as you know it, whether stars or planets. We are talking of a very different facet. It is not that 'physical' space, it is the level or frequency of the particular vibrations of the particular 'substance' that, to you, could look like a kind of mercury. Do you see what we mean?

NO RIGIDITY

BR- What do 'Beings' do there?

They have the choice and abilities to do what feels right at the time of their existence, **as their aim is to enjoy and experience the non-rigidity of their 'physical' existence**. Compared to yours on Earth, everything has that consistency and it makes it an interesting contrast, as the dissimilarity is accentuated according to the level of your thinking and the speed of your thoughts. All thoughts are fast but the delivery of the thought may be slower in some cases and the play with that level is what they use. We mean they are **playing with the different levels of frequencies of their Thought Power** and create as it is broadcast and beamed out.

So we have that kind of world which is not at all like the Earth. Some Beings may have gone to choose that, as it is a different experience from what they will have experienced.

But this is something we'd better not go into, as it is personal experiences, not general knowledge.

The others we could talk about is that on the **planets you know** of, or vaguely, **there are forms of life but they are no way near what you'd know in Earth life.** They don't need to go and reproduce themselves as duplicates of Earth life if they want to be elsewhere. If they wanted to be like that, they'd go on the Earth! That is the place for it.

Since they want something different, it makes sense to be dissimilar, so the appearance and make up of those 'Beings' is of such composition that **your instruments would probably not even notice** they are there! It is something to think about.

'Life' is not an 'object', a seed or a drop of water. **Life is an Energy made of and coming from our World of Energy**, which is what everything consists of. Except that this Energy can reproduce itself in very different ways.

The joy of Creation and Creativity is in the multiplicity in all possible and even near 'impossible' appearances and existences. We know these words are nowhere near what is needed to explain. So to sum up: If you look within your Universe of your particular type of Matter, you will find (or would find **if** you had the right instruments!) places **beyond** your man-made rockets' reach, where Beings can exist in a 'solid' way, at least solid to their experience and realisation. But there is a multitude of worlds which exist and which have nothing to do with your Universe of your Matter. And there will be umpteen of all kinds because the key to existence is to want to Be**! The Urge to Be**. When you have a Power which is constantly pouring itself out, for the sole purpose to exist into different ways, who can say what will be creating itself next?!

The Thought, the Urge, the Idea which suddenly sprouts for 'something different', if sustained, will automatically lead to its creation in that way, the way it had been thought of, unless it continues and develops itself for even more improvements. So yes, **there are solid-like worlds, but of different Matter.**

PERFECT EARTH

BR- Our Earth must be 'one possibility' since Life on Earth went eventually 'wrong' due to Man's free will . So there must be 'elsewhere' the 'perfect' original Earth with Humans behaving correctly?

That is correct. You could say that, because all is possibilities and probabilities and a multitude of offside shoots. The Earth of yours was the prototype. It had been altered by wrongdoings in many ways. You are right about the probabilities of a 'perfect Earth', because that's what it is. The inhabitants have the same rule as yours but have followed it and thus live happily in the world of Matter, you know.

NO DISEASES OR DEATH

It is not necessary to 'die' as you know, so they pop in, have fun and pop out... like you'd do for fun into a sea or a pool, to enjoy the bathing and come out. They have gone beyond, or rather have **never** known, the existence of **diseases,** because **they have not created such things,** since they stick to the pleasure and fun of creating with their Minds (as was meant) but in a constantly positive way!

This means they do not need to 'die' because the body is old, decrepit or sick - they just pop out of their vehicle to do something else if they have achieved what they wanted to experience there. A similar but also slightly different way of living to yours.

BR-Could any of us Humans go to that 'Perfect' Earth?

That prototype has always been maintained in the Minds of all Humans. Those you know and those you don't know. So you could simply wish yourself there and find it with your Mind and Soul, rather than physically.

BR- Is it in 'my' current Universe? Could it be seen with giant telescopes?

It is not seen as it is on a different frequency. The Universe you know has many replicas in a way.

BR- Why, if it is the same kind of Earth and just the life and human attitudes are different?

My world is on a different frequency and you don't see it and can't live in it (as you are now). So the one we mention is on a **different frequency because the THOUGHTS of those who created it remained on a much higher and more**

refined level! We know there is an 'Earth prototype' which has always been in the hearts and Minds of all Humans, except that the moment they reach the Earth of Matter, they turn it as it suits their Minds, ideas and ways of living.

The little lady *(me BR!)* wondering about all this is in a world where People do get ill and hurt each other, because she has chosen to come and teach 'that lot'. But she could have gone to any of the other possibilities and certainly to the 'perfect Earth' if she had wanted! That 'perfect Earth' is not an airy-fairy imaginary world but one which has been designed with Matter as a 'seemingly solid' appearance. Those who need it feel they are touching and handling and tasting the new things they have created by simply wanting to be there. **What is different is their way of thinking.**

Those Humans of the Perfect Earth of Matter have **not** lowered their approach to debasing themselves as Spiritual Beings. They have stayed on a high level of spiritual thinking, i.e. **following the One Law of not hurting** other travellers. That way their world has remained one of Kindness and Compassion, filled with that special Light, full of joy and happiness.

If you wanted to know where it is in a 'space' of Matter, it would be on a different level of frequencies and wavebands, like you face if you look for different stations of different countries on your radio sets. As it is a world of 'Matter', it is still tangible in the same way as yours, but nowhere where your current telescopes would sense it (if ever they could be made!).

BR- Is it 'invisible' within our current physical Universe?

My dear, the idea of being visible or invisible is very difficult to discuss, since you are talking of visible to your human eyes or telescopes. This is so impossible to answer since you don't even see our present World of Light and

Mind... because the frequencies are far more refined than yours on Earth. The wavelengths are not really reachable, as an instrument would do if it was powerful enough.

The idea of that 'Perfect Earth' was where Humans etc. were supposed to live and experience that new condition, but since they used their Minds to create for themselves other parameters, other goals and focus, this **automatically altered the state of the world they lived in!**

BR- Why didn't Beings from your world always go to that perfect place?

The prototype was created in the Minds of those who wanted it. It was the place to have a 'solid' body of physical Matter which would provide ways of surviving there by eating and drinking. And even reproducing in a pleasant way.

But the aims had nothing to do with the above-mentioned. Those **physical activities, though possible and temporarily pleasant, were not the goals**. The goals had much more fun and creativity; it is and was to create environments but feel them as 'solid'; create situations but alter them at will; create objects and places.

The difference with our world is the fact that though the Mind creates, here it can change things very quickly by shifting its focal point and then the 'thing' created will disappear, as it has no longer been focused on, whereas with Matter, it will remain there - It may not last forever if its consistency is of metal or a substance which will not last endlessly, but it will survive longer than here.

BR- Your World is more beautiful than on Earth and feels real. So why go to that new place of Matter?

The beauty you experience in our world is far different from yours in that the frequencies you encounter feel different to you from what you'd sense here. As there is no way of showing you the comparison while you are on Earth, it will be very difficult to explain. We could tell your Soul when you come at night, but you won't be able to put that into human words for the next day.

Just an example: When you feel happy, you may say: "Your Soul is singing", as you feel you are lifted out of your flesh body. When **we** feel happy, we feel our Spirit 'singing' and expanding into a state of utter bliss.

You have a restricted experience and it is usually temporary. When the Earth and the physical senses were created, the aim was to give each participant a new angle, a new possibility for challenges. Those would be fun to do and expanding their Creativity and Mind Power.

If the Mind does not 'do' something, it goes stale, it cannot function! It has to be given challenges, or else it will want to create some itself for the sake of it. The Minds of **all Beings have an unlimited reserve of Creativity which is an Urge to do, to be and to create**. So the Will of those who chose to come to this newly built Earth as a challenge was happy as it was a new experience and a new way of doing things - Instead of what we could do here. It may not be a better way, it may not produce environments or other activities which are 'better', but they certainly are **different.**

A physical body used to carry out challenging actions, testing itself against others, made life far more interesting as a change, as a newly created creative moment, as an Experiment. Not a 'way of life forever', but a challenge of being in a different environment, new 'set of rules' and frame of Mind. All this mattered and still matters to those who choose to go on the Earth, you know.

On to the 'other' Earth, the 'perfect' one, there will still be challenges which will be far more fun, since those travellers will not know what diseases or accidents are. This is **because accidents only happen when there are imbalances within the structure** and combination of the Inner Self driving a flesh reflection of Itself. So you need not worry about unpleasant

239

happenings when the Soul is happy with its body and vice- versa. All is well in 'Utopia', the perfect world. That's where everyone was supposed to go and where everything was changed when they focused on the desires of the physical senses . Their loss, not ours, but it is a shame and a pity.

There is a final point to put across: All those who think they'll want to go to the 'Perfect Earth' when they go over to our world, after the flesh has 'died', will have a surprise, because they will have caused themselves a baggage of emotions, regrets or bad thoughts, no doubt. So they'll have to spend some 'time' here in our world to rectify, improve or readjust their way of thinking.

That's why it will not be 'just stepping out of your current world' and into a level of bliss and Utopia land. But it would still be possible for them to go if they wished to do so.

BR- Could my Mum and loved ones go to Utopia? Could she be too 'engrossed' there when I eventually arrive?

We need to tell you that 'perfect Earth' is **not for an everlasting stay**, but for a refreshing break of enjoyment and challenges. So, if your mother, say, wanted to go there once she's sorted out all she needed to grasp and cope with in our world, then she very well could, but she would certainly not want to be gone and focused elsewhere when you arrive here, as she's been waiting for this for far too long!

BR- Yes, but her focus and concerns may be different after such a while.

She will be here for you, don't worry! That's something which is certain; love does not 'disappear' like that. She wants so much to be able to show you around and help you settle! You won't have to worry about not having her there!

CONTACTS BETWEEN WORLDS?

BR- 1) Can 'Aliens'/dwellers from other physical worlds (Some say Sirius star) communicate with Earthlings?

2) Can Beings going to 'Perfect Earth' communicate with Earth sensitives & mediums?

That's when things become more complex. The problem with some People thinking they hear or see those who talk to them is they can mix-up their beliefs, or their fears at times, with the actual happenings. Some may well see or hear some other Beings talking to them who will be very advanced in the method of transposing thoughts into Humans' Minds. That's very possible as nothing is really 'impossible' (even if not advisable).

They think they talk to someone on some very distant planet or star - but that would be dicier, as being on a star or a sun will not be very liveable... so it would be a Being of Mind who does not really live on a star! If a distant Being from some physical world of different texture would talk to you, wouldn't you be pleased? BUT would you be able to test whether he was **really** from that distant planet, since you've never been to or seen the place?

So you'll then have the challenge to work out what the Being said and why and how he would know all that. What can he say about his 'planet', how can he describe it? And **what would be a good gauge to judge his veracity**? He may be real, but he also may not be, yet you'd have no way of judging and guessing. It may well be someone here (*in Spirit World*) who thinks he is bored with his surroundings and decides to play tricks on People on Earth gullible enough to believe him! There is the added problem of trusting the information whatever it is. Very awkward.

TRUSTWORTHY LINKS

On the other hand, when anyone you are acquainted with communicates and talks to you, you can check what they say, as you have known them. And those who come and teach you will have made a lot of effort to produce good evidential work over the years, to help you build your trust in them and understand that the knowledge you are given is trustworthy.

The communication you can get from our world will be as easy to get as from any other place when your friend or loved one had **his Mind focused your way.** If she/he is focusing on the new place (e.g. Perfect Earth) they won't be talking to you, but the moment they change focus and think of you or listen to you then there will be no problem.

****

CHAPTER 26

DIMENSIONS WITHIN YOUR MIND

The subject of our talk is other dimensions none of you are aware of. Not dimensions in the sense of size (like height or width), but **dimensions in the sense of other worlds, other vibrations, other planes** and realms, do you understand? They are real, they exist and yet you don't know about them really.

When one Thought appears, or a few Thought Powers 'gather mentally' to think of something more interesting to do (we are using simple words and images to help you all understand), when such ideas come together for the purpose of more creativity, then it is always interesting to follow the pattern and the build-up and continuity of the process.

One such 'starting point' was, or is, the **creation of a new dimension** where Beings there have the freedom to roam, we could say, in a totally different environment from what they were used to. Such a 'place' could be a **feeling of existing without having a 'body'** so to speak. This is **a delightful state** of being, because one is totally free from any constriction, restriction or limitation.

The Being would be as free as it wishes but the aim is to see what it can do with its freedom, using its forever existing Thought Power. The level of this world is within oneself, a feeling of being awake and aware, as you would term it, but without having to deal with a body. So **the level of existence is within the Self** and that is a plane and dimension people on Earth do not think about. They do not realise there are levels and dimensions within oneself, which **one can reach and live in!**

So, you can see that it is not always a question of Matter and touchable things and places which exist - it can also be within the Mind... Not just the Mind itself but worlds within the Mind. What is Mind? Mind is the power of the Creative Force 'Self', realising itself. **It knows it exists.** So a Mind is a reflection of the Thought Power which has always existed anyway, but within that power there are levels and dimensions.

A dimension is not necessary a place or just a level of physically measurable vibrations: it is a state of being, **different from other states of being**, that's all. So one state of Mind may have a totally different, attainable state and dimension from others' states of Mind, you see?

You need to grasp that **a Min**d, as such**, is not a Being** but a condition and power of Creativity. If the Mind is used a lot because it is active, it will create a lot; if it is not used a lot, it won't be so creative.

BR- But doesn't saying 'is used' imply a Being using it?

It is used in the sense of 'Creativity being used', making things happen more than elsewhere, let's say. So the Mind of one Being has different states to the Mind of another, whatever the Being is, whether 'Animal', Plant or other Beings from other 'planets' or dimensions.

The 'Animals' and Plants you know have a Mind of their own because they have the Creative Power within, of course! They would not exist otherwise! And they **have their own levels and inner dimensions to reach** which cannot be comprehended by Humans, most of the time.

To sum up: The Mind of most 'Beings' (wherever they come from or go) is a Power within, with multi-strata and levels of inner dimensions, which can be released from any link to any 'physical' or material body form (whatever it is there). We need to use words you know. So, the Mind Power, or Intelligence in that context, has that **ability to go deeply**

within itself and feel free from constraints. The constraints are usually caused by interaction with others, who or which are not at the same level and that causes friction of interaction.

ESCAPE

But the escape is wonderful for those who love to feel free! That's what is not always understood. The getaway within a Mind dimension can be of many kinds - it is not just with words and pictures, if you are from the Earth. It can be **feelings of elation, elevation, self-absorption, ultimate bliss in the sense of blending with the universally eternal Energies** with other similar 'Mind Powers', with all sorts!

Such dimensions have the ability to make 'People' (let's say, as it is more useful to you) lift themselves from one level of 'drudgery existence' to a much higher level; from one level of understanding to another; from one experience to a different one.

To those who have not tried it, it is unexplainable in words. It can only be lived and experienced. But for those who have had a glimpse of the upliftment of other dimensions, it sparks off the desire to want more, to want to return to it, or stay there, or find a state even more blissful and fulfilling than the one they've just been in or glimpsed at!

That is what we term **'Progress'** - upliftment, elevation, evolving, understanding. We cannot explain in words those special states which have no real 'place', in the same way as our present 'Spirit' world has no solid place, as you'd call it; it is an inner experience which has no physical dimension.

Dimensions are depths of inner, improved understanding and elevated experiences: in the sense of moving away from the known to the new, unknown, more refined, more subtle and more subjective. All this into **one big Feeling of Knowing and embracing that Inner Power one is made of.** All that is so hard to explain to people on Earth who have an Earthly material body and do not want to think beyond the flesh and the physical! But those who try to grasp the eternity of Existence and the reality of One single, mightily powerful, eternally reproductive Mind/Thought Power (Mind =Thought, remember!), well, those could perhaps get a glimpse of what we are trying to put across.

People who thought we'd talk about dimensions in the sense of planet-type things may be disappointed in reading this, but we can talk (and have done so) of other such dimensions and levels some other time, if you like.

That particular explanation today is for you to understand that the **planes one can get to in one's Mind are infinite** and have their own Creativity still intact! That means, as one goes into each separate 'present-at-the-time' state, **one is automatically creating some kind of world or state of being** and feeling. That may feel like what you call a dream, but this feels real at the 'time'. You may understand some of it if you relate it to **dream-like state** - they absolutely 'exist' to you when you 'live' them, yet you can get out of them when you switch your focus of attention to another state, can't you? You simply wake up!

So, it is with these inner dimensions: you live them; you find yourself creating and created in a way by your own Thought Power, you have access to Knowledge and Understanding you did not have before... yet which you have now, because the extension and upliftment and wider encompassing of what is experienced means you can grasp more -- like a child's Mind cannot grasp more complicated concepts until it is led gradually from one to the other.

THIRST FOR KNOWLEDGE

That is what goes on when people have a probing, enquiring Mind in our world. They have new interests developed gradually through their own searching, inquisitive Mind, thanks to their own creative-enquiring-thirst for knowledge and inquisitiveness! All that leads them to step further on the path of discovery, a path unique to themselves in a way, but which some may tread upon, at least partially or in the same direction.

That's where help can be given by those who know, or have an idea of, what you are experiencing at that 'moment'. Life then becomes even more exciting because these inner dimensions open the door to so much more, ad infinitum! That is why **some 'Beings',** as you call them, **have not bothered with the experience of Earth Matter,** because **they are constantly experiencing inner worlds that have no end and no self-destruction** (unless they wanted it to be so, which is rather silly!).

My dear, that was possibly a long roundabout explanation, but we wanted to make you aware of these states in a little more detail, so that you grasp and can try to make others grasp that **there is FAR more for a Being to do than wanting to incarnate on this Earth** and **then pass over to Spirit World,** as you call it, and that's it!

This is not what happens exactly and even **our explanations are simplified** because it is not fair (and not easy either!) to try to make Earth Minds understand something which has not been experienced by them. So we'll say many thanks for listening and we hope you'll be happy to have learnt something possibly new for you, but of great interest if you go into it, absorb it and have a good think about.

BR- Many thanks, it's fascinating. Are you 'Brother John'?

My dear, we have said it before, the spokesperson is only a Mind speaking into your Mind. All those around have as much to say as one single personality, or even more, as **all Minds meet to gather and bring information to yours**. We are all happy to talk to you because you want to learn.

My 'voice' so to speak, today, can be labelled Brother John but that is not what is important. **The message counts**, dear, **not the messenger**!

BR- I know, but it gives me comfort to 'label' you all: you are my real friends who teach me so much!

You can rest assured we shall always be your friends and we'll all meet again one day, in more real circumstances as you call it; though we do meet at times when your body has a rest, but you usually don't remember in the morning, do you?

You can take comfort in our presence, which will be eternal, as your and our Minds blend and will make one creative learning/teaching Mind Power out of our joint resources and interests. You can rest now and rejoin your Earthly world and activities.

****

*(11. 50 am - Those were 8 handwritten A4 pages, in 60 minutes, dictated in full flow = about 7.5 min **per A4 page**. It is fast and only restricted by the slowness of my hand's ability to write down speedily what they tell me!)*

Chapter 27

LEVELS

BR- What can you say about possible 'levels' in the Universe(s)?

Then I wait, relaxing my mind as much as possible. Suddenly and unexpectedly my hand seems to have the urge to draw large circles on the page. Traced lightly at first, then with determination it drew the middle sketch: a kind of large 'cup' within which one can see whirls of concentric circles; after which, it was back to surrounding it with wider and wider circles.

I feel if the page had been bigger it would have filled it and beyond! Then I heard their dictation:

All of them *(referring to the symbolic circles drawn)* expanding and retracting under the influence of Thought. Nothing else influences Matter. Thought does because Thought is a Creative Power. **There is no 'Matter' anywhere which can produce itself or other things unless there is Thought Power within its formation, even at the most infinitesimal level**!

You cannot find Thought Power in anything as an 'object'. You can only discover it by looking at **its results**. All of you have the results around you and all of you have that power within you. Why do you not see this?!

Lots of circles in this drawing means there are millions and 'zillions' of so -called 'levels'? That means in reality there is a constantly increasing number of 'levels'. We cannot say how many and we cannot say 'where', because all blend within each other. Yet they are **separated by the distance of the wavelengths** and degree of vibrations they are made of, or produce.

(BR's NOTE- I wonder whether some other mediums' 'Spirit' communicators forcefully stating actual figures (e.g. precise distances or fixed numbers of levels or 'spheres' or years), are still close to the Earth way of thinking and have not progressed enough to reach properly, deeply and further into the 'Knowledge Box', since my teachers insist that names and numbers are man-made labels!)

INNUMERABLE

You cannot see any of them, as such, with a naked eye of course and your instruments will not pick them properly. It is impossible to feel and sense 'levels' unless you are, like us, in that environment. We do not want to say there are 'no levels'. We want to say there are so many one could not possibly count them! Moreover **they have the fantastic ability to blend and merge with each other, yet remain separate!** You see, it's beyond man's grasp to comprehend the Power of Thought's abilities. It is not a machine making them, so the average Human Being will never accept it is possible.

BR- Please explain the 'cup like' central piece of your sketch.

You see, that small drawing is an attempt at schematising the basic concept of 'all within all'. We showed you that within, say, an atom, or a molecule, or a structure there are billions of whirls of Energy all linked together, yet separate. There are **no real limits** and boundaries between them or anything. Everything is linked. All blend yet all are separate in their own individuality. So the **Energy** going from one to the other is **the only real link!** The emanations of Energy.

As you look at the sketch (which is incomplete anyway) you have to grasp that from one 'line' to another there are, in between, huge uncountable amounts of Thought Power, which is Creative Energy! If and when that Thought Power is more focused on one 'realm', one area, than on another, the difference in the pull it may cause will have some repercussions.

BR- Sorry, did you say 'in' or 'and' the pull?

The difference that the pull of Thought creates may cause repercussions. (That should be clearer?). So the pull of this Power creates differences and these are variations that you may perhaps see on your screens and photos, if you **observe them as a magnified vision of infinitesimal happenings**, if your instruments are powerful enough!

But we cannot talk in figures or words, since they have no meaning for us, as you know. We can only tell you that the thing you are all looking for has **no physical substance** whatever machine you'll ever use!

CREATIVITY THROUGHOUT ALL UNIVERSES

We have one thing in common, all of us, throughout the universes. It is the power of Creativity, which is an eternal Force running through anything and everything which exists and will exist forever! There is not one 'thing' which has not been, or is not, imbued with that amazing and **wonderful** Power which has no name to us. The 'stuff' it is made of is the stuff of all realms, though it can be used at different degrees, or levels, or directions, or intensity.

An example may help, on a small scale: If you had a big cup with a liquid whirling in it for ages and ages, you would soon notice a difference in the composition and the direction of its molecules. You may even see it practically 'disappear' from the middle of the cup, to 'stick' itself to the side. You would see various happenings which have nothing to do with the original stagnant, fluid liquid you had put in the cup. It might even heat up and become a gas, depending on its composition! So this is just a very small, simplified example to make you understand that **all things can change under pressure** of one kind or the other. And the pressure and power of 'Thought' is endless and limitless!

THOUGHT IS A TRIGGER

So search what you like... but you'll all have to eventually come back to the fact that the Mind, as you call it, is the power behind all happenings. All things, in whatever universes and realms, have the power of Mind, of invisibility; and **Thought Energy is the fundamental force that triggered anything into action.**

Whatever you may call it in physics or chemistry, you'd have to come back to Mind Power! **That** is **eternal** because that's how it is! This is incomprehensible to Humans because they have ensconced their Minds within the realm of the physical world, which has all its limitations, boundaries and restricted senses (which usually do not accept what cannot come within their grasp!).

So, that overriding and pervading Power has various names, if you want to use words, but it boils down to the same thing: The 'stuff' we are all made of, in any world of any kind, the untouchable to you but real vibrations of what we call **Inner Creative Light,** that 'Mind' which has always been the tool to make anything happen, change, 'disappear' or 'reappear'! All the same!

If you sense the drawing you'll see what we mean, as a very simplified sketch of what can be done by Thought. All encompassed tightly, all expanding widely. All merging, all parallel. All so far and yet so near and all within the Thought of the thinker! All thinking, the thoughts creating more. All is one and one is all and yet everything is different... to be excitingly interesting and challenging, for the next thought to be triggered and creating more! What else can we say?

Nothing is static. Everything is moving forwards, backwards, inwards, outwards... but there are no real 'directions' in worlds of merging and blending of powerful and subtle Energies! Is that any clearer? If not, try and think about it?

252

PART 3

FEARLESS LIVING

*"To condemn without knowledge
is the recipe for perpetual ignorance"*
(Erbert Hubbard)

Chapter 28

TUNING IN IS ESSENTIAL

Lots of people don't know what it is like to tune in to their own Higher Self. If only they could understand the usefulness and the great need for it, they would do it more often! It is essential to 'recharge one's battery' and one's knowledge by being aware of what can be achieved when **tuning in to one's Higher Vibrations, to balance out the pull of the lower, heavier, Earthly vibrations of Matter.**

When the Mind is not too active and rests enough to pick these vibrations, it acts like a magnet with the rest of the Being's vibrations, those areas which are not easily within reach usually. The attraction is emphasised when the Mind calms down even more, then the reception is really good and facts and advice can come more easily than usual. It is of paramount importance for people on Earth to try to do it periodically: because it is **no use living on Earth as an Earthly Being and forgetting their true origins**, since, anyway and automatically, they will all have to go back to their original world!

An example might help make this point clearer: If the Soul of a man was **not replenished regularly** by the latent energies within it and by the surrounding energies of this world, his Will to be that 'man' would perish slowly and **would fade out.** If the flesh Being on Earth, who has that Soul as a driving force, does not receive the invigorating Energy necessary to keep it going in this world of Matter, he too will fade away.

The Soul needs replenishing and the Earthly Being representing it needs recharging. All need feeding from the Higher Energies of this world of ours. So why ignore them when they are the Source of Life for all? It is of utmost importance for people on Earth to understand that unless they take time out to feel their Inner Self and reach to it, they'll be losing out in the long run! **The Soul needs to WANT to energise its flesh body**... otherwise the Soul will decide not to do so anymore and **the body of flesh will die**, which means no one will be left on Earth to play with the Earthly activities that person thought were of great importance!

Another point is the fact that energising is good but keeping the link through one's daily activities is even better, because **guidance can be at hand any time.** So being aware of one's link and using it to one's and others' advantage means the person's dual Energy make-up is far more fulfilled than if it stayed simply on the level of Matter, on Earth level. It is so important, yet few seem to know or bother about it!

HOW TO TUNE IN

How can we encourage people to do so, without looking as if we are interfering with their Free Will and their enjoyment of the life on Earth they chose for themselves? It is only a question of guiding them towards methods which are suitable for each individual as there are several ways of doing this, but in the end it boils down to the same result. Yogi or Buddhist, ascetic or frugal, happy or not, all have to listen within, to feel the presence of their own Self in a much higher set of Energies than their flesh body can provide. You have many methods to link up to that source, but the basic mode is to look for the silence within, when the Mind is not talking to you.

Look for the quiet zone within, which is where the hub of those Energies' Life Power resides. Reach it, keep it going, listen within and believe you can get to it. Be still and at peace in that frequency zone. When you have found it, you will be more able to get back to it more often. Then the power **will**

surge forward and fill you with renewed Energies. So well that you'll feel 'a new person', with ideas and inner strength you never knew you had!

When you find them and experience all these, you'll want to go back to that wonderful source time and again, so that your whole Being is renewed, refreshed, re-energised for the tasks ahead. All who have done so have never regretted it, because to maintain a link between the world of your Origins and the world of the Experiment is the **true path** to follow.

The 'Experience in the World of Matter' is exactly what it is called - an experiment. An experiment ends one day, whereas the Eternal Source World never ends; it can only feed those who can receive it clearly. Those who don't will struggle and suffer more. It is essential to feel close to one's origins to keep the Power within going and act on it. If you feel the Power within, you'll be able to use it and direct it where you want, as long as it is for the good of yourself, others and Humanity.

POWER ONLY USED FOR GOOD

An act meant to harm will not be done out of Mind Inner Power, but out of the negative side of one's Self and that's not the same thing at all. The negative side could not exist without the positive being there too; there is no light without shade and no shade without light. You can't create shade if you don't have a light to light up the rest.To harm others wilfully in order to give pain and torture is **not** part of anyone's plan!

If some 'Animals' eat others, it's because they have been created and brought up to eat each other, for special reasons, **not** because they want to harm. *(See ch.11 'Animals: Their Identity & Reasons')*. It is therefore **certainly not part of the Human race's pathway plan.**

CONSTANT HELP WITHIN REACH

When you have reached your Inner Source of Power, you can tap into it at will, any time it is needed so that there is always a way out of problems and situations which occur unexpectedly. If one wants help, **help is there all the time**. NO need to be 'religious' and believe in any kind of goddess or helper or supernatural power: you have your own Inner Power to help you and you should be able to reach it whenever you need to, if only you have practised getting hold of the key to open the door to it.

Mind Power is what you have before birth, what you are born with, what you have after death of the body. You have Mind Power, is that clear? If you did not, you would not exist either in our world or in yours! We are all Mind Power. This means the intense Energy you are all made of and so are we in this world can create, alter, attract other Energies, resulting in many different possibilities.

A man who has 'lost his Soul', as he thinks, has **not** 'lost' any such thing because he still exists! He has **lost the capacity to tap into his Soul** or Inner Self. If he did not have that 'Soul', he would not be where he is, whether in your world or ours! **Nothing can become non-existent!** To be 'non-existent' does not exist in our world. Nor in yours either, because if something did not exist visibly and materially, you may think it is 'non-existent'... but, in fact, **its Energies are still around,** whether you see them or not! Therefore, this has no meaning anywhere.

VITAL CONTACT BETWEEN MINDS

A Mind has a power which all Minds have - that's why there can be contact between them. **If there was no contact, you could not cohabit on the same plane or planet.** You need this contact whether you are aware of it or not. Why? Because **a Mind is fed by Energies from other Minds and similar**

257

sources. A Mind cannot simply be a powerful beam without receiving other beams from elsewhere and be even more lit up and re-energised. It is all part of the plan. As a Mind surfaces to send its beams out, others receive it, react to it and are activated by it. **You can receive actuation from far apart energies which lock onto yours and you don't even know it's happening**! As a Mind receives, so does it send! This is what is constantly happening within your world, and also in our world and many others!

THOUGHT FASTER THAN LIGHT

You can reach other Beings with your Mind faster than you can with your phones and other gadgets. **Nothing can beat the speed of your Mind and Thoughts.** If you were not able to do that, you'd see the world would not function as well as it does. If you play a tune loud and clear, you'll reach other people's ears, but it does not mean they'll want to sing, or sing it, or know the words. They would have to **want** to reach or follow it. In the same way, you can send thoughts to people, they'll receive them, that is certain, but you cannot rely on them obeying your mental instructions, or wanting or following your suggestions or even reacting to the reception of what you sent. It's all to do with the Free Will everyone and everything has! Nothing can break that down, as a spiritual Being, you have Free Will to choose which way you go and act.

So, that can be a great bonus or a hindrance to one's progress, according to what is done with or without it. A normal 'accepting' Mind will be more aware of inner impressions and its links with the outer world, but others may not be so. Therefore, you'll have all the differences of opinions and the arguments and the reactions which create disharmony. Because one can **only have harmony if Minds agree with each other**, not if they disagree. This is food for Thought, isn't it?!

Chapter 29

YOUR MIND IN CHARGE OF YOUR HEALTH

DISEASES

Let us make one thing clear: Diseases do not 'happen'! Diseases do not come, uninvited, to attack you. All diseases are attracted to you by your depressed way of thinking, your negative 'down' attitude. This is a mightily important fact of life which goes against what you have been brainwashed with. You cannot comprehend illnesses and diseases if you, Humans, think of them the way you do. There is no way a disease attacks you. It comes because it has been brought on by factors around you which caused it! It can be bad sanitation, of course, but that will be because the whole area is in a deprived region, say, and people have nothing better, so they are all upset by it and probably wish they were dead. Their dejected mindset will be the 'shaking' factor and the magnet to create illnesses.

BR- But, say, if I forgot to wash my germy hands before eating, I could become very ill.

You cannot be ill unless there are **weak points** in your **inner body,** which will then be **reflected** onto the flesh body, so that becomes ill - meaning if you have no hygiene and let the body be swamped with dirty water or other 'germy' environment, you may not become ill at once for it.

But **if your Inner Self is sad, dejected**, upset, churned and unhappy...then there will be 'gaps and cracks' in its inner/emotional construction. And if there are gaps and cracks in its structure, those **will be reflected as gaps and cracks in the physical arrangement of the flesh body**! THAT REFLECTION is what causes 'diseases'!

This is an important point: If you have **any** kind of inner imbalance as emotional or mental upset, that trouble will

definitely be mirrored in the flesh. So wash your hands by all means and 'don't tempt fate' (by that I mean put everything in your favour). BUT no matter how many times you wash your hands and keep things clean etc. if you are **miserable inside,** you will have such a lot of emotional unsteadiness that your flesh body will be tilted out of balance!

That's why, if it's not germy water 'attacking' you, it will be a fall or something else which will reflect the inner unevenness! There is no way any of you can escape that!

TALK TO CANCER CELLS

Did you know that **cancer cells in a body have their own Mind?** Reminder: Your own Mind is a Creative Force which can do anything! All Minds have that Creative Power

DISCLAIMER: Brigitte Rix and her Teachers in the Spirit World cannot be held responsible for patients' decisions regarding their own treatments. Patients must discuss it with their doctors. This text is for information only, regarding the true cause and very essence of diseases.

within themselves, but it needs to be applied with a direction, an aim, a goal, a purpose that triggers even more power somehow for the Creative Urge to take place and succeed!

A Mind of mighty Creative Power is the tool of a 'Soul' (no matter who or what it is) to guide it on its creative journey. It may be stalemate, or start slowly, or zoom madly, but it has power and it has aims within somehow.

The **disease was created by some dysfunction or misalignment of the emotional and mental body** with the physical cells, as well as caused by silly, wrong or unhealthy ways of living, as we'd call it.

If your Soul does not want it anymore, you can reach the cells' Minds with yours and **tell them to stop,** because

260

YOU no longer want the illness! (Yes, you may have **subconsciously wanted it** and not realised!). Then the cells can respond to your request.

If you send them the signal: "STOP. RECEED. DISAPPEAR", it will happen, **unless 'the Soul of your Soul' wishes to leave the body.** The Soul of your Soul meaning your utterly **inner** wishes, **your fundamental and Higher Self.**

So you **can** talk to the cells, if you don't leave it too late. Also, visualise anything you like, symbolising you are 'hoovering out/sponging off/blasting or dissolving away the unwanted cells or lumps. Then keep imagining and seeing your body clean and free from anything unwanted. As soon as a problem is spotted, it should be dealt with that way.

CONTROVERSIAL BUT TRUE

Treatments using chemicals are not the reasons for any regression or 'remission'! They may have killed a few cells of cancer... but that does not mean those could not reappear, because **what has been killed** is only the **physical appearance of the cancer cells, NOT their Inner Being and Mind**! Not the 'current' keeping them alive.

The very **CAUSE of the disease** (which is part of the Inner Self feeling emotionally and mentally unhappy about something) will not be totally cured by chemicals. Only a **turnaround of the patient's own mindset**, including their subconscious attitude, will bring about a healthy change because **that attitude is what gives life and feeds the deadly cells. Chemical treatments do not kill 'attitudes' and mindsets!** Your MIND triggered the illness. So USE your MIND to STOP IT!

YOU need to REACH the Mind of the cancer cells to say: "Please stop now! You are not needed, I have learnt what I need and I want to stay longer". If you don't, the body **will** succumb under their attack. It is all a question of manipulating

261

the Creative Energy within each and every thing. **A Mind reaches any other Mind, including the Mind of the cells in your body!** A 'superior' Mind is one which has practised and developed its skills at Creativity and reaching out.

A Mind that has no wish to multiply or conquer outwards will not invade others or harm or attack. A Mind which does not understand that by multiplying it can harm others, has not progressed yet. **A Mind receiving instructions from a superior or more knowledgeable Mind, will be able to react to it** and has the **ability to follow the instructions sent**, if they are given CLEARLY, PRECISELY and INTENSELY.

So please **send very precise, very clear and very intense thoughts towards the parts of your body you want to heal, or re-adjust, or cure.** This has the Power to improve the realignment of the inner subtle bodies and Energies, including tose of 'Animals' and Plants of course.

HEAL YOURSELF

YOU CAN HEAL YOURSELF if only you work at it that way! But it must be practised and done regularly with **the INTENSE DESIRE to be better, not only in the body of flesh, but also in the body of Mind and emotions** too.

If your emotions don't want to realign themselves, if **subconsciously** they like to stay out of alignment and to be in a turmoil (some people do like that, as they feel sorry for themselves and like to feel so, to make others feel bad or be blamed!) then the hope of improving the flesh body is practically nil! **It has to be done from the very Inner Self outwards**, reaching all the levels of the being. **THAT is how one gets healed.** So **do not expect others to do it for you, you must DO IT YOURSELF!** You'll feel the results as soon as you do it correctly. Then you can tell others. Then you'll know what we told you is correct and THE Truth. End of 'sermon'!

HUMANS' PITCH

Every single Being has its own attunement, its own resonance, its own 'pitch'. That's why if **you find at what pitch you function**, you can re-establish your health more quickly when it goes out of synchronisation, you understand?

You only need to rebalance, **realign the vibrations** which need to be in alignment. Once that is done you are all right and can be 'normal' again. Should you let the alignment go out of true, be uneven, then you won't be functioning properly. You can test and **check that with most of your so-called complementary medicine therapies**; that's what they are all about, whether one theory or the other, one therapy or the other. You cannot have balance if you are out of balance, can you? So we work at balancing the energies of the Spiritual Being, so that it can be in tune with the Energies of the world it is going to, in your case, the Earth material world. It's essential to 'fine tune' the balance of the mental, emotional and physical levels. It is not an easy task as every Being has its own radiation, its own magnetic field and its own pattern.

TRAUMA = LESS HEALING POWER

If you take an apple with a spoilt, damaged core, you cannot expect it to cure itself, as the heart of it has been attacked by some disease or some worm or insect. So either you cut up the apple into pieces and get to the core that way, or you drill a hole in one place and suck up, dry up and remove the rot. As you cannot drill without bruising the apple more than it was, you create even more trauma to its body. **More traumas mean** less strength, **less power to heal itself**. That's what drugs and too many operations, chemicals and scans with radiation may do: for example, badly affecting your immune system.

You must LEARN to use the Inner Power of Healing, the power of the Mind and Soul. That will reach within, from within, without having to cut up or damage any part of the flesh.

CHANGE YOURSELF

How do we know this? Because **we see it** happening in those who use it. If you want to be one of those who heal themselves from within outwards, follow the principles explained earlier and be of cheer as help is definitely on the way:

* **CHANGE your attitude.**
* **ACCEPT there was an inner problem you do not want anymore.**
* **LET the HEALING take place at its own pace, from within out.**

There will be times when you may doubt because you'll feel it is slow, but you'll see the results as soon as you feel calmer and peaceful within. So the best way to do all this is to start young and to start early in your life. That means **teach this to children** too! They'll have to focus within. **They'll have to learn they can trust their inner power.** Most will have felt it one way or the other, unless they've been tampered with by adults. Adults such as parents who don't believe 'in all that stuff', as they may call it, or who do not understand that all living creatures have that power and possibility of helping themselves.

So don't doubt, try instead.

Do not delay, act now instead.

Do not criticise, do and see.

Then you'll be convinced.

You can rest assured that a wish, well directed with intensity and determination, will always achieve something. You cannot lose, it's a winner at all times. Use your Mind to use your Mind Power. **Use your Mind Power to soothe your Mind and Soul, to heal the body** they affect when they are unhappy… and that will be the end of your problems.

(BR Note - Also see previous chapters on your life plan, choice of body, its health and your chosen challenges).

Chapter 30

MIND: NOT IN ONE 'PLACE'

BR- Some information was allegedly 'inspired by Spirit' as to the spot where the Mind is (supposedly) situated in the flesh body. Please confirm or comment?

LACK OF KNOWLEDGE

We must **repeat** here what we have told you before, as it is important to grasp it properly: There are often **pieces of incomplete information given out** by some other Beings who communicate with Earth people! Which means some Earthly recipients will sadly believe firmly what is given and the claim that "The Spirit World has spoken".

Unfortunately, those bits of information may be incorrect, or be right only at a certain level... but there may still be far **more underneath that has not been studied properly** and absorbed by those speakers in our world! As we said, this has done more a disservice than a service to Humans, as the speakers' limited absorption skills have transformed **a restricted view** into a wrongly 'final and authentic' piece of news and information!

So we remind you this is what we want to avoid doing! Therefore, this is why we all pool together as Seekers of eternal Knowledge, so that the questions you ask spur us onward and more deeply into the search for us to find and receive even more details.

SEEKING HIGHEST KNOWLEDGE

We've explained before that it is all a matter of intense focusing and of purpose of Mind, of 'Thought Querying Mechanism'. We have to tune in ourselves to much higher vibrations from where more detailed information can come through. So we need to pay great attention to what is being 'said', or rather what information emanates from these levels. Levels that we can reach with our Minds if we do listen within intensely and thoroughly.

We said the Knowledge provided can be attained at various deeper levels. Once you get to one level and describe it or obtain that type of information, **the next level reveals itself, being more concise or complex**! That then allows access to the sub layers! We pool together what we have individually received and grasped, as our joint comprehension is more likely to be correct than just one individual's.

We also told you that all Beings and Minds are fundamentally **ONE** big, gigantic, endless and limitless Mind Power, not many separate personalities, Mind powers/forces/Energies. So, we can all link to everything else. It has no barriers as such. If you think of the Mind as a generating power that is involved in everything that happens to you and around you, you'll see already what a powerful Force that is overall.

We need to point out that your medical world has **NO** way of finding the Mind 'in' the flesh body, because the **Mind is the Energy that keeps the whole body going** on this Earth of Matter. If the Mind did not have that overall Power and Energy, the flesh body would not function! This is what we need to make people understand. Make the whole world grasp that they are a product of their own Mind Power. Not the other way round! Their brains do not create their Minds. **The Mind creates every inch and centimetre of the flesh Matter.** It cannot be done 'from inside' it, as you cannot construct a car by sitting inside it all the time, can you?!

Anything a scientist **thinks** he can prove, **cannot explain what we see as real here!** What he does has to be with maths/equations or instruments. No scientist can call anything 'real' on Earth because nothing is really solid or tangible, since it's all an illusion, one big hologram you con yourself with. So, scientists won't be any good at answering that sort of question!

On the other hand, **we** can see things in another way, from a different and **far superior viewpoint. We see it happen**! You, Earthlings, do not.

MIND: NOT IN ONE PLACE

The Mind Force that is inherent to all Beings is **not in** a 'particular place' as such for residence in the body! It **may link** to your body at certain points, like a handle on a door helps open the door if someone turns it, but the person who turns it is not in the door or the handle!

If you want to understand the Mind Power that you all have, see what you do to your health all over your body, when you feel unsettled, unloved, hated, or have any other mental disturbances. **It will affect your whole body in general** and therefore disturb its equilibrium and balance. This in turn will cause a major **'earthquake' at the weaker points of the flesh that may have been ill-treated** earlier, because of various possible causes - wrong eating, smoking, physical accidents and so on.

So we know the flesh is only a tool (to live on Earth) which the Mind can affect and manipulate to try to heal it, if need be and if possible. But the Mind itself is also a tool! The Mind is not the 'Spirit Being', as you'd call it. The Mind is 'only' a fantastic Energy which the Being uses to direct its Will and see results from its own wishes and urges. The very definition of Mind is more likely to be a Creative Urge that is built in the fundament, the essence of every single thing and personality you can think of, or not even know about.

We have great reasons for being forceful about this, as we can see what happens constantly from and in our world here, a world of Light and constant Thought from the Light. This Inner Light which bathes and makes up everything that is

267

in existence, is the light of the Urge that fills any Being of any substance. It is what keeps them in existence as **they exist because that inner Urge is present** and has always existed!

It cannot be denied that the whole purpose of any existence is to promote more Power to self-reproduce and create more happenings, in order to enjoy the 'creative side' which fills every and any Being of any 'place'. That is what Creation and Creativity are about: that inner Urge has never stopped and will never stop. It is built into everything, as said before. Therefore, who want to state: "My Mind/Urge Power is in my toes or my chest?" It is even more ludicrous than saying the Mind is the brain! All are wrong!

YOU = A GIANT MIND URGE

You need to **think of yourself as a gigantic Mind Urge**, which has manifested itself into arms/legs etc., i.e. into a whole body which reflects the Mind Urge's own power, or its own desire for that particular life. The Being you see on Earth is the Being created by the Mind that you are. And 'you' are **not** the flesh Being! **You** are the 'Spirit' ethereal Being of Mind, who has projected that physical appearance of yourself as a tool. A tool for experimenting what it is like to be in a flesh body, to use it to be in a world of Matter that is totally different from the world of Mind and Light and 'non-physical ' surroundings, 'physical' in the sense you know it as. The Being you are is a Being of Mind Power and Creative Urge which transcends all time and places.

How you use that Mind Power (which is 'you') is up to you and is never-ending because **possibilities are constantly opening** themselves up at every step or direction your own Creative Power takes or turns to, so it is not a static state of things. All Beings have the same abilities. All Beings you see and all other possible 'Beings' you know nothing about! They all have that built-in Creativity.

268

This is what makes 'Creation' exciting! **As it changes its focus, you may say that looks like a 'beginning' or an end of something, but it is not** really. That can be understood when you look at a Being on Earth, say, a Human and you at last realise the flesh cover may have decayed but the personality is still alive and well, carrying on with its exhilarating discoveries in the potential of its own Mind tool and Being.

It is so exciting! We can't see why people are not more alert about this, more aware and more in tune with their own Mind Power and Creative Urge! All they seem to want is material goods. What's the use of that when you can change your whole life and world around you with your thoughts?! But that's another subject to deal with later. So be pleased you are a Mind Urge, a Being of Light and Thought. Thought creates. Thought is the Creative Power. **All thoughts create the moment they are produced** or even 'half thought'.

Everyone should be aware of what can happen with their thoughts and inner or disguised desires. Everything that comes out of your own Creative Power (which is your Mind) **will go on to create itself**, whether here or elsewhere. It **never disappears.** Have the courage to face up to your own Thoughts, because your thoughts become activated, therefore 'action'! If you think it, you have caused it to be created!

You cannot deny what you create because it is born of yourself! That is a frightening thought in a way, yet it should also be very exciting and empowering. That is all we can say for now, we can always broach the subject again some other time if you wish.

****

Chapter 31

ORGAN TRANSPLANTS

BR- Please tell me about organ transplants. Do they have any influence on the recipient?

As we see things, the transplant of things of the flesh has no influence on the recipient on a 'spiritual' level. The energies of the flesh do not clash with the Energies of the spiritual which have emotions linked to them. Remember that the fact a body of flesh exists is because the 'Spirit' person chose to have that particular body as a vehicle. If the vehicle is deemed not acceptable or not needed any longer, the personality will leave it for a trip back to the realms of Energies where physicality does not come into it.

The realm we exist in has nothing to do with the type of Matter you are used to. So, when a body of flesh is no longer any good to you, you can leave it behind and not focus on it anymore. **Focus is what helps keep it alive**; the focus of the **Will to live in it** is what will keep the personality attached to its flesh body. When he/it loses that interest and attachment, the link will break for good.

REJECTION

As you'll see with many transplants, some are accepted and some are not. The reason for this is that **the Life line/Energy - giving channels have not 'linked up' properly**, i.e. the donor's organ has not adjusted itself to the Life Energy of the body it goes into (the recipient). **It needs to be on the same frequencies**. If there is anything out of tune or out of line, it will not work and there will be no blending. It is an essential part of the receiving or losing out. If the donor is of a different blood type, the body rejects it outright. So, in the same way, if the donated organ does not resonate accordingly with the personality receiving it, the personality as a 'Spirit Being' will **not be able to 'manipulate' a link up** with that new organ.

*BR- So, will there be a need to 'analyse' and match donated organs with the recipient's vibrations? (Using such as Gordon Dalgarno's pitch seeking?) And what about the 'rumour' that the **donor**'s aptitudes, actions in this life and 'past lives memories' could affect the recipient?*

If a donor has not achieved his 'life plan' when he leaves his flesh body, the desire to fulfil it may well be left as a residue in that organ. That is a possibility of a longing. But if the donor had 'bad attitudes' or criminal ways of thinking, all this will create negative activities and Energies emanating from his organs and all cells! By their very nature, they would create a wall of 'negativity', not acceptability, i.e. the recipient's body and Soul would not accept it! Because you **cannot pass on 'nasty' attitudes** or thoughts since the **recipient's Soul and Spirit would not accept them**. Hence rejection of the organ!

This does NOT necessarily mean that an organ which is rejected signifies that the donor had 'bad' vibrations or attitudes! NO, it would only mean the vibrations' frequencies did not match, for many reasons. But when you ask: would an organ affect the person receiving it? Yes it could, in very small ways, possibly... but certainly not in negative ways, only positive ones. As we said before, the receptivity of a body to a donated organ needs to lie in the way the Spirit Being of the recipient's body accepts and can match the vibrations of the organ and vice versa.

If the Spirit Being cannot find ways of manipulating and handling what has been added to its flesh vehicle, it cannot help it survive. The organ needs to be on the very same wavelength (and other aspects about vibrations we cannot go into now! It is too intricate!) but basically that is why and how

271

the organ can or cannot be accepted. No one has found ways yet to match them for that. If someone can **learn to match spiritual vibrations with what is already there**, then the acceptance of a life-giving organ will be much easier.

WILL TO LIVE OR NOT

As with everything else, there are always possibilities. But if someone is absolutely intent on leaving his flesh body for good, then he will **not** get better and will not be saved by an organ! He will 'die' anyway and this will be blamed on 'organ rejection' by doctors. Yet it would not exactly be 'organ rejection' in this case but the Spirit Being **not wanting to stay on Earth**. Not the fault of the organ.

On the other hand, it may well be that a new lease of happier life could be offered to the patient, as he has a new, fresher organ which will help him live better, so that may **trigger his own Higher Self into changing its plan** for a while and staying in the body for the time being, for 'a little longer', as there is no time limit to be charted in eternity; no need to clock up time. If there was no urgency for the personality to leave the flesh and come back here, then it might well stay a bit longer and thus give people encouragement to share their body parts to help others.

BR- What is the Spirit World view on organ transplant?

As Beings of Mind and Light, we have no specific 'views' on transplants, as it does not affect us here. If you mean: Are there reasons why it is 'wrong' or 'right' to carry them out? Well, we'll say 'why not?' If you do some good to another Being, why couldn't you help them even after you have left your own flesh body, since you, as a Spirit Being, decided to discard it. There are no rigid rules against it or even for it, except that it may be seen as following the Law of the Universe: "Do not harm any Being and help them if you can". If you can help them then there is nothing wrong with that transplant. Nothing!

So, there is no worry about doing transplants or receiving them. You will NOT be turned into a monster or criminal if you had their organ! And you will not become, say, the best artist in the world either. Because after all, all your Being's own vibrations have to fit well with the new ones! So the new 'part' could possibly bring a lighter, or more cheerful, or a touch more artistic angle to your personality... BUT it does not mean you'll become the best player or artist etc in the world! It may enhance YOUR own innate abilities if you have any in that direction already and possibly 'encourage' them. But remember it is only ONE organ or piece of flesh, **not a whole** vehicle of flesh! So the influence would be fairly minimal, if there was one!

Conclusion? It is not to be worried or concerned about, as the overall Being has the upper hand on what it does with its vehicle - and the added 'spare part' has only a small 'role', is only a small part of it; it is not the whole vehicle nor is it the whole Being. Is that a bit clearer now?

SIMILARITIES?

BR- What about some allegedly 'studied' cases when a recipient supposedly showed similar tastes to a donor's?

The question about people receiving an organ and feeling or thinking like the donor is not too big a 'problem', as far as we can see from the information we received. If, say, a man was a 'bad' person (with nasty habits) it would make no difference to the recipient. It would not carry over from one body to the other the nasty attitude, because they were not attitudes of the recipient's Higher Self.

BR- The body is a reflection of the Soul, so organs may reflect it?

The basic personality is a 'Higher Self', who has **an aspect** of Itself projected as a Soul who is **intrinsically good, as it is part of a 'Spirit Being'**, which means Kindness and

273

Compassion. So the reflection of a **nasty attitude** (if ever there was such a reflection!) will **not be in the organ**. It cannot be because the Energy of the Higher Being within that Soul would wash off/ overcome the 'passing' nasty attitude, as it goes against what all Beings are basically composed of.

Little habits may have influenced a little **if it is part of the personality of the donor AND the recipient**. If the recipient was **ready to change** his habits on that not so important level, this could perhaps be a **trigger** for his own 'possibility', his possible taste or skill, to tilt that new way. But it is not to be worried about as far as getting 'bad influences'.

BR- Would transplanting a mathematical genius's brain (or other part) mean that the recipient could become a genius in Maths?

The transplant of a piece of flesh can carry only so much of the Energy of the personality.

BR- But isn't it said that every cell is like the acorn containing the whole oak tree? A kind of hologram?

The meaning of our message is: We cannot see why someone would become a totally different person **unless he wishes to do so and change.** If he wishes to change that much, from being useless at Maths to becoming a genius, he must have already had some 'seeds' of it within himself! He must already have that great possibility in his Mind and way of thinking and in the **abilities he chose to have before coming** to Earth.

Maybe he was a genius' before' coming to **this** life, in which case such a transplant (assuming there was some of that Energy in it!) would only awaken an old latent gift and reawaken his 'previous' abilities **IF** that's what the recipient would **want** for himself! No way could he become 'possessed' by another person's empathies or abilities or worse, hatred, because this is not the kind of thing the higher Self would accept to have - as it goes against the grain and the Law of the Universe.

HEART = ONLY FLESH

BR- Has the flesh heart got special energies (as some people say), since it is near the emotion centre/chakra/vortex?

It you think a heart of flesh (whether of a chicken or a man) would make a difference to the way a man becomes kinder or not, you are **wrong!** If he is kind in his behaviour towards others, it is simply because he has let his own Real Self come through, as all Beings should do! If he is nasty, it has nothing to do with the heart of flesh, it's to do with his Mind, his way of thinking, his attitude to life and others, his ways of reacting to what he may have suffered. So there is no way a heart of flesh could influence people to that kind of degree! They will not become a 'Mother Theresa' if they have a heart transplant!

They may no doubt get a new lease of life, from having been unwell to being well now and **that** may give them relief and gratitude for still being alive - so they'll be grateful to the donor. Their attitude to life around them may then change for the better. But that has **nothing to do** with the Energies and vibrations of the piece of flesh that moved from one body of flesh to another - his. Since the flesh is the reflection of the person who chose to have this body, when he built his vehicle for the Earth trip, then he will have built it in accordance with the Law of Compassion and Kindness to all. Therefore, **Kindness is part of it** and could 'influence' anyone - if you so believed - because it outmatches what the other person is composed of.

MIND TO MIND

If you want to talk of little habits, hobbies or new activities similar to those of the previous owner of the body parts, then it is a 'coincidence' which in fact is only a **merging of Minds at a higher level**. He may well link to the Mind of the previous owner who has made the gift of his organ, therefore he may be on the same wavelength, which could possibly create coinciding tastes and interests.

That is more likely where the link would be, rather than the actual flesh piece! Their link would be via the flesh organ, yet not actually transmitting the habit or interest via the Energy of the flesh but via the link of Mind to Mind - they connect to the other's way of thinking. Since all Beings are linked anyway and have been over aeons and distances that would not be any surprise.

This is what we'd say to those who enquire: Look for the link of Minds and Souls at the higher level, at the level of those Minds' and Souls' wavelengths, **not through the piece of flesh** which may break out and die, yet the interest in the hobby, say, would still be there afterwards. It would not necessarily 'die', would it? This is because the Mind of the donor and the recipient's Mind had a **link beyond the Earthly, physical aspect** of the body of flesh.

****

Chapter 32

VIRUSES DON'T KILL

BR- Why have viruses, germs etc? They cause so many tragedies!

There is no difference between viruses. They all have so-called deadly **results only** if the personality who gets infected **allows** it to happen! You will not catch a virus that will kill you, if you (as a 'Higher Self') have no intention whatsoever of leaving the Earthly world and coming back here! So that's the first aspect of misinformation we have to rectify!

You do not have viruses and diseases 'ready' to kill you unless you want to be killed and make this an excuse to leave the Earthly world! Why don't you just say: "I've had enough, I want to go?" without having to put yourself through the hell of being ill and traumatised by all the symptoms?! It would be so much simpler!

Even though each one might be what you call a 'virus' and has different characteristics, there is no differentiation, because it is still a **piece of engineering** by some sort of 'entity' who is trying to have some kind of experience in being 'a thing of Matter'.

It is not meant to be 'nasty' and harmful, it just wants to co-exist with the rest of the bodies manifested in Matter in this world of yours. But you have to understand that the combination and cooperation, or non-cooperation, of certain elements which constitutes both 'parties' (i.e. a Being in a flesh body versus 'viruses') will mean there will be clashes!

All these 'apparitions' (of virus, germs etc) in your world have **always existed** of course, they are not new. They were not as visible before, because you did not have the right apparatus to spot and examine them, until fairly recently. But if we told you that some 'germs' and 'viruses' are far superior to others and **of great use** to your society as well as your body, you'll probably not believe me!

NATURE'S PHARMACY

There are plenty of **micro-organisms which you have already discovered that have been of great help to Mankind** (*Just as he started saying this, I had a quick vision of Fleming's discovery of penicillin!*) so you can be sure there are plenty more you have not spotted, yet which will be helpful too!

You have not seen what is in all the plants' stems and roots! You don't know what's in all the tree barks! You are not aware of what lives at the bottom of the sand in the sea! So in fact, you Humans have very little knowledge about what those little 'nuisances' are or can do! It is just a question of people looking for them in the right places!

ATTRACTING YOUR KILLER

BR- So what about smallpox, AIDS, TB etc?

If you want to tackle one disease at a time, it may be harder to discuss as **we do not really use names and descriptions** for the variations taking place when **a body of flesh is 'attacked' by some Energies which it had attracted to itself in the first place!**

BR- Why?

You know very well why! You know that **all** thoughts are electromagnetic and will act like a magnet towards anything else outside their environment! So, **the body of flesh will be receiving what the mental side of the personality will have attracted to itself,** by behaving and thinking one way or the other.

278

As there are millions of billions of ways of behaving, if the thoughts were slightly or more negative than should have been, they will bend their Energy in the direction of something of whatever nature which has a similar resonance, a similar tone, as themselves. If a thought is negative, it will produce some negative results clashing with the electromagnetic field (and many other fields too!) of the personality. It is always to do with **Energies reacting with, or to, other Energies**! That's what **diseases** are all about!

****

Chapter 33

IMPROVE YOUR LIFE

Be aware of your Real Self. You cannot wear temporary masks and disguises and forget you are not those masks and disguises! Unfortunately, this is what most of you do, on your Earth.

WHAT YOU ARE NOT

You identify so much with the flesh body - which is only a vehicle for this particular and temporary life on Earth - **that you totally forget what you really are! You** are not the flesh parcel; you are not the camouflage; you are not a bunch of atoms and molecules - however cleverly they are put together!

WHAT YOU ARE

You are a brilliant **Being of Light** and Power of a Mind - an Energy force which is not tangible and is **not** situated in the flesh brain! The brain is used by the Mind to make itself heard, but the brain has no power - unless it hinders the Mind by being ill or injured, then the Mind cannot manipulate the brain for its own purpose.

A Mind has such power it can constantly create around itself what it thinks. It is therefore important to **think carefully** and be aware of what you have within you! Otherwise you are constantly at the mercy of your inner tool, rampaging without any control and possibly creating situations that you fear!

STOP CREATING EVENTS YOU FEAR

You are thinking about them so you make them happen... because the 'life power' of **a situation is created by the Mind thinking it.** The moment you lose interest, concentration and stop thinking about the subject, you withdraw that life power and the situation loses its strength.

* So, **you must NOT concentrate on something you fear to happen, as you will make it happen!**

* You must not focus on the disease: you must visualise the health state you wish to achieve.

* You must not think about someone being nasty to you; imagine them as kind, or at least neutral to you.

LIKE ATTRACTS LIKE

The Mind is an aspect and tool of the Soul. The Soul is the 'personality' who has chosen to be, for example, a Being of flesh in your world at this time.

A Mind has not got a personality itself - it is a Creative Power and can make things happen if it is directed powerfully towards a certain goal.

* It will attract positive energies if it is emitting positive thoughts itself. If people use their Minds for the good of themselves and those around them, the Mind will be strong and healthy.

* It will attract negative energies if it is emanating negative thoughts itself. **The Mind will be damaged if its power is used against the wishes of the Higher Self of the Spirit Being.**

If it is used to harm others, it will reflect on itself and attract negative (non-spiritual) energies to itself. So it damages itself by being a negative force - as that is against the fundamental, natural law of existence of a Spiritual Being: All Beings are basically good.

The Mind, **not** the brain, is the thinking and processing part of the Personality, which is a Spirit. Each one of us, being a Spirit, needs to express their thoughts by sending their Minds in the direction they want the information to go, whether to create something or to tell someone something. It is a tool within all of Creation. You need to have the right kind of Mind suited to your personality and to your needs.

ALL BEINGS HAVE A MIND

A Being of any kind has a **Life Force (also called 'Spirit')** within itself to make his existence possible, whether in the Spirit World or on Earth or elsewhere! As each thinks, each creates. As one creates, life changes. As life around you changes, experiences vary and provide opportunities for different possibilities of action. That is what Creativity is all about!

The Mind alone cannot function without being **driven by the Spirit Life Force.** A Mind is the 'engine' inside a 'vehicle' for transport, the Spirit Being, who must create what 'she/he' wants to create and decide to use that engine(Mind) to drive the vehicle or else the means of transport will go nowhere. But if the Spirit Being decides to use the Mind/engine to its full potential, it can do great journeys, with great speed and clever manoeuvres.

VISUALISE BETTER LIFE AND HEALTH

The power that people have is immense, yet they don't know it. If only they used it, life on Earth would be much different for all of you. It is far more important to **use your Mind Power to see how well you can influence Matter** than making machines and drive them to your own death. That was **the aim when you first came to Earth** - all of you. But that seems to have been forgotten as your material goods and activities tempt you!

It would be more useful to practise developing that power within, instead of trying to get more new 'toys'. You can always get out of this trap by loosening up your Mind and looking within, to find a more stable and secure environment based on the truths we have been teaching for aeons.

282

SUMMARY

1) As you grow up you don't always know 'why you are here'. The only way to know is to go within, because that's where the answer is. **All answers are within, because WITHIN is where you are - the Real YOU,** the total you, the You who has facets, one of which is the present person you think you know and are. With practice, it is possible for all to know how to do it. So learn yourself, then teach others, including youngsters!

2) The physical world was not created to be a place of misery and strife. The Earthly world was a place of enjoyment of another state, a different state of being - physical instead of 'ethereal', as you'd see it. It is not the same thing to be a Being of Mind in a world of Mind, as to be a Being of Mind in a body of Flesh in a world of physically felt Matter. As we explained before, the world of Matter was created by those who wished to go there, as an exciting experiment, to see how one could stretch oneself outside the world of Mind one was used to.

3) As the world of Mind or 'Spirit' and the Earth are linked up, it is not difficult to have a link from one to the other. But it is important to **realise that to focus on one only**, without paying attention whatsoever to the other, **has caused and will cause tremendous problems** and significant outcomes and consequences.

A world of Matter is made for and with physical things such as a Flesh body. A Flesh body has its needs, that's why it exists and how it exists. But **the bodily needs cannot be listened to exclusively, otherwise they will take over and override and swamp the Mind.** They will have the dominant 'card' as they are closer to you, the Human Being, than the Mind and Soul which you have to **find within.**

4) Your Mind will be clouded by the push, the desires which the flesh body will always put forward... and not just the body, the physical world too. You'll become programmed

283

to respond to these and will not be able to find your Real Self easily, the one inside, the one who should be governing the whole ship instead of the ship telling the captain what to do!

Make room for the one inside to surface easily and often, or else you won't contact within easily anymore. THAT is of the utmost importance. With daily or so practice, it will not be an effort and will be as easy as getting up or sitting down. You'll just need to decide to do it.

5) That way **you'll have answers to your inner and most immediate questions**! Answers to why you are on Earth: what life plan you had, what projects and **aims you had when you chose to come to this Earth.**

You came to enjoy it no doubt too, but to lead the way in one direction or the other, so that others can find their way back to the Truth, the real Eternal Truth... not what man-made dogmas tell you is 'the truth'.

"Carefully watch your thoughts, for they become your words. Manage and watch your words, for they will become your actions. Consider and judge your actions, for they have become your habits. Acknowledge and watch your habits, for they shall become your values. Understand and embrace your values, for they become your destiny." (Mahatma Gandhi)

****

Chapter 34

DISCOVER INNER KNOWLEDGE

As the pages unfold, you learn to know this book. As this book unfolds, people learn the Truth. As they learn the Truth, they will be enlightened by the Knowledge given and this will be a success of some kind, because its aim is to teach and open people's Mind and turn facts around which had been distorted. Look within for the **hidden Knowledge** you all have. Look and listen within to access it because no one outside will give it to you, you access your own personal knowledge.

When the Pharaohs of Egypt were on Earth, they thought they knew it all, because most of them were psychically gifted and had knowledge of other worlds and other dimensions. But as the gifts waned because material and physical pleasures and distractions took over, then the gifts which should have been bestowed to the leaders were passed on to others below in rank. That way the less famous could do things the famous ones could not. That led to jealousy, of course, often to murder, sadly. But this is not the point. The point is: **Open your Mind to knowledge and it will pour into you,** all of you.

That is the way it is meant to be, as long as you don't let others interfere. A child does not know any better than an adult at times, but most of the time **a child has a better link with his Inner Self** than an adult has - and that's why a child can so often be wiser than them. You can all lead your own life but you, with the Inner Knowledge you have, are more and better equipped than the average person, who is not aware of the amazing secret tools they carry everywhere with them.

SECRET TOOLS

BR- What Inner Knowledge?

Knowledge of everything which is beyond the material:

* You know there is a life after bodily death.

* You know 'Animals' have gifts and are Spirits, therefore should be respected as such, as well as loved.

* You know there is no one above anyone else, as you are all born equal.

* You know an equal cannot be superior or inferior to you, so you treat him as you wish to be treated.

* You know one can easily communicate not only with one's own Inner/Higher Self, but also with the realm of those who have gone ahead of you. That means no one is left uncared for.

The only way to progress is to get rid of the rut. If a rut slows you down, get out of it. The rut of daily life is one of the worst ways of never progressing in anything! So, the way to do it is to start from scratch and only take on what is absolutely essential. Reject the rest. That way only the essential is left and it won't be much. Eat, drink, sleep, breathe, wash, feed the animals. What else needs doing?

FOCUS ON ESSENTIAL

BR- Well, tidy the house at least a little, for example, when my mediumship practice circle members are coming!

The house could be a dirt floor and a roof of leaves and you would still have a 'circle' and people would still enjoy it and progress! So do not worry about the house.

BR- But it has to be clean!

The main thing is that their chair is clean, their glass is clean. Do not overdo it! Plenty of people have nothing and are still happy. Try to go for that, be happy with nothing or nearly! The Inner Wealth is what needs working on, developing more, studying, nurturing and enjoying. It is a kind of joy nothing on Earth can be compared to. The **inner joy of Inner Knowledge is priceless.**

Lots of pleasure for little cost! Suddenly the world looks brighter, the sun shines more, every leaf becomes a jewel and the dew is like the sparkle of a diamond... but inside the fire burns hotter and the Knowledge grows! Lots of people have turned to **Nature to find peace.** You should **all** do that and realise you have been wasting your lives looking for trivial pleasures which could have been greater if you had looked for them in a different place.

Nothing is worth spending time on which does not enrich your Soul. Your Soul can only be enriched with 'manure' of a different type; the source is not a horse, the source is **the fact one lives on!** And when you find out why and how one lives on, you'll enjoy more what you've got around you on the Earth... because **every molehill becomes a miracle and a wonder,** instead of a 'heap of soil' or trouble for a gardener proud of 'his' plants! So what! A molehill is much more exciting than a flower that has been forced to grow where it should not be!

Essential, essential, only the essential - that's what one should reduce daily life to. Then take off towards the real, valid stuff. You know what I am talking about. Let them all know. Points to study:

Mind over Matter

Looks after Knowledge.

Personality before looks.

Presences around self - all of you are surrounded by lots of 'Spirit' presences, by Beings and you don't know it! Therefore, link up more and see what there is to perceive with the inner eye and inner senses. All this should have been done ever since you were born, but it was subdued most of the time. All this needs to be brought up to the surface again!

Chapter 35

INVENTIONS

As Mankind started planning its journeys on the new Earth, it had to devise many projects suited to the environment and the abilities of a flesh body. So far, **no one had had a flesh body made of this particular type of Matte**r, so it was indeed a new experience, but as men and women went to Earth, tried their own designed body and came back to complain of the mistakes or misalignments, there was something else they had to take into consideration.

BODY'S LIMITATIONS

It was all very well to have a flesh body you could do what you wanted with, but it had its limitations. Let's say wanting to fly in a body of Earth size and shape was not practical, in fact impossible... but the birds could do it, so why not Men? It was a conundrum, as they wanted to **will** themselves into doing things... but those things had to be done, or be possible, within the parameters of the specifications of that flesh, you see! So the rest had to be solved differently. That's when their Mind Power had to be used to think of something different and invent, design and create it!

It could have been done more easily, no doubt, but that's how Men decided in the end to solve their inaptitude for things they could not do because of the body's limitations, they could only use their Mind Power to overcome them. So that's what happened when they tried to design plans and new items of many various types: from constructions to artefacts to use to help themselves, to many other things such as travel on a boat, or even later on objects on wheels to carry them from one place to another.

In other words, the inventions that sprouted over centuries and millennia have come out of the need of Mankind for objects to help them, which they could not have otherwise.

INVENTIONS USING MIND AND HANDS

Inspiration has usually been **given from our side** too, because they had to have some starting point, some direction towards which to find the necessary tools or systems.

But Mankind had to use its own Mind Power, therefore its own Creative Power, because any Mind is a creative tool. A Mind without that creative side is not a normal Mind!

So, we have those new Humans on Earth, with tools of wood, or metal or whatever else they started creating, making new things for the sake of getting more comfort in their lives. They used their Minds to design. That means they looked at the needs and **in their thoughts, they produced the blueprint**, the template of what they wanted. It could give a successful result, or possibly an inefficient result, if it was badly designed, because of lack of logic or attention to details (like not taking into account gravity or weather powers). They **had** to think about it first; they had to visualise what could be useful and workable.

NEVER DONE BEFORE

This may be obvious to you nowadays, but at the time **they never had to do such things before**, remember. Indeed, they'd been 'Spirits' in our world, that is to say, Beings of Light and Mind, who did not need to use their hands or any artefacts and tools to make things happen; they would just think of it strongly and it would appear.

So, the transition was a bit sudden for them, but **it taught them to use their Mind even more to make the result appear in a different way.** It had to be worked out **gradually**; calculations or combinations had to be thought out piece by piece and 'felt right' before they could proceed to the next step. This is how inventions came about - through the need to have more physical things to make life more comfortable from the point of view of those there. But had it been thought out differently; they would have made things in another way!

They could have ignored the need for physical objects and worked at making their Mind Power over the flesh stronger. They could have worked at it so that the flesh obeyed the Mind as much and more than it already does now. The flesh is intensely influenced by the Mind and the **Mind has to be at rest, otherwise illnesses will start cropping up.** So Mind Power is visibly, and well-known to be, a creator of illness as well as good health in the flesh body.

Therefore, why couldn't Mankind have worked more at increasing its power over the body of flesh? Say, to make it levitate, fly, do without food or drink... or even never die, if they insisted on living for ever, though that would be rather silly because the Earth Experiment is meant to be shorter lived than eternity!

This is what we are coming to - **the power of overcoming the flesh was and is there!** Few Men have learnt how to use it. Most have forgotten the inner and innate ability. It is latent in them; they simply have just not used it at all and let atrophy set in or even disappear! This is something sad in a way, as there was a gift and a skill they could all have used! Instead, they went towards using their hands and thoughts to make objects of various sizes and goals.

FIRST HUMANS' AMAZING GIFTS

When the 'first men' came, they **could indeed 'fly'** but only over short distances, just going from one place to another nearby without walking. They **transcended the body's weight, they lifted it up with their powerful Mind** and they were able to move about that way. Much less tiring physically!

They could also stay for a long time **without eating or drinking**; they had this ability. They had not lost it even a few centuries ago. There were still some people who could do that. Now I am not so sure but they'll be few in numbers, if any.

So we want to point out that, if they could do it then, why couldn't Mankind do it now? All it takes is practice! It would reduce or cancel all fuel bills and worries. It would allow crops to grow without being destroyed for food. There will never be enough food if you keep growing it for breeding 'Animals' as well as for People.

You cannot keep eating 'Animals', as Mankind has to go back to its original and pure plan of "not hurting anyone". So how can you keep killing them, or worse, eating them alive? This is nonsensical and the **result will be more diseases, more upsets mentally and physically**, more unrests across the populations, because the Souls themselves will feel ill at ease, unhappy, 'out of sync' with their flesh body, which they had originally designed to fit like a glove.

Now the 'glove' wants to take over and go in a totally different direction from the original plan - the need for inner and outer balance. Make people understand and we'll begin to be on the right track.

BR- Is there any chance for Mankind to relearn those skills?

The practice needed could take a whole lifetime, so I doubt many will take the time and trouble to get into it, with the dedication needed for its development, you see. It is of the utmost importance to be still within for long periods of time, to be well balanced emotionally and spiritually as well as physically. So there will be no hope for most of Mankind at the rate it is going on nowadays! It may be possible for a few Beings who have worked at it from a young age somewhere, but few would do it as things stand!

There is hope, though, to have more coming back to Earth to emulate and encourage those who may want to learn that, but it must come from within. If one does not **have that built-in inner desire**, it would take more than a lifetime, so what's the point of not succeeding? Yet there is a halfway measure.

MIND POWER OVER MATTER

The halfway measure is to tell yourself: 'All right I would have liked to do that (absence of food and drink and levitation instead of walking or driving) but I can't as things are, so I'll **cut down on my excess attention to physical needs and pleasures and concentrate more on my inner needs'**. Those are the need for utter calm, utter peace of Mind, utter blending with the world of Mind and Light (or Spirit, as you call it) and make the **days more useful in a spiritual way** than in a physical, materialistic way.

The material side of the worldly life can easily be taken care of, as long as you have enough decent and basic food to sustain the body healthily (and it does not need meat from dead 'Animals' for that! You can have other means of feeding yourselves!). So, the Mind side can be worked more on and that should be easy enough as you relax increasingly more often. But what's the use of it, you will say? Well, it is obvious: The use of developing your Mind is for your own good as well as others.

You can ask some 'superior' Being to 'make things happen' for you and others and hope it listens and that works eventually, or not! Or you can definitely hone **your** own Mind Power to the extent of sending your powerful energies towards goals you want so much - that success, that health recovery.

When you start having successes, then you will know you are on the right track and doing things correctly. So that's why it is always, always useful to spend time quietly, in silence or in Nature's silence full of its own Energies. When the silence breaks for you to 'hear' an inner voice, or 'see' a person you've never seen before or for a long time, then you'll know you have started using the power of your Mind to overcome limitations caused by the flesh body! From then on, you'll believe more perhaps in sending thoughts to heal others at a distance and to **make things happen for you and others,** if they allow it and don't hinder it by not being of a negative nature! Isn't this worth doing?!

****

Chapter 36

QUIET DAY

Any 'Animal', even a tiny insect or anything you can think of, does not worry about its daily life in advance; it lives it day by day, moment by moment. It does not think: "Oh dear, what is going to happen **if** I don't find food?" It thinks: "I am hungry, I am looking for food." Once it's fed, it thinks no more of food or tomorrow's meals! It does whatever next thing it may want or feels the need to do.

But Mankind is not like that. They all worry about "What is going to happen, 'if this' or 'when that' happens?". Yes, it may be good in some respects, but it is not good for the inner thoughts within, for the calm within. It is impossible to be serene, tranquil and peaceful within with such thoughts, you see?

An insect has peace of Mind, no matter what. It does its things and it is at peace. The only fear it may have is only when it faces an aggressor or a danger, but not before and Mankind should do the same. If all did it, there would be more peace within each one of you and eventually less stress all around.

WHY IS MANKIND SO STRESSED?

Because they all worry about what they could have if xx, or cannot have because of yz. They don't enjoy what they have now, by comparing themselves with the less fortunate. Instead, they compare themselves to those who seem to 'have more'. More what? More **material** goods, isn't' it?! More peace of Mind is not what they compare themselves to, is it? Do they want more peace within? More spiritual links? No! People think they have less or more than the ones who are 'richly endowed with material goods', wealth, riches of the temporal world!

294

None of those who worry are people who fret about having less peace of Mind than a peaceful contemplating person with stillness within! They want a tumultuous sea, full of boats with noisy engines and full of gold, instead of having a peaceful lake for a Mind. They want to be rich, famous and wealthier than others... and that's all we seem to see going on in this world!

BR- But some people worry more about health, about their family.

The worry I was talking about is the concern about wanting more wealth and material goods. We know some worry about health, loss, disasters and that is normal. We are talking about the **unnecessary concern about material life and goods**, as that is something that can be got rid of easily. Much more inner peace would then be achieved if one did away with that side of things.

When Mankind stops that way of thinking, there will be more peace of Mind, that's our message. When that is achieved, we'll see more people listening within and **discovering a vast array of inner wealth**. All that is needed is a bit of peace and quiet inside. The results will be superior to whatever physical and material goods you could acquire! Let's be honest, what can a new TV have compared with **communicating with your Higher Self, with your family in our world, with sages ready to pass on Knowledge** with answers to profound questions? There is no comparison, is there?!

A DAY INWARDS

So let's start by putting Mankind on the right path by suggesting they **have one day of quiet thinking,** one day of pure reflection, silence, inner listening. No thoughts of goods, of riches. **More inwards watching** rather than watching the TV. More inwards listening than to the radio, records etc. **More inwards talking** than outwards chats about nothing to talk

295

about. That's what we suggest. Perhaps Mankind will start remembering the days when it was normal to do that throughout the days and the weeks... but that goes back to a long, long time ago!

Anyone ready to have a go at a profound quiet day will benefit from it immediately! No surprise, because **all they want and need is within,** wanting to come out and be reached, but they do not realise or have forgotten! All they need is a day within, a day inward, a day of peace and quiet, a day of television off, noise off, quiet reigning**... so that the Inner Voice can be heard**! Then when they hear it once, they'll never want to lose it again or switch it off in favour of some trivial programme. You'll see, all of you, you'll see... so why not try it?

✴✴✴✴

Chapter 37

PEER PRESSURE

Peer pressure has existed for nearly as long as Mankind has existed. It can only be put down to Ego exerted by those who have too much, onto those who have little and are frightened of their own thoughts, beliefs and habits. They can be influenced to do what others want them to do, or are influenced to behave in ways unnatural to them, but they do not wish to stand out as different from those who bully them. So the pattern is set when others order and the meek follow!

SOLUTION WITHIN

But it need not be like that, if only the so-called 'weak' ones could understand the power they have within themselves. **All they have to learn to do is listen to their Inner Voice.**

The Inner Voice at first will be Fear, no doubt, as Fear is what governs most of Mankind, but beyond the Fear there is the real Inner Voice of the Spirit, who is the real person. If that person can understand and accept to rely on **their own Spirit** voice, then they'll know they need not fear the bullies or the neighbours' opinions and they CAN indeed stand on their own two feet, to have their own opinions and stick to them. That's not easy to do when you first start, but the (Universal Spirit) Law is: **Free Will to all.** So why should you be subjected to someone else's ideas, influences, opinions and threats?

STAND UP STRONG

You can stand up to all this by saying: "We all have Free Will, we can all choose what we want to do and I choose to do such and such because that's what I want to do at this particular time of my life". That's all.

So, all of you who fear, do not be afraid of letting your own 'Spirit within' give you the inner strength to oppose those who cannot be as spiritual as you. You are being 'spiritual' because you have a link with your own Spirit. Once that's established, you'll find you'll be helped all along and will never look back.

YOUR SPIRIT IS SAFE

You are first and foremost a Spirit Being! Nothing can harm the Spirit. They can harm the body, even kill it, but will never touch the Spirit because the Spirit of anything and anyone cannot be harmed, in as much as Energy cannot be destroyed!

Someone said: "You can only change its form, it can only change its forms, but Energy will never disappear or be destroyed"- that's what you must remember. (*Obviously referring to a statement about Energy, made by the French scientist Lavoisier*).

WHAT WILL PEOPLE THINK?!

Since **YOU are pure Energy,** why worry about some small-minded little bullies, or even simply narrow materialistically-minded people, who think they have the answer to anything and everything! In fact, a lot of this happens regarding material activities rather than spiritual ones. But even there, you'll find people wanting to leave a particular group of worshippers, because they don't like them, or don't agree anymore with what is being done there... yet they **don't dare** to! They feel they 'have to' carry on because of 'what other people would say or think'! Make your mind up, my friends who are being influenced. Make your mind up to be your own Self, and let the others swim in their personal little waterless pond, while you can have the oceans to be free in!

FREEDOM = NO LIMITATIONS

You can only win! **To be free means you are not limiting your way of thinking or living.** You do what you mostly want to do and the feeling of freedom and peace of mind you'll gain, from within without, will soon show itself in many ways! It will reflect in your behaviour, your health, your way of speaking and thinking... and your life will have a different sparkle you never knew could exist!

All it takes is **to listen within, find the strength** which is given to you from your own spiritual core. That is the Real You, who has had enough of seeing the Being you are on Earth led by the nose by some unthinking creatures who need to rectify their own judgement and actions! But that's their own problem!

A bully, or an overbearing acquaintance, can ruin or limit the life of a decent person who has not listened within deeply enough to find the strength to say: "Let me be me! I am me, you are you. Good-bye, see you in heaven!"

Excuses to do otherwise may be: "We can't, we'll be laughed at. We're not strong enough, we'll be beaten up, we don't know enough to change to something else..." WHY?! Why can't you resist the temptation to be weak, when being strong brings so much gain? Being beaten up in some sad cases is indeed a great threat, but human laws are there to protect you, even if it may mean to lose materially, like moving house. Be on the right side of your Earth laws and you'll always be on the side of Spirit, **unless of course the Earth laws were wicked, in which case this is where the pressure is!** So you'll need to find the strength to go within yourself, to dip into the font of strength - your own Spiritual Being - which had perhaps been smothered by the nasty behaviour of others.

Have faith in your own spiritual side because **no matter what happens on the Earth and even 'death',** your own Spiritual Being will always win, you understand? It will always win the battle if there is one, because **YOU will always survive,** no matter what. So why worry so much?

RIGHT PERSPECTIVE

See things on the scale of Eternity - that's the only scale to compare and view things and facts by. Only Eternity can give you the right perspective. Can a needle lost in a haystack be of urgency, when the Earth whirls round the sun across the sky and when the stars hurtle across space... and when centuries of your 'Time' see events which at times are unthinkable or unspeakable of ?

Look at Life with an eye on Eternity. Look at Life with both eyes open to the reality of Eternal Life, before and after this Earthly, possibly troublesome, life. **Life on Earth is meant to be temporary!** Why not **think differently** and decide this Earthly life may have problems, but the Inner Voice of Spirit will guide you, so there is no need to fear?

Could Spirit's advice be safer than neighbours' or peers' opinions? Could it be sounder and a more interesting path to tread than copying, like a sheep, what others do, so as to fit within **their** pattern and way of thinking and behaving? Of course, there is no question it is!

Therefore, go ahead, take the bull by the horns, find the peace you need within, **do your own thing, feel better for it!** Realise what others do may suit them, may even make them (temporarily) happy, but **in the long run you will be the winner because you will achieve peace within** and no doubt succeed eventually - in a spiritual way, not necessarily materially.

****

300

Chapter 38

TOLERANCE & FREEDOM

The main point we'll discuss now is the extreme lack of tolerance all over the world. As people do not accept others' views and want to impose theirs, there will always be a war between two or more factions, because you cannot have Peace where there is Intolerance!

Intolerance leads to bigotry and nastiness, closed-mindedness and selfishness as well as arrogance. All these are **fuel to hatred and racial discrimination**... but discrimination has never been a bed from which Peace could rise. It is still running strife across your world of Matter and that will go on for a long time, until the majority of people open their eyes to the harm they are causing with their stupid behaviour.

If Man**kind** was **kinder** (!) it would be so much better. Yet all they have to do is return to the Source they come from; within them is the place where Truth and Light reside, but some will bury it so deeply they won't see or even know there is a spark there waiting to be reignited! Let the spark out, let it shine and it will light the way of your thinking towards Right Doing, Right Behaviour and Right Thinking. You cannot ignore it once it's shining and you cannot let it die because that flicker will never die. It will only lie dormant within your Soul until you decide to look for it, or look at it, or realise it is there.

WHAT IF IT WAS YOU?

Intolerance is not so difficult to combat. All that is needed is a mirror within you: "How would I react if it was done to me? How would I like it if my words were crushed to have others replacing them, even though they might be totally wrong as far as my thinking is concerned?"

All you need is to **put yourself in the place of others**. If you have never tried doing so, especially with those you try to crush, why not have a go? Why not play a game with yourself and be the 'victim', be the 'wrong one', as you'd perceive it? See what happens when someone else, who does not understand your views, not only blocks them in many unfair and devious ways, but also attacks you for who you are, without even listening to your point of view and your possible ideas? Why not follow **their** train of thoughts? Why not see what it would lead to?

Why not accept that sometimes **old, well-rooted ideas may be wrong and distorted** and it is just possible that new fresh 'blood' should be injected in the whole system to revitalise what has been stagnant for so long? **Stagnation is close to death and rot.** Who wants to have stagnant, rotting ideas? Who can even imagine that would lead to new growth?!

It's impossible to obtain new shoots from a rotten flower; it needs fresh air, sun, warmth usually; it needs Energy to get it going. No corpse has ever come back to life as a physical Being. It has to be revitalised by changing body and shape. Ancient Ideas are the same!

CRUSHING LIES

We cannot let the brothers of our world become slaves and victims of the Earth world. We cannot stand by lies and deceits and close our eyes and say: "That's their problem, we are safe and sound here", because we all care for all of you and we cannot let LIES which have built up over centuries become fake 'solid truths'! **They have only been manufactured and concocted out of greed, spite, ego, wickedness and - more important - intolerance and evil thinking!** The ones imposing these lies now are people who cannot see beyond their very limited way of thinking! If they could see past it, they would not hesitate to reject the very things they are now imposing, or trying to impose.

302

DANGER OF MATERIALISTIC LIFE

Another point is that as Mankind 'progresses' (in the material sense of developing more technology, more weapons, more artificial ways of finding pleasures and distractions) the inner gifts are squashed. The spiritual ways of thinking are switched off; **the inner person disappears in an array of material goods and superficial activities. Look for the spark within** that you never knew you had. It is still there but you'll have to look for it. The good news is that if your **desire for its discovery** is strong enough, **that** will light up the spark to such an extent that it will shine brightly enough for you to pick it out of the inner darkness you have drowned it in.

Let the light shine out, so that once you have lit yourself up within and re-established who you are and what you are in a spiritual sense, you can then shine that light to light the way for others to find what you have found. **That way Light will come back on the dark world you live in.**

NO BLOCKAGE

Too many lives are wasted by ignorance, selfishness, greed and intolerance. **Intolerance is a closed door**, a blank wall you don't write on. It is concrete in a flow pipe, it is a blockage to new ideas. It is impediment to development. It is 'impossible' instead of 'possible'. It is negativity itself. Nothing good comes out of negativity! Out with the negative, in with the positive and open mindedness driven by the light of understanding and compassion. Openness is what allows light in, what makes ideas grow, flourish and bloom and what produces new seeds for more ideas to grow and blossom: not being blocked but being nurtured. Allow that to happen and life will be totally different all over the world.

Why fight your brothers when you could spend that Energy building together a happier, more comfortable world? That is the question!

OPEN-MINDED BALANCE

Indeed, many intolerant creeds in your world are led by an inner sense of what is right and by the shock of seeing basic virtues damaged. If a woman cannot behave decently in public, it can outrage some people, who see her as a wanton who puts physical pleasures first. She would "not be fit to be a wife and mother" and also would give a "bad example" to young ones coming behind her. But the **limits of that intolerance have to be set**.

It's one thing to object to wanton behaviour, it's another to barricade all women behind bars and walls and wrap them in clothes to hide every part of the body and forbid them to grow mentally and intellectually.

A balance has to be attained in all things; nothing out of balance will ever work or achieve anything. Balance and equilibrium are delicate mechanisms which keep things going perfectly when they are well set. But if you tip the scales one way or the other, even by a fraction, then you'll find disaster and calamity instead of a smooth, balanced running of things.

You can all wake up to the fact that **closed-mindedness has never brought new ideas to the forefront.** Closed-mindedness has prevented new inventions from developing themselves, from progress being made and it has caused misery, stagnation and suffering!

NO RELIGIOUS FACTIONS

Churches, religious organisations and spiritual movements should not be factions. This information has been going round the world in various heads for some time, but no one, or few, are trying to implement it, because it has so much 'controversy' in the very fact it should bring various 'factions' together.

They should not be fighting! They should all be on the same side of the 'fence', as you call it, to face the materialistic world and make a united stand, to **resist the pressures of the physically inclined world**. A world - where what one has 'outside' is more urgent and worthy and pleasant and precious than what one has 'within' - is a very poor world indeed!

All it has to do is pay attention to the voice of Wisdom within, to find its way back to the Truth. Unfortunately the voice of Wisdom has long been squashed time and again by the desire to have fun in a physical way.

There was and is nothing wrong with enjoying the pleasures of a beautiful world, constructed for its own enjoyment, but there is a fine line between that and giving it free rein to take over one's life and make you forget your origins to the extent that the law, which had always and forever existed, seems to remain unheard, like a cry in the wilderness.

As you progress in our world, you are encouraged and helped to remember that One Law fundamental to all living Beings: **You cannot hurt other**s. You cannot take life away from others, because they selected to have an existence on this Earth and it's wrong for anyone else to remove that right. You cannot take away anyone's life as they have **chosen** to be there for their own trip, their own creative expansion. Every single Being is entitled to be allowed to fulfil his/her/its wish in the first place.

NO RIGID MAN-MADE LAWS

As Mankind links up again gradually, one way or the other, with the 'Great Unknown', as they call it, in various ways, it is a special trip which has to be respected. All religions have tried to go back to what they believe to be the true source of Existence. But they have often failed to fulfil the rest of the equation.

If you listen within, you have to listen all the way - not a little bit here and there and **NOT add your own man-made rules** around it! That is where things went wrong

305

many times in various ways. As men imposed rules for their followers to obey, so they made rigid what should be fluid; they made harsh what should be loving; they made closed-up and closed-minded what should be open-minded and free!

Freedom of Thought is important because, by being free to think for yourself, in a free environment, with free-thinking people around you, you have more easily **access to the deeper levels of your Inner Being**. When you can do that, you then reach to the levels where Truth lies, because Truth has a Light of its own which cannot be extinguished when it shines.

The level of Man's thinking is very important. If you think in a kind way, you will get kindness back. If you think harshly, you will get harsh words back. You have to be mellow and willing, open to suggestions and open to others' ways of thinking too, because you cannot impose your own views on someone who has his own. All are equal. **All People, all Beings are equal.** So why should one impose himself onto the other ones?

EXCHANGES & BRIDGES

If Unity and Peace are to be found and achieved, it can only be done as One Voice talking in the same direction - not two voices talking at each other in an aggressive way! **Exchanges are vital; not imposition**, not dogmas, not ruling. Exchanges. That's what the word means - 'changing for another thing'.

So, changing for another's views empowers you to open up and see the other person's point of view and ideas; empowers you to feel what it's like to be in his mental environment. Then you'll see there are some good points, no doubt, here and there if not everywhere. When the good points are noted and understood, it will be a sign that you two have got **some things in common.** Note what they are, as they are important. No doubt the other party will think the same about yours: "We have that side in common, that aspect".

That will **start building a bridge**. No one has ever crossed a raging river in the air; it has to be via a safe and firm bridge. All bridges can be built if people are prepared to bring their own bricks and stones, placed in the right direction and if they are willing to make some cement together. You do not build half a bridge. It has to be built from both ends and you'll **meet in the middle.**

That's what needs doing - any opportunity to bring people together, to make them reflect upon what needs doing and can be done will be a useful stone placed at the right place, in the correct position as well as direction. As Minds open and build that mental bridge, you'll see loathing and hatred diminish gradually. It can only be done by those who are prepared to open their Minds to other ideas. Those who have closed them before even starting won't have much or anything to offer!

It has to be made clear that **no one is there to impose anything** on the other, but to simply demonstrate what they believe and why they believe it is good. And when the other party thinks: "Ah! Such a point has similarities with ours", it will be the starting point on a long road ahead, but a road leading somewhere, hopefully!

Bring people together to exchange ideas. Bring Minds together to feel the differences and iron out the difficulties when they can be ironed out. Base the facts you give on Truth rather than on hearsay.

HOW CAN TRUTH BE GIVEN?

By demonstrating it, by having facts, witnesses, evidence, renewable evidence, always **fresh evidence. Do not just rely on old stories which have lost their power** because the witnesses to those events are not present, so no one is here to back them up.

Make the wall between the two groups fall, one brick at a time. Or at least make peering holes available here and there, for them to see the Truth in all its sincerity, pushing through at every opportunity. That's the way to **build a bridge of Understanding and Knowledge of the Unknown.** People fear the Unknown, in whatever shape or form. They fear what they hear in the dark, they fear what they cannot hear in the dark, they fear all which is unfamiliar. That's why it is called 'the Unknown', because they have not become familiar with it.

It's simple to make it a little more familiar, just show it as it is - without frills, without disguises. Just as it is. Explain, prove, repeat, reassure and let them talk too. Let them express their inner fears, as this is where they are - inside. So let those apprehensions come out and stop them eating people up from inside. When that's out, it won't be hidden anymore and it can be faced with an antidote - a fact or a proof which will start hopefully to disintegrate or start crumbling that unfounded fear. Because **fears are usually unfounded** - they nearly always are!

They are dreaded because there have been stories told, or panic spread out by other people who too fear the same things! Or else **Fear has been managed and mongered by others wishing to manipulate people's Minds and lives!** That's why there have been so many religions to empower those in charge and bring down to heel many unruly crowds, but it has often got out of hand!

There comes the crunch: When a religion has got out of hand, it cannot be controlled by the spiritual side of Mankind, **it is directed by man-made ideology and rules.** This means **Truth is squashed to be replaced by imposed dogmas,** exaggerated and imagined 'facts' or overemphasis of minor points. Those divert from **the one fundamental Truth: All Beings are equal**. All men, all women, all children, all 'Animals', all plants are equal. That means they are all

Spiritual Beings who have chosen to come to Earth and cannot be forced to leave/die because others want them to! They should be helped to live better if they are in dire need, they should be understood if they have problems.

ALLOW PEOPLE'S INNER POWER

Finally, people should be allowed to listen within to the silence which contains all the truths of millenniums and millenniums of centuries and **free to grasp that they have an inner guiding Power** they can trust.

You cannot eradicate worldwide Knowledge of the Truth within. It is within your Soul. The 'physical you', your body, is only a representation and visual tool of your Soul. It is only an outer shell to live in this material environment. You can act from within if you use your Mind Power, but have you found it? It is within you and has more power than many of your machines as it can reach farther, quicker, for longer lasting results. A power that needs no other fuel than being listened to and **used with intense desire for doing good,** so well that if done regularly, it builds its own reserves, becomes stronger and more effective. What for? To rebalance your emotional and physical bodies and restore your health; to make the correct decision and good events happen; to create peace within you and around you; to send healing and blend in harmony with the rest of the world; to reach for the highest Knowledge. You are all creative Beings with a mighty tool!

****

PART 4

IMPROVE THE WORLD

*"Our lives begin to end the day we become **silent about things that matter.**"*
(Martin Luther King)

Chapter 39

WARS' EFFECT ON SOLDIERS' SOULS

When you have wars on Earth, lost lives arrive here, lost in their Soul and Mind because they could not see why they had to die for nothing in the end. 'Lost lives' mean lost Souls and destroyed homes or families.

We know we cannot change things from our world. It can only be done from within the hearts of each man and woman on Earth: to want peace at all cost **without** giving in to going to war and smashing the adversary into submission, because you have superior weapons.

CANNOT CONDONE WARS

Because of that, all **those Souls feel they have been cheated**, yet they did opt to die for the cause, otherwise they would not have chosen to be there! If even one war made a difference to the world, one could praise it... but no war has ever made a real difference to your world. It may have changed things in as much a party, or a man, would not reign or would reign over others, but it's not what **we** would call making a difference to the world!

BR- Some people would say: We would all be Nazis or there'd be no Jews left, if there had not been wars recently...

In a nutshell, **whatever gain you may 'gain' on Earth will not be 'gain' once back here, because you'll see the folly of your actions;** the kindness of some people versus the abominable horror of all these killings. **You CANNOT CONDONE WARS.** War has NO place in our world.

No justification. No 'raison d'être'. Whatever reasons Mankind invents to justify a war **will not withstand a jury in our world**, against war.

SOLDIERS' SOULS SUFFER

You cannot **comprehend the harm it does to a Soul to have to go out killing** or, worse, to choose to go out killing others for the sake of a 'cause' or a political party, or some belief ingrained or implanted into his Mind by others. Because **NO baby is born wanting war!** He comes from the Spirit World; he would not want war; he would want peace and fun and kindness to himself, that's all! No man can justify war.

Make the world understand the validity of what we are telling you. We are telling the Truth for the world to know, as the Truth has not always been told before.

KILLING A REFLECTION OF YOURSELF

The man who went to war to save his country from being invaded by other men from other races, or a race, **has not done himself any good in the end**, sadly. He may have done what he truly believed was 'good for his Soul' because he was being good and brave to save his country from what he saw as a 'bad fate', but he has not! Because the Truth is **no one can kill others, no matter how great the 'cause' is.** The cause is only man-made or thought out by Man. Since **a Soul is the same as another Soul, the killer is killing a reflection of himself.**

One way to look at it is this: Think of a mirror and attack it every time the mirror's picture or reflection looks like you! Wouldn't that look or seem ridiculous or foolish or even mad? Well, that's how we see it from this World of Light and Love.

INCREASING THE DEBT

When you kill another, you add to your own debt and faults and lessons to learn. You also add to all **the debt of other people you encourage to fight!** Their debt will partly be caused by you pushing them to go and fight - if you are a/their leader - and partly by their own lack of spirituality and awareness of the reality of the Souls' link. **All Souls are linked to each other,** as one strong bond unites them. What is that bond? The unity of Love, Caring, Compassion and Creation. All that is one thing - one cares and one creates. One creates, therefore one cares. One cannot create without caring.

BR- What about bad thoughts?

You cannot create bad thoughts out of Love, of course, but if you have bad thoughts about or towards someone, the feelings behind are strong. Those strong feelings have been caused by some inner emotions which were or are directed in the wrong direction. Feelings, emotions create! Therefore, make sure they always are positive and 'friendly' rather than 'unfriendly'.

ENEMIES WILL BE FRIENDS!

Men were and are constantly sent to war to kill others as the ultimate deterrent. But that does not work in the end, because killing the body does not kill the Soul or the Spirit of these 'enemies'! These 'enemies' may have been, or will be, the best friend you may have or have had **one day**! Why? Because **sooner or later you do meet again,** all of you, somehow, to **recycle** all those unexpressed feelings or distorted feelings or fears that have caused the wars in the first place. It is imperative to understand that no one can kill others, no matter what.

SELF-DEFENCE

BR- What if a mother with her child is being attacked by a man with a knife and she has to kill her attacker?

The solution to this question is this: If you have a situation where no way could be found to avoid such an act, it may be understandable to save your own life to protect, say, your children from a dire situation without a mother, as you said. But **the stain will remain on the mother's Soul until she is able to remove it herself** by having many excursions

314

into her Soul and her other lives, which will have to be planned to extract, remove and eradicate that dreadful mark, that stain. It will have affected her life as far as this life is concerned, but it will also have affected and **will affect the rest of her other lives**, one way or the other... because the spiritual nature of her own Self will have to suffer from the consequences! Her own Soul and own Spirit would **not** agree to such an act and will mourn the accidental succession of events leading to it.

So, in the end no one wins. No one is safe from ever killing someone without tarnishing his or her own Soul. As no one can do that, as explained above, then the wars waged all over the world at all times are constant blemishes on the surface of the Earth, on its own Psychic Energy, on the Soul of Mankind as a whole and on each of its individuals - which means a dark cloud cannot be lifted so easily when it is constantly reinforced, thickened, accentuated and reactivated.

NO LAWS MUST PUSH WARS

Laws leading to wars, therefore murder and killing, are laws that should be banned. Man-made laws should be there to help Mankind stay or be steered onto a more spiritual pathway, so that it finds its way back 'home' where it came from. Mankind has, on the whole, forgotten **the original plan of being on Earth** for fun, for the joy of Creativity, for the sharing of its inventiveness, for the upliftment of being able to do something different, yet **governed by its Inner Knowledge.** If and when the Inner Knowledge is drowned or removed or forgotten, how can Mankind go back home easily and safely without having spoilt its own spiritual path?

The fact of having laws against spiritual teachings and laws acts against the fundamental principles you were born with and came from - **no one is above the other, no one is different, all are one, one for all.**

SOLUTION? INNER KNOWLEDGE

An Inner Self is the best guidance you could all have for what is right or wrong to do. It has alarm bells inside you, you **know** it is wrong. Yet with unfortunately too much practice at ignoring it, you all grew to ignore that inner bell signal and go ahead with what the Mind (led by the physical needs and wishes) makes you **think** you want or have to do.

No one is safe from being driven by the physical desires, or the Mind's ego trips, which lead to disaster. No one is safe from this, you can all fall for it, because you all have become so engrossed with the Earth Life! It has built up such a momentum that no one can ignore its call and passions, its desires and its hatred, rising from strong emotions which should not have the place they have. So if no one is safe from this, **the only salvation and solution is** the escape route always in existence: The road to **Inside Knowledge**, the path to Home Truths, the Inner Knowledge you had before you came to live an experiment once more! The Earth experiment is what it is : ONLY an ex-pe-ri-ment!

That means it is not an eternal way of life, it is a **temporary** situation made-to-measure to try out certain criteria for certain reasons. But if you let the experiment get out of hand without following the safety guidelines, you are bound to hit many pitfalls. You'll have dreadful, eternal results if you constantly cause yourself pain, remorse, hatred of others, which will inevitably turn into hatred of yourself sooner or later.

So why do it? Why not start the other way round? **Start with thinking: What is the spiritual solution**? What is the way to apply one new set of rules (i.e. the spiritual ones) to set them against man-made rules that are badly made, non-spiritual, 'Earth conflict orientated'? Those human laws or ways of thinking were developed from inner selfishness and ego, or cruelty, or sheer stupidity at times too!

Narrow vision of what could happen is often the result of self-centredness and impatience, or stupid behaviour.

BEWARE OF WARMONGERS

A leader cannot think he is a great leader if **he sends his countrymen to their own Souls' destruction** or damage by ordering them, for whatever reason or so-called 'cause', to shoot, kill, murder and endanger other lives. No matter who the others are!

As already said, the **'other side' of a war is a bunch of people just like your side** and they too have narrow vision leaders sending them to maim, shoot, kill that 'side' that **you** represent!

NO WINNERS JUST LOSERS

No one can or will ever win in the end. That's all that can be said and repeated. We can only talk to you all from what is seen from our perspective. Remember, our perspective is much wider and broader and eternal compared with yours and your leaders' narrow, restricted point of views! You cannot see beyond the fact a hill is being attacked by the enemy!

Those in the Spirit World can see lots of hills attacked, at the same place, over thousands of years of your time... and each time the murders of both sides **have NOT solved the problem of the same hill being wanted** and being captured by various groups over centuries! But those who killed others will have **lost their peace of Mind; their Souls will have suffered and may still suffer** from the trauma of realising what they each have caused - the death, the damage, the hurt, the trauma of, or onto, someone else's life.

That cannot be forgotten or forgiven by anyone else than yourself, to yourself. You cannot exonerate yourself as easily as someone else may possibly pardon you, because no one knows you better than yourself in the end, on the grand scale of Eternal Life. **That is why it is so painful for you if you have caused harm to others** - even to just one other - as it may take you ages, in your terms of Time, to come to terms with it and try to wipe the slate clean. So think what would and could happen if you have caused the death of many, of millions? You may not have enough 'time' in Eternity to recover from that!

All this to say: **Thou shall not kill because thou killest thyself in the end.** You definitely harm yourself.

****

Chapter 40

DISTORTIONS & TROUBLES CREATED BY MANKIND

We have here a gentleman who wishes to speak to you. He has been in our world for a long time now and knows more than most of us. He has a special interest in the way **Mankind has distorted what was originally the Truth of existence on Earth.** The Truth being: One is always a Spirit, no matter what shape or body one has chosen to have within that particular 'span-time' on Earth. *(Sudden change of communicator).*

Mankind came to Earth of its own volition, one by one - as part of a great trip into an Experiment not done before, as the Earth was a new venture and trial. So, we in the 'Spirit World' (but we call it: the 'World of Light and Pure Truth') saw to it they were as safe as possible. They were being guarded and guided at every step. As the venture was so new, no one was certain what the next step and venture might be!

As some faltered, they were soon shown the right path, not as an imposition but as supportive guidance. It had to be so. We could not let newcomers to a strange new world struggle on their own! So, that's why they had a link to their origins, their own source, their world of Light, where they came from and belonged to.

The lifeline was inner communication; **the communication and link they had in their Inner Self, within themselves.** They could connect with us, or concentrate on their newly-formed Earthly world and adventure, in a physical world not encountered before!

All went well for quite a long period of your 'time', but gradually there were a few 'false steps', a few hiccups, more of them increasingly apparent. Then, over time, there were adventurers who decided that the Earth, the physical world, was far more fun and tempting than the one they came from! It had its faults, but to them it had **rewards which they could not resist**. This is where all the new problems stemmed from.

A man cannot easily resist what he sees with his flesh eyes or feels and perceives with his other senses... whereas a different concept is needed to be applied in our world. A physical world has not got the same aspects or temptations as the world of Mind and Energy, which can offer more but differently.

So, because some faltered and let the physical senses take over, life on Earth started changing its focus! From being a link between two worlds, **the body became a centre of attention and temptations.** That is what caused millenniums of **problems and diseases** and torments and 'Soul searching', when in fact the Soul has always been there, if it had not been hidden by bodily pleasures and attractions.

FIRST RESCUE

When it was realised in our world that we had a new problem creating itself, we let those who wanted to go back to Earth make it their project to teach those already 'over there' what they had forgotten or were forgetting! We wanted to remind those in that physical world that they had a very strong, vital and essential connection to the very Real World of Light! Where they lived was a world of illusions, of man-made inventions, of Mind Power succeeding in creating Physical Matter, of experiments to see how far and well it could be done, how varied the experiments could be and so on.

So the 'venturers' who went back to Earth had a big task in front of them - trying to reopen the eyes of those who were blinding or had blinded themselves with Earthly pleasures. They had to gradually set a number of 'rules' for

320

guidance, to help the forlorn ones find their way out of the mist, fog or darkness into which they had plunged themselves. That is what is **nowadays called a 'religion'**!

WHY MEN CREATED 'RELIGIONS'?

This guidance was **not** meant to be dictatorial or authoritarian. It was simply meant to reopen eyes to what they had forgotten or wanted to forget out of convenience! The importance, you see, was not so much the fact they had given priority to their flesh desires and impulses. The importance was **they needed to let their Soul, their Spiritual Aspect, through.** They had to remember the 'rule' or directive was: "Do not hurt others in any way. Help them instead, when they need it"! So, not hurting others meant that **wars were NOT part of the programme on Earth,** were not planned or meant to be. They were not what should exist or ever be considered as an option!

That is why you had all these 'holy men' coming to the Earth as volunteers to spread the word again, to remind people what they had come for in the first place - to experiment for the fun of Creativity; to test the possibilities of manipulating Matter via the extensive use of one's Mind Power, which everyone has. It was NOT to exploit or grab others' abilities, goods, personal possessions or even physical bodies! That was NOT part of the plan; never should have been.

When a man started thinking back to his own origins, he reflected: "Oh yes, that's true. I was a 'Spirit', I chose to make a physical body to use in this Earthly world. That is correct. I wanted to see what I could do. Now I have let my physical senses take over and lead me, instead of me leading them! That's where I went wrong!"

That way he would find his way back by turning within, listening more to his Inner Voice, Inner Self and feelings and all would be well. But if another one thought:

"This 'preacher', this man telling us we are mad to concentrate on our life here and enjoy its physical pleasures, is an arrogant spoilsport! He cannot tell us what we can do. I have come to Earth because I enjoy the diversity of its offerings and possibilities! I am not going to let that go now, I am here as an adult. I had to go through childhood first so that I could enjoy my adult activities. Now I am here, I am staying and doing as I please. That man is a pain, an interferer, a do-gooder who wants others to be as boring and lifeless as he is!"

Make that remark be multiplied by thousands and millions and you get the result of centuries (of your 'time') of religion and anti-religion. The 'religious movement' was originally started to say: "Listen within, do not look for eternal happiness in flesh and physical activities or you'll be lost and disappointed'". But unfortunately, within that movement too there gradually were splits, a little here and there.

WHY SPLITS?

It all started because one fellow thought he would add something to the 'rule' to reinforce it, to drive the point home, to make sure the followers would adhere to it. It may have been with a good intention but gradually it distorted the original purpose! This is why nowadays there are so many 'angles within angles within aspects' of some religions or faiths! This is very unfortunate because it can **confuse thoroughly those adhering** to it and make them lead a life which has no real link with what was meant to be given originally.

As time went by, the sections turned into factions and factions always argue with each other or fight each other. Therefore, groups of people (who were 'Spirits' in our world wanting to go and help the Earth!) have become groups of Humans fighting each other, sometimes to death, horribly attacking each other... in order to spread the word: "Thou shall not kill, thou shall help each other!"

This is the most illogical and absurd aspect of all **religions based on man-made additions** to the one primary guidance: "Have fun during your Experiment in Matter and with Matter, but do NOT harm others nor let them be in the lurch." That's all that was required. Remember, you have a link within yourself to reach your own Eternal Higher aspect, Higher Being. That cannot let you down if only you learnt to reach it, feel the guidance and let yourself be guided by the real inner voice of what is good - not be guided by the thoughts of a Mind affected by ideas created on Earth by other Beings who have forgotten the basics of **all ethics and rules of spirituality.** These are:

- There is no one superior to any other.

- There is no harm that shall not be regretted later.

- There is only caring and compassion as guidance during your adventures with Matter in a world created basically by yourselves, as you are all part of the world of Creative Light which we all live in on this side of Reality.

The Reality that one lives on is a real one. The Real Life is here with us. On Earth, you have only an aspect of an experiment which has to come to an end sooner or later! You can't be left playing about with Matter as Matter has limitations in itself, it has a limited 'span', a limited 'shelf life', as you say nowadays. It is essential to comprehend this point.

All that religions have done and do is try to outdo each other, most of them anyway, when they **should link up and add their positive sides together** as one great wave of Thought. You are what they preach about; you are of the Spirit World you came from. You are part of it from the moment you came to exist to when you go back to it. There should be no break, no division and no separation.

You are a Spiritual Being, whether in our world or in your physical and temporary world.

BE THE CHANGE YOU WANT IN YOUR WORLD!

What you do in either world should not make any difference to the fact you are a Being of Energy, Light, Love and Compassion and most of all Creativity! If you create a world of Thoughts around you in such a way as being constantly surrounded by negative thoughts and feelings, you cannot be surprised to have negative greyness around you! You asked for it, it came at once. It has sprung from your own personal and private thoughts! You cannot escape this FACT!

On the other hand, if you use your own creative Power, which is led by your own thoughts, to fill your Earthly or spiritual world and surroundings with Light and Love and fun and interest and discoveries, then you will enjoy a life of eternal life of positivity, not negativity. **You will reap what you have sown**, it's as easy and as simple as that.

So, religions have their good points in a way, but not as they have become nowadays - all scattered, all turning their back to each other or denying the existence or acceptability of others. This is not what was meant. People have to be reminded of their origins in the World of Light, where they 'fly' back to, when leaving the Earthly physical body.

It has to be said, because so many have completely and totally forgotten the essential truth: "Thou art a Being of Light, thou art not a Being of flesh! That is a temporary setting to facilitate your manipulation of Earthly Matter." Now we have that set out as a basis, we'll need to analyse each one to see how they could come back to that basic principle and let some of their man-made concoctions go.

HOW TO PREVENT WARS OF RELIGION

The new way of seeing things to save the world from Wars of Religion, which have constantly plagued it for centuries, is to open the doors to all and say: "Look at what can be done if we **pull our resources together**, by understanding what Mankind is primarily!"

Mankind is a group of Beings who have chosen to come to Earth, for their own personal reasons and desires, to investigate the possibilities of manipulating Matter with the use of their own thoughts. Yet many and most, if not all, people will definitely have forgotten that source. **They will not even know they can** and constantly do that with their thoughts! They have no idea it can be done and do not see how on Earth they could do it!

It's quite understandable because it is difficult to see out of a pit when you have fallen into it, or out of the gunge when you have fallen into a mire. So the main points are:

1- LISTEN TO YOUR THOUGHTS
To make people listen to their own thoughts and see where it takes them:
How often **do they think positively** in a day?
How often do they think negatively in a day?
Have they lived a 'pleasant-cheerful-all-goes-well' day?
Or have they constantly hit problems whether minor or major?

This is the first step: Analyse **your** own thoughts and see whether YOU have **sent positive or negative waves of Energy around you.** THIS is what you have to understand; THIS is what you must look into and at; THIS is where you start to stop passing the buck and blaming others and the rest of the world! You **have to look at yourself**. No one needs to know, so you could be honest if you wanted to be. It is **the only way** to start changing yourself!

If your life is upside down, or your health not good, then you'd need to go back in time to see where and when you started being like this or like that. The reason being problems

325

(whether material, health or other) escalating from one stumble to another, from one grumble to another, from one row to another, from one resentment to another! All of **these create a web of negative attractions**. Attraction attracts! It attracts what it knows, what fits with its own, what is similar to itself.

So if you want to be surrounded by sunny surroundings, do not attract fog, clouds or storms. Let the sunshine into your life, even if there are problems. You can sort out problems better if you see them clearly in daylight, not in the middle of a snowstorm or a foggy day! All is symbolic of course.

First examine yourself to see where and how you let yourself down by forgetting that **you are the Maker of your own life**. You create and have scores or trillions of **possibilities** around you, like butterflies and moths floating around the light. If you leave the light on, the butterflies and moths will be attracted to it. Make sure the Light is a positive one to attract the right type of possibilities and make them happen! That is the starting point. When you have analysed yourself, then you can start changing and altering your way of thinking, your attitude to others, your pattern of speech, your conversations, your doings and sayings.

We cannot control that from here, we cannot do it for you, we cannot make it happen for you! YOU have to build or **rebuild your bright light within your mindset.** Think negatively and your body will respond negatively, because your flesh, your **physical body, is the mirror of your emotions and way of thinking.**

It cannot be repeated enough times. It has to be understood. It's no good saying: "This is rubbish" if you want to alter your life experience. You won't alter it thinking that way! Instead, you'll dig yourself in a little deeper, in your dark hole of inner mental misery and negativity. So the choice is yours. Try it, instead of rejecting it.

2- SCIENTISTS AND THE MIND

An example of total rejection is indeed the 'scientific' mind, also the so-called 'atheist'. He does not accept anything which is beyond the ordinary and the visible to his eyes. He needs to analyse, calculate and be proved it is right and repeatable. Unfortunately, **he does not understand the importance of his own Mind Power** and that's where **his** stumbling block is even bigger!

So, as a 'scientist', he will have an extra task to tackle, which is to analyse 'what' and 'where' his Mind is. That is, he must not think it has to do with the brain, it is NOT the brain that does the thinking, but he does not know or understand that. This is where the problem is for him, even before he does try to tackle anything else!

3- REJECT MAN-MADE DOGMAS

There are various parts of human society which have nothing, yet everything, in common. They fight each other at times, however they do not see how much in common they have!

It would be so essential to get rid of the dogmas, the rules, the aspects which Mankind has added to the age-old principles that all deep Knowledge comes from within and is an innate gift, if only people reached for it and listened to it. That's where the levelling can be done - accepting you all have that gift, **you all have the Power within yourself**, whether a Christian, Muslim, Buddhist or Atheist.

You can all listen within, but not with rigid **ideas imposed on you**, with a fresh outlook if you are able to start afresh to see what is offered around you. Only then will you be able to look at things more objectively! Express yourself as a Being of choice, not a Being of imposed ideas. You all have an option:

*Be yourself, which is a spiritual person with no ideas imposed on himself.

*Or be a person who is only a robot, reacting to and following orders by some other robots, who have made mistakes in the first place! Mistakes made when they **concocted man-made regulations** which do not fit in with the basic principle - Spirituality, which 'religions' should all be about.

To be spiritual you should not kill, you should not harm, for whatever reasons. No excuses, no invention! Just be a Being of Light, reflecting Light onto others and be understanding. That's all. It will make a difference to **your** life when you start that way.

No religion was supposed or meant to exist at the 'beginning' of the Earth Experiment, simply because **there wasn't any need for it.** A Being of Light does not need to be told he is a Being of Light, whether it is in his own world or when he wants to go and play with physical Matter elsewhere! He has that at the core of his Being.

It's when things started going wrong against the very basis of spiritual behaviour that 'religion' started appearing in the hope of straightening the paths of those who wandered off it. But the problem nowadays, as well as long before now, is that few want to learn to listen within themselves. Many have rejected what they knew in the first place.

What a waste of Earthly time and Energy! You could do so much more with it! So much more good for yourselves and for other Beings in your physical world.

SUMMARY OF SOLUTION

* Know that you are all scientists and physicists at core: You can all do things that you are not even aware of doing!

* **All** Beings in your Earthly world are Spiritual Beings who have come from a world of Light and Mind Power to a physical world of Matter to learn or practise and enjoy manipulating that Mind Power, to affect the energies of Matter. **You** affect your environment, your relationships with others, your future,

your past as well as your present, by the way you think or not.

* Individual Beings need to look into their own way of thinking.

* **Churches of all descriptions must look at ways of blending with others** to bring a common denominator back in focus, as it used to be right at the very 'beginning'.

* Leaders in charge must be willing enough to **look at the source of their dogmas** and beliefs, their rules, the changes made to them way back in the 'mist of Time'. Accept that at some point there were things done which **went against** the very principle on which all 'religions' were built:

- Having a Light within oneself, having a Soul.

- Having a link with their Light and lighting the way ahead of oneself and others, but with caring and compassion as a base.

* You have to help everyone look at themselves.

It is there that you will find what made the difference, what caused the rifts and where the healing and blending could be achieved. You cannot heal sores that refuse to accept they are sores. You cannot heal someone who won't accept he is ill in the first place. It is not something that can be done overnight unfortunately, because the rules, regulations, dogmas are deeply rooted as said before.

* Look within. Talk. Compare. Add or retract, subtract. Remove superfluous additions or even 'garbage'. To what you find, add more caring, understanding and spirituality. That means: **Others before Self, because Self can only grow in stature and power thanks to its reaction to others.**

A tree cannot grow on its own; it needs to absorb water and minerals from the ground, sunlight from the sun. It breathes in carbon gas as it gives out much needed oxygen to its surrounds. It does not harm its surroundings; it blends with it and thus grows stronger and taller. **Be the same with your spiritual growth.**

****

Chapter 41

DROUGHT, CHILL & DOOM

The pen neatly draws a kind of translucent cloche shape, then starts the first word as I hear English spoken.
When the wind rises and blows the dust off the surface of the Earth, the world will know there is another king coming... The King of Drought! The drought, which will cover the Earth for quite some time, will cause a lot of unhappiness and misery, as water will become so short as being invisible to those seeking it. That drought will be a warning of things to come, sadly for those still there.

It is a warning as Mankind, over the ages, has not listened to the many voices cautioning it that it is destroying the Earth it has built for itself over aeons. So the **drought** there will be a warning, because after the drought, there will be the opposite - the **freezing cold,** with plenty of water but frozen, to be had only if melted! That will remind them the extremes of temperature had been forecast long ago by those sensible enough to see the damages caused by excesses and selfishness!

Why can't it be stopped now, you'll say? Well, it won't because it is too late for a start. Too late as the clouds have been formed and created as layers obliterating the right rays the Earth should receive! The sun should be warming but not cooking you dry. The rain should be coming but not drowning you. The warmth should be just right but it won't be anymore!

So what can you do? Warn them over and over again. It might eventually reduce a little the intensity of the trouble but it won't annihilate either of them. They are on their way. Their course cannot be altered!

Perhaps an extra warning could be of help, you'll think? But it is not as easy as that, since it takes decades to build up and therefore decades to last. That is what is sad, as it **had been forecast**, had been guessed at, **had been inspired** (by those in Spirit World), yet none of those who could have done something listened! And now some try to listen, but it is too late in a way! Very sad.

BR- (Puzzled by the unexpected and unusual monologue) - Who is speaking?

As we speak, we listen to one another and to others above and beyond our own knowledge. That way we have constant communication at all 'levels', as you'd call them. **We can only receive the highest and the best**, as you required.

With that purpose in Mind, we gather information that might be useful to you, to pass on to others. Sadly this one is too late for successful results to be felt; you can only possibly soften the outcomes here and there - but there will be **terrible times ahead for those in hot countries** and that is where the sadness we feel is centred. You can only receive our condolences for the plight of the Earth to come. That's all that can be said.

(After hearing this unexpected powerful flow, I realise the cloche shape drawing is symbolising some kind of 'greenhouse effect').

****

Chapter 42

EARTHQUAKES & UPHEAVALS PREDICTIONS

BR- Please clarify the concern about Yellowstone and other upheavals? Also, why do some governments stack up food, body bags etc?

The answers will have to come from beyond our own field of information, as this is specialised knowledge regarding the Earth's Magnetic Field.

BR- Did I hear this correctly - E.M.F?

Yes, the **Earth's Magnetic Field** and the attempts from within the Earth to rectify all the imbalances that have been imposed on it. It is of vital importance to grasp those points! The Magnetic Field of the Earth has been **seriously attacked from all angles by the various apparatus Humans have** floating **above it**, in the atmosphere.

If the field had not been damaged, distorted and displaced at times, it would not matter so much. But because the EMF has been tampered with, whether voluntarily or not, then the whole structure (which was built aeons ago to a very finely tuned balance) is now in a helter skelter state! It has been damaged and it is trying to rectify itself... so this is an aspect of the problem, or rather one angle.

EARTH PSYCHIC FIELD

The other one that could be pointed out is the **inner core field**, the 'psychic field', the sensing side of this marvellous creation we built aeons ago - the Earth. The Earth was and still is built by waves of very subtle energies, all blending together to create a mesh of fine energies; ultra-fine vibrations that keep the whole structure vibrating at the correct rates and maintain it in its place, though, of course, it is moving across 'space'.

The importance of this is that the moment the slightest disturbance is inflicted upon this structure, the repercussions cannot be prevented and it vibrates through its whole being, right through its whole body, if you see what we mean?

The echoes will unfortunately be felt physically as huge reactions of plates moving and earthquakes, which will result with devastating effects at times.

AMERICAN CONTINENT

You've asked whether there is something afoot about the US government seemingly stacking food etc. We have no recorded information about this as such. But we know that **there will soon be a devastating natural disaster** throughout the American continent, because that's where the underlying plates will collide again.

BR- What will trigger it?

It's been on the cards for a long time but this is unfortunately a mighty one... which will make people think twice about everything!

BR- Can you explain this statement please?

Those kinds of events are always traumatising to the population, whether to those who are enduring the events or those watching pictures of the events. But the result will be that **people will then pull together much more** than they have done before. There will be heroic acts and defences against such elements will be thought out and turn out to be **good ideas.** Defences **against leaks** of dangerous fumes and gases, leaks of gas underground, leaks of water in inhabited areas. Programmes to **strengthen buildings** to a degree not thought out before- community spirit pulling together so much more than they have done before.

There will be **a new way of thinking** burgeoning at last! They will see that their materialistic goods are no help in the case of disasters! They will think of what really matters in the Earthly world, such as friendship and love - you can keep them in your heart. You need not have goods of any kind to have love and friendship. You also have to look after those in need near you. You cannot let People or 'Animals' suffer when there have been catastrophes all around. You have to learn to **share** with them whatever little morsel you have, instead of keeping it just for yourself and let them die of starvation.

All those little things are going to start reopening the road to an improved way of thinking. There will not be any major 'enlightenment'; no one will come out as a 'Messiah' or 'Saviour'. But deep within each, or nearly each, person there will be a **reassessment of values and priorities**. And if that carries on, then the floods and earthquakes will have really been worth it, as there was and is an immense need for a revaluation of what matters in life, in the World of Matter! No more selfishness and greed. Make room for generosity, selflessness and sharing. That's all that is needed and life will be much happier. So let's go back to telling you what we can see so far, until or unless things change drastically, which is most unlikely!

NEVER SEEN BEFORE

The one outstanding point is the **magnitude** of the shaking you will all feel! **The Earth will shake** at a very great level indeed. That movement will be from the whole core outwards; it will start deeply inside and will move and vibrate outwards so that the whole outer mantle will have repercussions of what is going on deeply inside. You will see **things you have never seen before**: Colours in the sky, light underground, tumultuous seas uncovering deeply kept secrets.

BR- What do you mean about colours in the sky?

It will be an upside down effect and experience. We mention those so that you recognise it when you are told it's happening. We want you to know we told you the truth when others tell you it is taking place.

That is what we are shown. There will be **strange lights** coming over your world, but there will also be some unknown lights under the ground. We cannot see what they are exactly. They appear to come from machines underground trying to work out what the Earth is doing when it acts that way, but they will not help; they may **make it worse**, because there will be repercussions and reactions to their own magnetic effects. So, the whole world of the Earth will react to what is done to it voluntarily or involuntarily. That's all we can see so far.

You *(me, BR- in UK)* have nothing to fear personally. You will not be hurt at all. But you will know **of many people going over to our world** because of the traumatic events. When that happens, you will have even more reasons to pass on our message to those who, hopefully, will listen. Our message that **greed and self-centred materialism are of no value** and their effects are very bad. Whereas concern for others and trust in a happier world when over here, will give people faith in themselves and hope for the future. We cannot see much more than what we see for now.

BR- Can you see which countries will suffer?

There will be many areas affected because **the seas will move** at a higher and faster rate than normal. So many will be drowned or swamped. But **you** will be safe, as we told you.

BR- I was more thinking of my brothers, rather than me.

We cannot say about anybody else, because we are not focusing on them at the moment. We are sure we can say that the part of the world of Earth you live in is safer than the part of the world your little brother lives in, because he is nearer the sea than you are. *(New Caledonia - near New Zealand in the Pacific Ocean)* But we know you'll be all right because you have a very important job to finish and **you** will not go until you have accomplished what you have come for! The rest of the population of other countries cannot be accounted for in this picture. We do not see everything in detail. We are just focusing on what you are asking.

BR- Will the majority of the Earth population vanish? Some people fear it...

As you ask this we look at the map of 'happening' or **'more likely** to happen'. This is a hard question because **no one 'disappears' (that means leaves their body) unless their Soul wishes to leave the flesh!** So, we'll say we don't know for sure, simply because **one cannot be sure what people are going to decide** years or even months ahead! It can be changed at the stroke of a wish or urge, or if the body of flesh is so worn out there can be no 'miraculous' recovery.

So we'll say, we cannot see, so far, the whole world population annihilated, as you say. But it's not to say there won't be many, many casualties! It will mainly be in the regions where the 'quakes and floods will occur. It is the **main continent of North America,** as you see it, which will have the main trauma.

But there will also be other places in the world which will have their own upheavals - because it is not possible to move one part of the underlying crust, without affecting the other parts as well and having **repercussions on the whole surface** one way or another! It may be seas as well as ground.

It is more dangerous to live in towns, because you have buildings that fall on you when you have a 'quake! If you were in the middle of fields, you would not feel the trauma as much (unless you had a crack opening beneath you of course!).

Will HUMANS LEARN THE LESSON?

We are more concerned about seeing whether people will accept to learn from the lesson the Earth is giving. If they don't learn, there will not be any improvement, will there?! So we hope they will start thinking afresh, so that a new life can be given both to the Earth world and to the people and other Beings living on it.

BR- Some fear a catastrophe at Yellowstone in the USA. Will there ever be a huge ash cloud/no sun?

Essentially no. We do not seem to pick up anything like that. Of course, there could always be a possibility of it happening... but if we focus on what you are asking, we are trying to see the likelihood of it and we cannot see it happening... **so far.** It is in the interest of Mankind to feel its way out of all this.

BR- How will it do that?

It has to **reassess its aims and goals.** It has to weigh up what it has been doing so far and why it's so bad most of the time!

BR- Are governments wilfully creating and manipulating 'quakes or hurricanes etc. and directing them to certain countries, such as in retaliation?

That's what you may hear. That's what many people may say. We have not got, at the moment, any such information on our own 'inner screen'. There may be some manipulation of electromagnetic and other, fields. That is within the capability and skills of those who know how to handle them!

There will always be some people using their own knowledge and the technology available to dastardly ends! But we do not see such acts standing out in our vision of events, so we could not give you details on that, 'for the time being' - except we have no 'time'. We try to focus on **ever-changing maps of probabilities,** which are not always 'correct' **if** the subjects change their perspective, wishes and aims! We are **at the mercy of Humans' Free Will, which changes everything** of course!

CATASTROPHIC REPERCUSSIONS

So we can only say there will be, certainly 'fairly soon' within your time frame, **a catastrophic happening in the region of the American continent.** The Northern one, but the Southern one too will react to it, of course, as both are linked up! Then, at the same 'time', more or less, there will be **repercussions** underneath the surface of the Earth world which will reverberate all over the surface where cracks and weak points exist. That will create water flooding, lava flooding and terrible problems for those living there, as you can presume. If there were no Humans living there, you'd barely notice it. If it was in a desert area, say, you would not know of it, or hardly. It would not matter so much, but because there will be lots of people suffering from it, it will cause a lot of heartache, grief and concern.

But we hope the outcome of it will be, in the end, better communication from the hearts, between Beings. People will learn to go **back to the basics of caring for others** rather than thinking of themselves first. And that is the end of our profound sermon!

You can rest your hand now for a while. You have been very active, taking all that down in writing and we are pleased you could ask and we could answer in a fashion.

****

Chapter 43

NOAH'S ARK

The knowledge people so want can be obtained through meditation, through listening within, by anyone wishing to learn. All they have to do is listen quietly and have the inner desire to learn more. So here is a sample of what they could acquire if only they paid attention to what is taught within, rather than **what old books told them they should believe!**

An ancient story is the story in the Bible, of Noah and his Ark. He has made a boat to save Humanity i.e. himself, his family and a few 'Animals' from the Earth. That was a noble gesture indeed! But was it true?! NO! No man could take all the 'Animals' on one ship and let them be and not have epidemics, murder or whatever. You can all guess **it is not true**, yet you have people pretending they found the Ark wood, the Ark plans, the Ark remnants and all that. What does that prove? That people are making money out of others through a fairytale some wish to believe. It would have been and would be **more beneficial to Humanity to try to understand the morale behind the fable!**

REAL MEANING!

A moral quite visible if you only try to look. A single man building his own ship, whether with help from his sons and daughters or not, is still an incredible achievement and that's what has to be seen: With a big effort one can achieve something. If you want to reach safety, you make an effort. So to reach safely the Other Side of Life, you should **make the effort now** to build your 'passage ship', your own ark, by starting constructing, plank by plank, the Knowledge you need to have to make your journey easier and your understanding clearer!

A ship is a means to travel. The journey over to here is not a long way, yet it is if your Knowledge and Understanding are so non-existent that to you 'that country', the Other Side, is as far as China was in the olden days, or even more!

* **The planks are facts** - facts given in hard wood by Spirit teachers wanting to help you cross over easily and without fear.

* **The nails** are given by us each time we talk to you **to implant that Knowledge** hard and fast in your Mind, so that it stays forever, not just in this Earthly life but the other ones too.

* **The mountain** the ship rested on supposedly **is the safety of the arms of those who love you from here.** We are all around you to protect and help you every step of the way, so you are lifted up over the worse flood or disaster just in time, if only you let us do it with you.

* **The dove** bringing you peace of Mind is the dove of Love and Compassion, Caring and Healing.

* **Knowledge** is healing, Knowledge is uplifting, Knowledge is enlightening, just **like rays of sunshine** after the stormy day has battered you.

* What **Noah represents** is the **Man who trusts in his Inner Knowledge**, in his advisers within, so that he followed the advice given, the inspiration brought to him in his hours of need before, during and after. As he listened, he grew more confident he could do it. As he built it, he felt it was right and he knew it was when he finished it, because the boat floated and took him over the waves of a turbulent sea and raging skies.

* But **the 'Animals'** don't make sense, you will say?

No, they do make sense, in a way, because that fable invented by Mankind tries to explain how **the first men on Earth welcomed other Spirits** who wanted to be on Earth too **and helped them be passengers on that new venture**.

The fable is a mixture of wanting to travel to the World of Spirit and travel to the world of Matter. If Matter matters to some, they have to be helped to survive the pitfalls of its world

340

by being taught they come from Spirit. Then they'll understand more how to cope in it, how to still behave like Spirits should (i.e. in a caring, loving way towards other passengers on the trip). They'll also grasp how to be able to enjoy the Earthly life they chose to go to, without overstepping the limits which could be dangerous: An elephant on a ship is a big responsibility, a giraffe on a ship causes problems, an ant on a ship is no trouble as such, yet could be if it decides to bite and be a nuisance!

So all these little details were **symbolic of how one has to think of others;** take care of each other; match others' needs to one's needs without interfering either. **Elevating one's Mind** over mountains caused by problems **is like elevating the Ark** over that so-called Mount Ararat! If it had not been left high and dry, it could have fallen on its side and been destroyed or damaged, or it would have been swept upside down by the waters receding to wherever they were going. So, the whole story was an allegory, a symbol of what can be done for Mankind and by Mankind.

The first episode mentioned was to make sure Mankind dropped its **ludicrous search for a non-existent boat** which can only exist in people's minds! Of course, if some of you wish to make money out of others by pretending you found the wood etc., go ahead! Let us hope no one will be foolish enough to believe you! But the story has so much significance it would be a shame to reject it altogether! It is a tale of trusted servants of the Light and Truth which reigns here.

It is all that and more, of course. More in that once you have learnt to listen, learnt to trust, learnt the Wisdom and the facts, the Knowledge and the rules of caring for your Soul and others, **then** you can go ahead on to the longest or shortest trips you like, because you are well equipped. No one was better equipped than Noah, apparently! Well, no one would be, or will be, than those who **have faith in what is taught to them from the Higher Side of this Life.** That is what we wanted to tell you. Pass it on, let them know!

The 'man on the boat' was a brave, wise man indeed, hence the big beard. The ship was definitely a safe ship; it had planks of hard weather-resisting wood made by Spirit. The facts were drilled in, implanted safely in his head and his heart and his family's too because he made sure they knew what to do, how to do it. They were good people, caring, loving to each other. They had pets indeed! Hoards of them: The 'Animals' of the world, who were, like them, **travellers on that trip, not slaves, not being used, not being killed and eaten!** They were simply passengers, helped to travel over the rough seas towards an unknown land!

But the adventure, though risky it seemed, was in safe hands since it was guided by 'those above', inspiring the ones 'below'. And that's what life on Earth is about and what 'Life ending' (the passage over to Spirit World) is about - all together helping each other. **All those facts got mixed up, disguised, entangled, misunderstood,** but finally, worse, became such a fable. Money makers thought: 'Great! Let's con them to say we found the boat's remnants!'

Ah well, we would have a laugh here too, if it was not so sad that the Knowledge inspired via this story had not been lost for good, obviously! So now is the time to start **reviving it** in your sad world of wars and despair, loneliness and fears, troubles, diseases, murders and searches for something missing no one seems to put a finger on. Yet where it is, is WITHIN. That's where they'll find what they need and miss - within! **The source of all Knowledge is within each and every one of you all**, but few listen and heed what is given, or few look for it or wish to get anything beyond their Earthly activities.

An ant, an elephant and any Animal, all are the same Spirit in a different disguise. Why make distinctions among passengers on a trip? You travel, they travel. You go for your reasons, they go for their reasons, to wherever each one is going.

WHY has someone suddenly decided that the trip was only a pleasurable experience for some, at the cost of the lives or comfort of others?!

WHY should some take over the ship, or train, or plane and make half or more of the other travellers work or slave for them, or be eaten, or killed for pleasure, simply to either entertain or satisfy the lust for food or taste buds or the selfishness and ego of others?

No one can take over the life of anyone, no matter whether they are insects or big 'Animals'. You cannot decide that you don't like So and So and kill or torture them for that reason! Just as **YOU would not want to be killed, tortured or used for whatever reason, no matter how 'justified' that reason is, according to your murderer!** Wouldn't that be correct?

So, make life easy for other passengers of the Earth trip, just as you would like them to make it easy enough for you. An insect can be 'a pain' for you at times, but it has its reasons for being here and can also have its uses for plants etc., so do not judge anything by **your limited standards and vision!** Wait till you are in our world to look at the wider picture of what Creation is all about, then you'll understand the magnitude of it and its intricacies. After that, you'll realise there is no room whatsoever for killing, destroying, rejecting or using other creatures. That's all that can be said.

All who judge now will be judged afterwards... but much harder! And **the judge judging you will be yourself,** as you come here to look back at what you have done during your journey in that particular life. No one judges more harshly than oneself; it is amazing but it is true!

(11.29pm - All the above was not prompted by me at all, as I had never read any such information anywhere and was not interested in the Ark! This was unexpectedly dictated at a constant steady flow, without any hesitation, as fast as my writing hand could catch it!).

FINAL PAUSE FOR THOUGHTS

Yours is a world of doom and gloom as it is at present. This is why we all need to unite and make a big assault on the causes ruining the wonderful Earth Experiment, which could have been a total success, if only Humans had not failed it! So we suggest you all try and pull together in every corner and niche you live in and see what you can do. Help protect Nature and its inhabitants, help protect your Earth soil and its surrounding air. Then also work on people's attitude. Help them get rid of their fears and conduct themselves in a more caring and less self-centred attitude.

If you do that yourself, individually, it will soon reflect on others, starting with your own children and family. Place your friendship amongst people with the same likes and objectives. (Not those with the same cars and fancy gadgets and materialistic goals!).

We can see the world changing already indeed. Not fast. But there have been quite a few major turnarounds. Such as the USA having a 'black American' president! Something which would not have ever been dreamed off a few centuries or decades ago! So that's an example. But you cannot rely on just a few sparks. It's the whole world which must be shining again, as it should be. We suggest you always **focus on good news.** Do not pass on bad news unless doing so helps fight the cause of the trouble.

YOU ARE NOT ALONE

You have done well, all of you who care about your world. You have done well, all of you who have understood that everybody lives on after the passing to our world. So keep placing your trust in those in our world who look out for you. Remember **none of you is abandoned** and you are looked after. If you feel your life is hard, look within yourself in case

344

you are doing things which you are not happy with and you could change. But **if it is your life plan**, then take strength in knowing that simply **doing your best** in as kind a way as you can muster, **will help your Soul grow** and shine and will give you inner strength.

Always trust in your guiding Friends from our world. **Learn to tune in** to them, so that you'll then never feel alone and you will be inspired as to the best path for you to follow.

LIGHT UP THE WORLD

We see the Earth world with lights all over, like a dark night lit up by illuminations. Those lights are every single one of you all who shine with your kind hearts and Souls. **You are illuminating your corner of the world**!

You can then **spread that light by living as decent spiritual Beings** and doing your very best, so that you too obey the one and only 'law' which is Pure Kindness and Compassion: "Do not harm any other Being and do your best to help those in need". You cannot do any better than this, my friends. We know you are kind. May you do your utmost to shine your light over your world. You will then '**be a star**' doing so!

****

"The only thing necessary for the triumph of EVIL is that GOOD people do... nothing!" (Edmund Burke)

"Today is the First Day of the Rest of your Life!"

Please visit my website for further knowledge:
www.italkwithspirits.com

THE PERFECT GIFT

(Entirely dictated to me at high speed, without any hesitation, by my Spirit Teachers).

Creation… Creation…Wonderful Creation!
The joy of putting together
The most exciting forms to express Life:
Millions of flowers, millions of plants,
Millions of animals, millions of birds,
Millions of little creatures, larger ones too...
The joy of thinking: "What's the next one?"

The scenery to act the play,
The play of Man on Earth,
Had been designed for Joy,
For Health, for Food.
But the Fun is on our side:
Creating the World and its facets,
Like a diamond for You,
For those who'd appreciate...

But not all understand!
Many just look, not even looking!
All is left is Dust, Death and Drought!
Why spoil this World of Colours, Sounds and Smells?!
Why ruin this Beauty, this Jewel, this Pearl?!
How could you be blind to what had been given?
This World is priceless, nowhere is the same.

You have machines, you have toys,
You have tools, you have homes;
But you have no means of creating this:
A Tree... a Cat... a Fish... a Bird...
You can't make a Sea, you can't make a Sky!
You can't make Fire out of nothing!
You can't make a Leaf or a Flower!

Where are your tools, your machines and your pride?!
You have nothing; you think you are All!
Your pride is trivia... You face a Marvel!
Why waste it, you mere Humans?
Who made your world?
Not you... WE did.

Respect what you are given,
Respect the signs of Life,
Which are shown in myriads
Of shapes, sound and scents.
You are crazy! The Woods are magic,
Oceans priceless, the Sky is awesome!

Open your eyes... your Inner Eye,
And see what truths are shown
In the wonderful World of Nature alone!
The search for God, the search for Life,
The Search for Cures, the search for Health,
The need for more... will be no more,
As all is given in the World you own!

****

© *Brigitte Rix*.1998

Ley Lines sketch 1 – Chapter 23

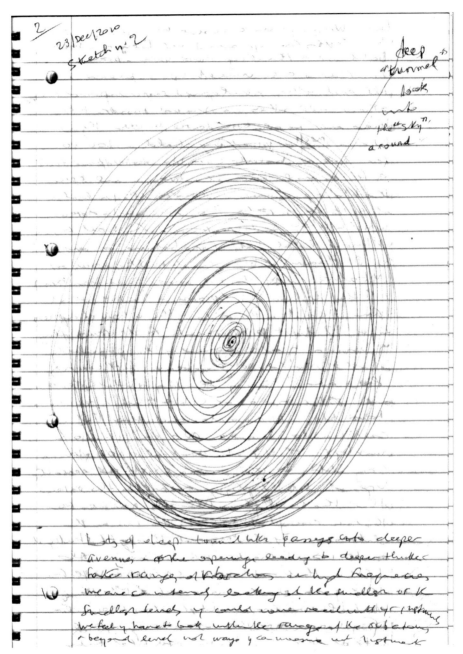

Ley Lines sketch 2 – Chapter 23

Sunday 19 December 2010   8:45 am

(Q) About so-called "Levels" & number of them?
9:48

Levels Sketch – Chapter 27

350